PRAISE FOR *GAME PI*

"Dean's clear passion for career assessment and deep com
back to his field are evident in this book, which offers a c
structured process for leveraging career assessment met
clients develop their own game plan. Readers receive valuable help in the
subtle art of integrating and interpreting assessment data, with all its ambi-
guity and complexity. In addition, the book offers a true insider's view by
sharing Dean's personal journey, insights, and perspectives."

—**Tamara Nelson**, PhD, LP, founder, CareerMoves

"*Game Plan* is full of practical advice, easy-to-use forms, and real-life
examples to help readers apply the material they've learned. The end-of-
chapter observations and questions nicely summarize content and get readers thinking about their own style and how to use it to best advantage with
clients. Whether you're new to career assessment or an advanced practitioner, you'll learn something from this book."

—**Jean M. Kummerow**, owner and consulting psychologist,
Jean Kummerow & Associates

"Dean DeGroot has an established reputation as a premier career counselor, coach, and mentor. He's conscientious, detailed, systematic, and,
importantly, caring in his work—all characteristics reflected in the book.
Game Plan provides practical and common-sense assessment strategies
based on Dean's work with clients and his support of his colleagues. It's
for both career counselors who want to grow their expertise and practice
and those aspiring to be a part of this life-changing profession. I guarantee
you'll be glad you have it in your toolkit!"

—**Sandra Krebs Hirsh**, principal, Sandra Hirsh Consulting, co-author
(with Jean M. Kummerow) of *LifeTypes: Understand Yourself and
Make the Most of Who You Are*

"I especially enjoyed the case studies, which offer rich examples of how
assessment can be applied in our work with clients. Dean and Liz have done
an excellent job of making complex topics approachable by breaking them
down into step-by-step components. I will use these ideas in my own work
and also recommend them to colleagues."

—**Paul Timmins**, executive director, University of Oregon Career Center,
and former president, National Career Development Association

"Rarely do we get an inside glimpse at the work of a master career assessment professional, but that's what you'll find in *Game Plan*. Drawing on his extensive experience as a career counselor and psychologist, Dean DeGroot shares his wisdom about what really works with clients seeking new careers and lives. With real-world stories, practical tools, and a step-by-step process, the book fills a real need by adding practical advice and color to existing textbooks on career assessment."

—**Kate Schaefers**, executive director, University of Minnesota Advanced Careers Initiative

"If you're a new career counselor or thinking of becoming one, you need to read Dean's book. It's practical, organized, and chock-full of useful and usable information. Reading this book will help you deepen the learning for your clients. The processes and tools that Dean generously shares will provide the outcomes you and your clients deserve. I wish I had had this book when I was starting out!"

—**Barb Krantz Taylor**, MA, LP, licensed psychologist and principal consultant, The Bailey Group

"I especially liked chapters 2 and 3. Chapter 2, Exploring Your Strengths, offers great insights on self-assessment and introspection, helping readers reach their own potential so they can better help their clients. Chapter 3, Building Your Network, shows how minimizing fear and maximizing risk can lead to a stronger, more collaborative network. Highly recommended."

—**Sharon Givens**, chief executive director and founder, Visions Counseling and Career Center, and president elect, National Career Development Association

"In *Game Plan*, the authors make a unique and timely contribution to ongoing discussions around career assessment and the world of work. In particular, the chapter on workplace bullying addresses an important issue often overlooked in other career resources and dialogues."

—**Michael J. Stebleton**, PhD, associate professor and coordinator of higher education, University of Minnesota–Twin Cities, and co-author of *Hired! The Job Hunting and Planning Guide* (4th ed.)

GAME PLAN

An Insider's Guide to
Effective Career Assessment

Dean R. DeGroot and Liz Willis

with a Foreword by Bruce Roselle

Innerview
PRESS

Game Plan: An Insider's Guide to Effective Career Assessment
Published by Innerview Press

Print ISBN 978-0-578-98993-8
E-book ISBN 978-0-578-98994-5
Library of Congress Control Number: 2021919859

Cover design by Christian Storm
Page design by Beth Wright, Wright for Writers LLC

For questions or comments on the book,
contact Dean DeGroot at dean@innerviewconsulting.com.
For more information on the book, including where to order,
visit careerassessmentguide.com.

For my wife, Liz Cole-DeGroot, and daughters, Sarah and Anna, who have added meaning to my life.

—Dean DeGroot

For my husband, Tony Bergmann-Porter, whose love and support have made my life as a writer possible.

—Liz Willis

Contents

FOREWORD

Knowing your game plan is essential to living the life and engaging in the career for which you were designed. However, most people do not take the time to think through this question thoroughly; rather, they just step into the next thing, and then the next thing, and eventually call it a career. Those of us who help people think through their work and life decisions recognize the critical need to have a plan and work it over time. In *Game Plan*, Dean and Liz provide a simple, practical, yet comprehensive formula for helping others create their own powerful, winning career plans. Within these chapters are the detailed steps, structures, and strategies that all career counselors and coaches can use to optimize their results with clients.

Some of our clients suffer from irrational fears and faulty beliefs that have undermined their career thinking in the past. Others are relatively naïve about the world of work and the level of education and experience different types of jobs require. Still others have grown up thinking they can be anything they want to be, regardless of their intelligence, talent, and drive limitations. These issues propelled me years ago to apply assessment tools on the front end of career development and also in my leadership consulting. Though there are schools of thought that encourage clients to explore their own personal narrative and use that to envision their next career move—and I have used these in the past—assessment data that gives clients a realistic picture of how they stack up to norm groups often provides the needed breakthrough. Dean's assessment process allows for both—clients explore their personal narratives but also find enlightenment and new opportunities through formal career testing.

If you're new to career counseling and coaching, and especially if you're new to career assessment, *Game Plan* will speed up your learning process by bringing together a range of tools that would otherwise require much time to source and learn. Also, because the book is full of stories about actual clients—with their issues, process, and results—you'll quickly see the rationale behind and efficacy of the tools that are presented. Some of you who are more experienced will have already developed your own versions of these tools, but even experienced practitioners can benefit from the insight and experience reflected in this book. If you're a leadership consultant like me, for example, you may tend to approach career and leadership conversations from a broad strategic framework, which can come across as too vague and ambiguous for some clients. When that's the case, you can use the practical tools in this book to augment your work.

In reviewing the book, I especially enjoyed Part 4, Career Stories and Transformations, including the Q&A with Dean. Having known Dean for more than thirty years, I've had the pleasure of seeing him grow in experience and model the lessons he shares in the book. I've watched him work with clients and colleagues, seen him lead our local career development association, and witnessed the caring, responsible approach he brings to his personal and professional relationships. Most important for this book, I know Dean as an insightful psychologist with deep knowledge of career assessment and its application. By reading *Game Plan*, you stand to learn a lot—about yourself, your colleagues, and the clients you serve.

—Bruce E. Roselle, PhD, LP
　　Author of *Vital Truths* (2002), *Fearless Leadership* (2006), and *The Fraud Factor* (2016)
　　February 18, 2021

PREFACE

Today it seems both natural and inevitable to be publishing a book on career assessment for career counselors and coaches. But when I look back to when Liz and I first began talking about a possible writing collaboration, I was pretty sure any book we wrote would be aimed at people looking for career advice, not career development professionals. In fact, our early efforts were headed in that direction, with one idea to offer career and business strategies for people over fifty. However, once we began thinking about career assessment as a possible focus, the value of writing a book for career counselors and coaches became increasingly clear.

In 2007, Howard Figler and Richard Bolles published the second edition of their book for current and prospective career development professionals, *The Career Counselor's Handbook*. In chapter 12, somewhat deceptively titled "How to Use Career Assessment Tools," Figler warns against using such tools altogether. He believed that both clients and career counselors were too dependent on them for guidance. He felt that clients had more than enough self-knowledge to guide themselves—it just needed to be drawn out. That was the counselor's proper role, he believed, not administering career tests. So if readers were looking for practical advice on using career assessment instruments, they would need to look elsewhere.

I bring up *The Career Counselor's Handbook* not because it's a bad book—I own a copy myself, and many people, including some of my colleagues, recommend it to others as an introduction to the field—but because it represents a missed opportunity to provide practical, from-the-trenches guidance on career assessment instruments. That's where *Game Plan* comes in. Despite an ongoing debate over the value of formal assessment tools like the Myers-Briggs Type Indicator (MBTI) assessment, Strong Interest Inventory assessment, and other instruments, practitioners like me use them every day to help clients. And to learn our craft, we need practical guidance, something I wish I'd had a lot more of earlier in my career. While more academically oriented texts on assessment are widely available—and I point out several good ones in Appendix B—practical advice on learning about career assessment and integrating it into your practice is surprisingly hard to come by, at least in a form that's convenient and comprehensive.

Finally, just a note on how we chose to write this book. With the exception of chapter 13, in which Liz offers thoughts on her own experience of assessment, it's me who'll be speaking to you from these pages. But the work is a true collaboration, with Liz contributing research, developmental editing, and writing to the book. Although she's a writer and editor and not a career development practitioner herself, Liz believes strongly in assessment and the insights it has given her, which you'll see reflected in her chapter. In fact, when she first came to me for career counseling back in 2000, she was already a huge fan of assessment, proudly announcing her Myers-Briggs type and eager to learn more through further testing.

Both Liz and I wish you success, and we hope you enjoy the book!

INTRODUCTION

***Game Plan* is meant to help career** counselors and coaches as well as graduate students in counseling to expand their knowledge of career assessment practice, both as a set of tools for working with clients and as a possible career focus. If you're a student or recent graduate in counseling, you may have learned about career assessment in theory and even practiced it to a certain extent, but your understanding and experience may be limited. This book should make it more real for you and fill in some of the practical details missing in more academic texts. If you're a career counselor or coach thinking of adding assessment to your offerings or expanding what you currently offer, this book should accelerate that process for you.

Career assessment—the use of formal and informal techniques to explore interests, personality, and other factors in order to help clients make better career decisions—is an exciting skill set to develop. It's also a viable way to specialize in your practice. To me, nothing is more rewarding than seeing clients grow in self-awareness and take positive steps forward as a result of the assessment work we do together. And specializing in assessment is one of the key reasons I've been successful in my career. Not only has it brought me great career satisfaction, it's also resulted in numerous career opportunities beyond client work, including outplacement, selection assessment, and training projects. But it took years to gain the career confidence I have today.

For some reason, perhaps because we help other people with their careers and therefore think we should know it all already, we tend to shortchange ourselves when it comes to our own career development. But to help our clients effectively, we must first attend to our own needs as professionals. In Part 1, "Assessing Yourself and Your Career," we begin with the topic of specialization in assessment, specifically the use of formal tests. We discuss what it takes to be a go-to person in this area. If you don't currently focus on assessment yourself—and not all career counselors and coaches choose to do so—you'll get tips on how to collaborate with others with that expertise. We'll also talk about your own self-awareness and development: the sweet spot that will best use your strengths, the most effective work environment for you, and how to identify your leadership style. Finally, chapter 3 discusses networking and learning about assessment through professional associations and mastermind groups.

In Part 2, "Assessing Your Clients," I walk you through my assessment process, including interview questions I use with clients, the specific battery of formal assessments (tests) I draw on, and special worksheets I've developed to help clients capture their thoughts and consolidate what they've learned. One of the biggest challenges we have as a career counselors and coaches is getting our clients to fully realize the benefits of assessment—that is, to process what they've learned, take ownership of the information, and move forward confidently. The chapters in Part 2 offer a way to meet that challenge. In chapter 8, for example, you'll learn about what I call the "game plan," a simple template clients can use to capture criteria they need in their work to thrive. Getting clear on these criteria is the prize for doing assessment well, which is why I named the book after the plan. An important takeaway from Part 2 is that assessment is not a "one and done" event in which clients passively receive test results; it's an ongoing process in which they're invited to explore their past, present, and future and what it means to them. Creating a game plan is the ideal culmination of that process.

Part 3, "Assessing the Work Environment," is all about *context*: we may be perfectly suited to a particular role or career, but if we find ourselves in the wrong company, or being bullied on the job, it's going to be hard to succeed. So chapter 9 explores work values and job satisfaction, which I measure through a special tool called the Career Compatibility Scale. Chapter 10 addresses workplace bullying and includes a personal story of my own experience with bullying. Chapter 11 is all about communicating job fit based on assessment findings. By providing us with key insights and language, assessment helps us communicate our strengths more effectively.

In Part 4, "Career Stories and Transformations," we begin with case studies: stories of seven former clients in various stages of transition and crisis who found new direction through assessment. In chapter 13, Liz, a former client and my collaborator on the book, offers an analysis of her experience in career assessment and how it affirmed her long-standing goal of being a writer.

Chapter 14 is a Q&A on my own career, including how I got started in the field, how I came to be focused on assessment, and how I determined the kind of clients I work with best. Together these chapters provide a rich picture of how assessment can support and propel a career—whether it's experienced as a client or pursued as a practice.

Part 5, "The Quick-Reference Toolkit," is a convenient guide to solving common assessment issues and questions. Section 1 features five key tools I use in my assessment process, each of which was developed to solve a particular coaching or assessment challenge. In Section 2, I describe six exercises I've found handy to use with clients when they're feeling negative or stuck in some way, or need additional career guidance. In Section 3, I walk you through the process of managing career assessment instruments, from purchase to cost recovery, including tips on working with test publishers.

It's important to note that this book is not intended as a general introduction to career assessment or career assessment instruments. That ground is extensively covered in more formal texts and reference books, including publications by the National Career Development Association. (See Appendix B for details on some key texts.) Instead, *Game Plan* offers a unique, behind-the-scenes, highly personal look at assessment as a practice and a specialty. It took me years to develop the right interview questions, decide which assessment instruments I wanted to use, and fine-tune my process so I could get the results I wanted with clients. I'm excited to share that hard-won wisdom in this book.

Finally, a quick note on terminology: As a student or working career professional, you may already be familiar with many of the terms I use in the book. However, to ensure there's no confusion, I've included a glossary of assessment-related terms in Appendix A.

A SPECIAL NOTE FOR INSTRUCTORS: USING THE BOOK IN YOUR CLASS

If you're teaching an introductory or advanced course in career counseling or coaching, *Game Plan* can be used as supplemental reading, helping students envision working with clients and managing assessments in their own practice or professional role. In presenting to classes on career development and assessment, I have found that students are hungry for real-world information, the kind they usually don't get a lot of in courses focused on theory. *Game Plan* is intended to meet that need, providing readers with helpful tips and observations from my practice, and filled with details of my own experience as a career counselor and coach.

With its thematic arrangement, the book allows you to focus on whatever is of most interest to you and your students—your students' own career development (Part 1), client career assessment (Part 2), special issues related to the work environment (Part 3), or career stories and case studies illustrating the application or study of assessment (Part 4). Part 5, "The Quick-Reference Toolkit," can be used to focus on specific challenges or tasks students may encounter in their practice, such as signing up with test publishers to deliver assessments to clients.

One feature of the book you may find particularly helpful is the reflection questions and tips at the end of each chapter in Parts 1 to 4. These are intended to get readers thinking about various topics in the chapter in terms of their own professional experience or study. Here's an example from Part 1, chapter 1: "Having a network of colleagues whom you can refer work to, and who can refer work to you, extends your capabilities well beyond what you can offer yourself. What other counselors and coaches could you partner with in order to create a more dynamic experience for the clients you serve? If you are currently a counseling student, ask your fellow students what they think their focus might be."

Finally, because *Game Plan* reflects my own experience as an independent career counselor, coach, and consultant—and is therefore limited by that experience—I felt it was important to also provide readers with a broader view. In Appendix B you'll find overviews of several career assessment texts, many of which address important trends that may be of interest to you and your students. For example, the National Career Development Association (NCDA) has for years published a guide to career assessment instruments that offers not only detailed reviews of those instruments but also foundational chapters on emerging trends and issues, standards and competencies for practitioners, the use of computers in assessment, and multicultural considerations in assessment. The latest (seventh) edition of this guide, titled *A Comprehensive Guide to Career Assessment*, has a global reach and has chapters (as part of its online component) covering career assessment in Asia, Australia, Canada, Europe, the Middle East, and South Africa. For more on this guide and other NCDA books and periodicals, go to ncda.org and select Publications.

Part 1

. . . .

ASSESSING YOURSELF
AND YOUR CAREER

Chapter 1

. . . .

SPECIALIZING IN CAREER ASSESSMENT

I've called *Game Plan* an "insider's guide" for a reason. Career assessment work can be a bit of a mystery. This chapter sheds light on what it's like to specialize in assessment—that is, to regularly use formal assessment tools like the Myers-Briggs Type Indicator (MBTI) assessment, Strong Interest Inventory assessment, 16PF Questionnaire, and other career assessment instruments as part of your services to clients. That's followed by guidance on self-assessment for career counselors and coaches (chapter 2) and reaching out to others through networking (chapter 3). Whether or not you decide to specialize in assessment, these chapters will help you get a better sense of your overall strengths and direction.

In this chapter we'll first look at some of the benefits of specializing in assessment, should you choose to do so. Second, I'll walk you through several examples of colleagues with whom I collaborate in my work, some of whom have an assessment background but prefer to outsource the work. Finally, we'll take a look at what it takes to be a "go-to" person for career assessment in terms of knowledge you must have and investments you must make.

If you do decide you want to specialize in assessment, there are two other places in the book where you'll want to spend some time. First, in chapter 6 I describe the battery of tests I use and also offer tips on how to learn more about assessment instruments, especially if you're just starting out. Second, in Section 3 of "The Quick-Reference Toolkit" (Part 5 of the book), I walk you through some of the procedures for purchasing and administering assessments, including working with test publishers, reducing your expenses, and recovering costs.

THE BENEFITS OF SPECIALIZING IN ASSESSMENT

Regardless of your field, specialization allows you to get noticed and stand out from the crowd. It's easier to get referrals, because when people think of your name, they automatically think of your expertise. I love being known as the "test guy" in my local market. It's a big part of my brand and a badge of honor for me. When people call me for assessment, I feel I've earned their trust and respect. I take pride in being a trusted professional who can reliably provide value to clients.

Recognition as an expert and development of a clear brand is just one benefit of specializing in assessment. Here are some additional benefits to consider:

- Clients respect and value assessments expertise.
- You'll find consulting opportunities in related areas.
- You'll gain an enhanced understanding of assessment technology.

When you're able to make formal assessments easily available to clients, who expect and value this service, you gain their trust. In addition to asking about credentials, clients frequently ask me about which assessments I offer, how long I've been using them, whether I've been certified, and so on. My knowledge of assessment leads to regular referrals from colleagues. I've also had clients do testing with me and later hire me to do similar testing with their kids.

Once you've mastered some key assessment instruments, you'll find opportunities in outplacement, selection assessment, training and development, and other areas. Most consulting opportunities I've enjoyed have been directly attributable to my ability to offer assessments. These projects can last for years and add significantly to your income. (Consulting engagements tend to be more lucrative than regular client work.) For one project, I provided training services to a leading Minnesota health care provider over a three-year period. Another multi-year project involved doing selection assessment—helping the client hire and promote employees—for a Fortune 500 company.

Finally, when you use assessments frequently in your work, you gain a special knowledge and appreciation for what goes into them and what's required to create them. And this could even inspire you to try creating your own assessment products. I likely never would have created my Career Compatibility Scale (CCS), a work values and job satisfaction assessment tool, without having knowledge of how career assessments are researched and put together. I discuss the CCS in detail in chapter 9.

WORKING WITH COLLEAGUES WITH COMPLEMENTARY SKILLS

No matter how well equipped we are to provide assessment services, none of us can do it all. In my own case, some of my career counselor or coaching colleagues have experience with formal assessments but want to focus their efforts elsewhere when working with clients, so they may refer clients to me for career assessment only. Others might practice assessment and have subject expertise or competence I lack, so I refer clients to them for both coaching and assessment. Still others don't practice assessment at all but have deep knowledge or competence in a particular area that I lack, such as social media. In those cases, we refer clients to each other for specific services.

For example, my colleagues Pete and George have both referred clients to me. Pete is an executive coach with deep expertise in positive psychology. He occasionally has me do career assessment of his clients so he can focus on coaching them. George, an executive coach who works with individuals over age fifty building encore careers, sometimes refers nonexecutives to me for career assessment. I have occasionally worked with executives but generally prefer working with individual contributors (like technical professionals and project managers), so occasionally I refer clients needing leadership coaching or development to Pete and George.

My colleague Ann happens to love working with clients who are transitioning from the military. This is a specialized area where I feel I am less competent and experienced, so I would refer transitioning vets to her. And because Ann is a licensed psychologist skilled at assessment, she takes care of that, too. Ann might refer clients to me if they fall outside *her* subject expertise.

As a LinkedIn expert and former recruiter, Lonny provides important expertise I lack. While I do help clients gather information they need to prepare strong LinkedIn profiles as part of my assessment process, Lonny is the expert when it comes to the marketing and technical aspects. So I might work with clients on coaching and assessment but send them to Lonny for in-depth help with setting up their LinkedIn profiles and with marketing themselves. Lonny in turn refers clients to me for career coaching and assessment.

I've worked together with Bruce, a psychologist, for over twenty years on a variety of projects, including selection assessment for a Fortune 500 company. In recent years, Bruce has focused his work on leadership development, helping individuals and teams perform at their best. Since much of his time is spent managing his consulting firm, conducting workshops, and traveling for speaking engagements, he sometimes refers clients to me for career counseling and coaching.

For over ten years until she retired, Sandy routinely referred clients to me for career work (interview, assessments, career focus), while she attended to their emotional well-being through her expertise as a therapist. This was an enjoyable, mutually beneficial partnership and one where our complementary skills were put to good use.

There are many more examples too numerous to mention here, but you can start to see the possibilities for collaboration and referrals. These kinds of partnerships are particularly important for those of us who run solo businesses or work in small consulting firms. We can't do it all, and we create win-win relationships and results when we partner with folks who have different niches or areas of expertise.

Special Referrals: Sharing Client Work with Colleagues

When a colleague who's the primary coach or counselor requests my services to do assessment work for the client, we create a collaboration based on our different insights and contributions that can benefit the client.

In a typical collaboration, my colleague will do some kind of interview or needs assessment with the client. They will let the client know what they can or cannot do to help based on the client's request or situation. If they determine that the client might benefit from some kind of assessment (for example, career, IQ, personality) that they either cannot do or do not wish to do, they might then contact me. Of course, before they do that, they will ask the client if they are willing to work with another counselor.

If the client agrees to see me, I'll conduct an initial interview to get a sense of what they are doing with the primary coach or counselor and what I can do for them—a clarification of my role and professional boundaries with respect to their relationship with their primary. Depending on what I discover from this initial inquiry, I might do my whole structured interview (see chapter 5) or an abbreviated version of it. Or I might do some hybrid of that and other questions, depending on the situation. (Sometimes issues other than career are involved, like major life transitions.) This helps me confirm what kind of assessment is needed.

While this work is going on, the primary coach or counselor and I might talk on the phone and share insights. (We will ensure that the proper releases of information are in order in these cases.) For example, when Sandy sent me clients for career work, she and I would talk about their progress during the engagement.

With this kind of referral, the client usually pays me directly for my part of the service. In some situations (outplacement projects, for example), the primary consultant gets the entire fee but pays the counselor or coach directly for services performed based on time and materials. Often, that's a situation where the client's employer is picking up the tab.

These partnerships are a great source of satisfaction for me. I feel flattered to be called upon to assist, and I know I'm adding value because clients benefit from the wisdom of two different counselors with insights to offer—insights arrived at in different, but complementary, ways. After I'm finished working with a client, the primary counselor and I will often compare notes on themes and characteristics that jumped out at us. It's fun to be able to discover an attribute or piece of information my colleague wasn't aware of, because this information can then be woven into their work with the client. This kind of synergy is very gratifying.

INVESTING IN ASSESSMENT SERVICES AND CAPABILITIES

If you're willing to build solid credentials and have a passion for helping clients find direction, specializing in assessment can be a viable route for you and help you brand yourself and your services. But to be a go-to person in this area, you do need to invest in the necessary training and resources, what I like to think of as an assessment infrastructure. Here are five key strategies to set yourself up as a go-to person for assessment:

1. Establish accounts with reputable test publishers.
2. Know and follow proper standards for test administration.
3. Pursue ongoing training to refresh your skills and stay up to date.

4. Extend your capabilities by networking with colleagues.
5. Commit to improving your overall assessment process.

First, once you create accounts with test publishers and purchase inventory, you can provide your clients with instant access to career assessment tests. Most of the tests I use come from the Myers Briggs Company (formerly CPP), and I have tests already in the system I can administer when needed. It's just a matter of providing the links and passwords to clients. If a colleague sends me a client who needs to take the MBTI assessment, it only takes me a few minutes to get the client set up. For details on how all this works, see Section 3 of "The Quick-Reference Toolkit."

Second, providers of career assessment services are expected to know and follow the correct protocols for administering and interpreting career assessment tests. So once you're up and running, you'll want to adhere to the standards. These are generally set by the publisher and may differ from one test to another. Other guidance comes from state licensing boards and associations like the National Career Development Association (NCDA). For more information, go to the NCDA website, select Standards, and then click on Career Counselor Assessment and Evaluation Competencies.

Third, it's important to pursue training to stay up to date and in demand. As a psychologist in the state of Minnesota, I'm required to complete 40 CEUs every two years. But beyond that, I try to stay current with any new developments that arise, particularly those that relate to the core tests I use. This increases the value I add and gives me continued confidence that I'm providing the best possible service to my clients.

Fourth, be sure to tap into the expertise of your colleagues to extend your own capabilities. My assessment infrastructure includes my network. Having a robust network means I can extend what I offer to clients beyond my own services, and colleagues can do the same by referring clients to me. They add to my own capabilities and know-how by being open to questions and offering their insights on complex assessment situations, such as unusual test patterns or varying test results from multiple instruments. (See chapter 3 for more on networking.)

Finally, strive to continually improve your overall assessment process, which will also include informal assessment techniques such as interviewing and client worksheets. I consider my larger career assessment process—from the structured interview to the game plan—to be the heart of what I do, and I'm constantly looking for ways to make it better.

REFLECTING ON CHAPTER 1:
SPECIALIZING IN CAREER ASSESSMENT

The NCDA lists assessment third in its list of minimum career competencies for career counselors (see ncda.org, Standards). However, the reality is that not all career counselors and coaches choose to focus on assessment. If you haven't already, consider researching career development professionals in your area to see who's doing what.

Specialization in formal assessments can lead to opportunities beyond working with individual clients, such as work in selection assessment and outplacement. If you're not yet familiar with these professional services and what they entail, consider doing some networking and research. (See chapter 3 for tips on networking. Also, see the Glossary in Appendix A for definitions of these services.)

If you are currently working as a career counselor or coach but not yet using career assessment instruments such as the MBTI assessment and Strong Interest Inventory assessment, have you found that clients are asking for these services? If so, you will find lots of ideas in this book on how to get started. If you have clients who are asking for formal assessments but you'd rather *not* conduct that work, to whom might you refer them?

Having a network of colleagues whom you can refer work to, and who can refer work to you, extends your capabilities well beyond what you can offer yourself. What other counselors and coaches could you partner with in order to create a more dynamic experience for the clients you serve? If you are currently a counseling student, ask your fellow students what they think their focus might be.

To be a go-to person for assessment, you need to build certain capabilities, as discussed in the last section of this chapter. If the idea of specializing in assessment is appealing to you, what steps can you start taking now toward that goal? Write them down. Also, consider writing a game plan (see chapter 8).

Chapter 2

EXPLORING YOUR STRENGTHS

Several years ago my mastermind group decided to read *The Mindful Coach* by Doug Silsbee. In the book, Silsbee presents what he calls "the seven voices of the coach," which are actually seven *roles* coaches can play during a coaching engagement: Master, Partner, Investigator, Reflector, Teacher, Guide, and Contractor. Each entails what he calls "aspects," or functions, the role carries out. So, for example, one function of the Reflector is to provide "direct and honest feedback."

When my group read the book, one of our goals was to identify which of the roles sounded most like us and which we most wanted to play. For me, the Partner and Guide roles really felt "on brand." The Partner role is all about structure: being clear about how the engagement will work, who's responsible for what, and when decisions should be made about what comes next. The Guide role is all about action: deciding, in consultation with the client, what needs to be done and then doing it. These roles are in keeping with my assessment process, which is structured and action oriented. Knowing that this works for me is both comforting and satisfying.

When I first started out in private practice as a career counselor and coach, I used to take on almost any project or client, which sometimes worked out but just as often left me feeling stressed. It took years before I was able to establish a brand and a niche I was comfortable with. For me that was being the "test guy" who works best with mid-level, mid-career professionals and technicians. It was a huge relief to finally figure this out and not try to be all things to all people. Better to find a role that comes naturally than to force yourself into something that's against your nature.

If figuring out your strengths and ideal niche has been a struggle for you, don't worry. It does take time, but it *will* come together for you. The strategies in this chapter should help. It also helps to find out what others have done. In Part 4 of the book, "Career Stories and Transformations," you'll find a Q&A in which I share my own career history, including why I decided to focus on assessment as a specialty.

UNDERSTANDING YOUR SWEET SPOT

Your sweet spot is where three things intersect: your strengths or gifts, your passion, and what the market needs. It's a good way to think about what kind of clients you want to work with. Let's say you have a knack for and interest in business; perhaps you earned an MBA at some point. You're also passionate about helping others grow and develop. In the business world—particularly today—there's an ongoing need for coaches and counselors who understand business and can help develop business leaders. In fact, several of my colleagues work in this area.

My own sweet spot? I enjoy and am good at assessment and analysis. I love helping people manage career change and other difficult transitions, particularly those working in technical or frontline positions—folks who work hard but don't get all the attention and don't enjoy all the advantages executives and upper-level managers do. While what I do is perhaps not as hot or prestigious as leadership coaching, there's a steady demand for my career transition and assessment services. I especially enjoy working with people who want to refocus and are motivated to change.

Here are three recommendations for determining your sweet spot:

1. Learn more about yourself through self-assessment.
2. Consult with colleagues for additional insights.
3. Pay close attention to what you enjoy doing.

In Part 2 of the book, I describe the assessment process I use with clients. Consider trying some of these tools as part of your own self-assessment. Answer the structured interview questions. Complete some of the tests from the core battery of instruments if you haven't taken them already. Complete the information processing worksheets. Write a game plan. All of these tools will help you get to know yourself better, as well as give you a feel for how you can use them with your own clients. I've also found certain books to be critical for developing greater self-awareness and self-confidence. See the sidebar "Five Key Books for Self-Development" for titles I highly recommend.

In chapter 1, I discussed how I work with colleagues with complementary skills. Collaborating with colleagues can tell you a lot about your own strengths, because they often see strengths in you that you can't easily see in yourself. In chapter 3, we'll delve deeper into networking, which I've personally benefited from in my career. My participation in a mastermind group, in which we regularly compare skill sets and service offerings and support each other in taking on new initiatives, has been particularly beneficial.

Finally, when you are working with clients and colleagues, pay close attention to what you most enjoy doing. *The Mindful Coach* is a good resource if you're interested in exploring your strengths as a counselor or coach. Determining which of the coaching roles you do best can help you shape your own assessment process. I'm most in my element when I'm partnering with and guiding my clients to success by encouraging them to act. When are you most in your element?

. . . .

FIVE KEY BOOKS FOR SELF-DEVELOPMENT

I like to think that we're on something of a parallel track with our clients. To help them, we also have to help ourselves. And some of our best inspiration comes not from books written for us as career development professionals but from books targeted at a more general audience. Here, alphabetically by author, are five books I've learned from myself and frequently recommend to my clients.

***Designing Your Life*, by Dave Evans and Bill Burnett**
I love their bias for action and emphasis on work-life balance. And as someone who hates to put all my eggs in one basket, I appreciate their idea of building multiple prototypes over time as needed. There's more than just one path that's possible. I worked through both their "Good Time Journal" and "Odyssey Plan" exercises and learned a lot from each. The journal,

which I kept for a couple of weeks, helps you track your actions over time to see what gives you the most energy. With the Odyssey Plan, you plan three alternative lives for yourself using notes and drawings on a timeline—a great way to combine logic and creativity in one exercise.

Working Identity, by Herminia Ibarra

I like her idea that we not only "work our identity"—take action that determines who we become—but by taking that action create an identity that's more meaningful to us. In other words, we find congruence between what we do and who we are. In the game plan (described in chapter 8), I have clients work toward determining what criteria they need to thrive in their lives and their work. We build these criteria both by thinking—analyzing insights from the interview and from test results—and by doing (homework). Ibarra stresses taking a number of small steps to build confidence, something I endorse and follow in my work with clients.

Repacking Your Bags, by Richard Leider and David Shapiro

I find in my practice that many people are overburdened by trying to carry too much in their lives. The authors talk about focusing and de-cluttering our lives in terms of three key "bags" we carry: place (where we live in the world), relationships (people we care for and identify with), and work (how we make our living). When we only carry what we most need or want, it moves us from a place of unconscious acceptance to a more intentional state. In the game plan, I explore similar ideas—the what, where, and who of what we need to thrive, but with more focus on career and work. *Repacking Your Bags* is broader in scope—about life in general.

Callings, by Gregg Levoy

Levoy talks about attending to recurring themes or "boomerangs" in life—thoughts, situations, or feelings that keep coming back over time. He suggests that we receive messages or "callings" regularly, but that we may not pay close enough attention to them. He invites us to be aware of these callings, sort out the question (or questions) behind the message, and make a conscious decision whether to act on the calling. In the same way, I believe that the assessment process brings to awareness recurring themes and encourages the client to invite those themes into their life in some capacity.

Learned Optimism, by Martin Seligman

When we or our clients are going through difficult career transitions or exploring career possibilities, we need resilience in order to withstand uncertainty, disappointments, and other challenges. Those of us who are optimistic will persist and move forward; those weighed down by negativity may not be able to act when they need to. The book shows how to build resilience by overcoming and dealing with negativity. Not only has it helped me personally, but it's also been key to my process, especially elements like my structured interview and exercises I use when clients need a boost in self-confidence.

Interestingly, not all of the authors mentioned here are champions of assessment or career counseling and coaching in general. In two of the books, in fact, *Designing Your Life* and *Working Identity,* the authors are quite skeptical about career counseling and assessment in particular, believing that true wisdom comes only from taking action and seeing what results, not through career testing and heartfelt discussions with counselors and coaches about what it all means.

I agree with the authors on the importance of taking action, which is one of the reasons they're included in this list. However, I also believe that career assessment provides important fuel for thought and discussion, which can then propel clients to action—*educated* action. Too often clients haven't really thought things through or are paralyzed by confusion or self-doubt. Often they lack a firm grasp of their true strengths and weaknesses. And sometimes we as their counselors and coaches are in the same boat! Let's use whatever tools we can to build our own self-awareness so we can better help our clients.

DETERMINE THE BEST ENVIRONMENT FOR YOU

There are many possible work environments to choose from—university career centers, schools, workforce centers, private practice, consulting firms. Each environment will be different in terms of the roles you get to play, your level of interaction with colleagues, the pace of work, the extent of control you have over your schedule, and other factors. One of the most important factors, of course, is clientele. If you're working at a university career center, students will be your primary clients. If you're working at a consulting firm, the companies the firm provides services to are likely to be your primary clients. And so on.

I have found that working in private practice, along with frequent collaboration with colleagues, works best for me. I'm free to use whatever assessment tools I want, which is not always the case in other environments. I get to control my own schedule and decide which clients I work with. There are tradeoffs, of course. While my college career center colleagues have a built-in network—other counselors, professors, academic staff—I work alone and so must create my own network. They also have built-in clients! But on balance, I love my work as an independent.

Here are some tips for determining the best environment for you:

- Know yourself in order to know your environment.
- Understand what criteria you need to thrive at work.
- Study what your colleagues are doing and why that works for them.

Consider what we talked about in the previous section on finding your sweet spot. Knowing what that is will tell you a lot about what will be a good environment for you. In my case, for example, I'm good at assessment and analysis, and I enjoy using those skills to help my clients. Again, working in private practice has given me the freedom to shape my own assessment process and use whatever assessment instruments I deem appropriate. And, as I explained in the previous chapter, my specialization in assessment has resulted in many successful collaborations with other consultants. What do you most enjoy doing, and what kind of working environment would best allow for that?

Another good way to determine your best work environment is to write down your criteria for thriving in your work. In chapter 8, you'll learn about the game plan, a simple template for recording your work needs in three areas: *what* you do, *where* you do it, and *whom* you work with. Having some clarity in these three areas can go a long way to determining which environments would allow that to take place. To take an example from my own game plan—you'll find it in chapter 8—I enjoy working with both individuals and organizations, and my private practice gives me that flexibility.

Finally, for comparison purposes, think about what some of your colleagues are doing and why that works for them. One of my colleagues, Vic, is a director of career and professional development services at the University of Minnesota. An extrovert with a big heart, Vic loves working directly with students and helping them find their true selves. He's also a voracious reader who enjoys sharing what he learns through blogging and classroom presentations, an excellent fit for a learning environment like a university. Vic has spent most of his career in academia, and every time I see him, he seems passionate about his work and more committed than ever to helping his clients.

A great way to compare notes with colleagues is through a mastermind group. See chapter 3 for more about building your network.

DISCOVER AND HONE YOUR LEADERSHIP STYLE

Years ago a colleague who works in leadership coaching and development made a comment that I thought was profound at the time and has stuck with me ever since. He said that we're all leaders, but some of us just don't realize it. It's easy to believe that there are leaders and followers and that most of us fall into the latter category. But the reality is much more interesting and nuanced. We're all leaders in our own right; we just need to discover what that means to us personally and where we can make our best contribution.

I believe that as career development professionals, we are by definition leaders. Any career in which you are helping to shape someone's future is a leadership role. At the same time, we are no different from our clients in that we're obligated—if we want to be successful—to become as self-aware as possible and use our gifts wisely. And that includes understanding our leadership style and how we lead best. With that in mind, here are three strategies to try:

1. Use assessment instruments to examine your leadership strengths and style.
2. Adapt your assessment process based on your leadership strengths.
3. Take risks that enhance your leadership potential and understanding.

Earlier in this chapter I suggested you get to know yourself better by trying some of the assessment techniques recommended in this book. Using formal assessments can be a powerful way to examine your leadership potential. For example, the California Psychological Inventory (CPI) assessments are often used for that purpose. With the CPI, high scores relating to dominance, responsibility, self-acceptance, and empathy are often associated with success in management.

Having taken the CPI (most frequently the CPI 434) several times over the years, my own scores, while rising over time, have stayed in the moderate range. This is consistent with the collaborative style I prefer to have with clients, as well as the Partner and Guide roles I tend to play. Both of these are also consistent with my overall assessment process, which stresses client input and responsibility and lots of action through homework and the completion of a game plan. For more on the assessment process I use with my clients, see chapter 4.

Finally, taking some risks and stepping out of your comfort zone will help you further develop and hone your leadership potential, as well as see yourself in a new light. Back in 2000 I took on a leadership role that was a stretch for me at the time and tested my self-confidence. I've never regretted it, because it immediately expanded my network and opened up new opportunities for me. For details of that experience, see chapter 3.

REFLECTING ON CHAPTER 2:
EXPLORING YOUR STRENGTHS

What have you learned about yourself so far that will help you determine your sweet spot—that point where your strengths, your passions, and market needs intersect? One of the recommendations in this chapter is to learn more about yourself through assessment, including trying some of the assessment tools in the book. Based on any self-assessment work you've done to this point, what have you discovered?

Think about any counseling or coaching work you've done with clients in your current business or role, or in your practice sessions or internships if you are studying for your degree. What have you observed about what you particularly enjoy in your interactions with clients? What role (or roles) do you most enjoy? Reading *The Mindful Coach*, which we discussed in this chapter, can be helpful for thinking about the role or roles you most want to play in your work with clients.

The environment you choose to work in—private practice, university career center, school, workforce center, consulting firm—can have a major impact on how happy and successful you are in your work. What kind of environment is best for you? If you are a working career counselor or coach, are you happy in your current environment?

In this chapter I recommended that you observe your colleagues and think about why they are well suited to their particular environment and role. What can you learn from colleagues who are successful and happy in their work? If you are currently a student, what have you noticed about your fellow classmates in terms of their strengths? Consider getting together and comparing notes.

As a current or future career counselor and coach, you are by definition playing a leadership role. With that in mind, how would you describe your own leadership style? If you're curious about your leadership potential, consider getting tested in the California Psychological Inventory (I recommend the CPI 434), a respected leadership assessment instrument. Find someone who's trained in the CPI, and hire them to administer the assessment and provide you with feedback. It can be an effective way to get deeper insights into your leadership skills and also experience how assessment results are communicated.

Chapter 3

. . . .

BUILDING YOUR NETWORK

One day early in 1994, while browsing through an association newsletter, I came upon a short article about Richard Bents. At a recent meeting of the American Society for Training and Development (ASTD), now the Association for Talent Development, Bents had presented on German-American leadership and business practices. I'd visited Germany a few times and even lived there briefly, and I was intrigued by what I read of Bents's work. Although somewhat apprehensive, I picked up the phone and called him, and we set up an appointment to have lunch.

Since that time, Rich and I have worked on many projects together, including two consulting gigs in Germany. In June 1997, we organized a German-American business partnership conference in St. Paul, Minnesota, which was followed by a series of monthly business meetings over several years. In 2010 we launched the Career Compatibility Scale (CCS), a work values and job satisfaction assessment tool. (See chapter 9 for more on the CCS.) In 2012, one of Rich's clients, a medical equipment manufacturer, was entering a busy hiring phase and needed assistance with selection assessment. Rich alerted me to the opportunity, which resulted in a three-year project with the company.

I met Rich by taking a risk—I reached out, not knowing if anything would come of the effort. Of course, meeting Rich all started with my ASTD membership and that newsletter article. In our field, as in many professions, belonging to professional associations can be a major boon to your career, connecting you with influential people, keeping you up to date on developments in the field, and alerting you to new opportunities. So in this chapter I want to look at two ways to get out there to connect and learn: first, by joining professional associations, and second, by forming or joining a mastermind group.

Before we go further, there's another point I want to make about reaching out. I have found that connecting with others can lessen fear and anxiety, which tend to increase when you're isolated from others. In fact, one of the presentations I most enjoy delivering, "Fear Busters: From Apprehension to Connection," is based on that premise. Whenever I've presented it to career counselors and other career development professionals, it's been well received and generated lots of interesting conversation.

The key message in "Fear Busters" is that keeping yourself isolated from others will tend to keep you stuck in place. When you're isolated, you may lack the kind of focus you get from interacting with others. You may also lack the kind of support and problem-solving assistance that comes naturally when you reach out to your peers. Worst of all, keeping yourself isolated can heighten fear. When you connect with others, you open yourself up to new options and ways of doing things, which can make you less fearful and apprehensive about the future.

JOINING PROFESSIONAL ASSOCIATIONS

Over a thirty-plus-year career, I've belonged to and benefited from a number of professional associations besides ASTD—the American Psychological Association, the Minnesota Career Development Association (MCDA), the Minnesota Professionals for Psychology Applied to Work (MPPAW), the National Career Development Association (NCDA), and the Minnesota chapter of the National Speakers Association. While I have since dropped some of these memberships—some became less relevant or essential over time—the collective benefit of having belonged to these groups is immeasurable. Association memberships can result in friendships, referrals, and professional opportunities; a rich array of learning and educational options; and opportunities to serve in, and benefit from, leadership roles.

One of the greatest benefits of belonging to professional associations is connecting socially. My MCDA colleagues, whom I fondly refer to as my peeps, are a rich source of friendships, referrals, and professional opportunities. It was an MCDA colleague who recruited me for what became a multi-year project doing selection assessment for a Fortune 500 retail company. And it was through MCDA that I first met many of the members of my mastermind group, which has been meeting for well over a decade now. MPPAW is particularly relevant to my interests in formal assessment, and over the years I've developed some close ties with members of the organization, some of whom have developed their own assessment instruments for the corporate sector.

Associations are an important source of learning and education. Through scheduled events and publication programs, they can significantly expand your knowledge of career counseling and assessment. At MCDA, for example, I've attended presentations on formal assessments given by others, including by MBTI assessment expert Jean Kummerow, and presented some of my own. Through MPPAW, I've had exposure to the technical and research aspects of testing as they're applied to work settings and human resource management. (Hogan Assessments, a pioneer in assessment and workplace performance, is one of MPPAW's sponsors.) And through my membership in the NCDA, I receive the *Career Development Quarterly*, which frequently covers career assessment instruments in its articles.

Finally, taking on leadership and mentoring roles can boost your self-confidence and expand your visibility and networking opportunities. From 2000 to 2001 I served as MCDA president (see the sidebar "Becoming a Leader: A Personal Story"). While president, I had the opportunity to shape many MCDA offerings to better address the needs of independent practitioners, which were underserved at the time, and some of these offerings involved formal assessments. Later, from 2009 through 2010, I took part in a peer-coaching partnership through ASTD that involved working with a PhD student on career assessment—coaching her on interviewing, career assessment instruments, and goal planning for clients. We both learned a lot and grew professionally through this partnership.

BECOMING A LEADER: A PERSONAL STORY

Early in my career as an employee and later as a solo career coach, I really didn't give much thought to the role or value of leadership in my day-to-day activities. Intellectually, of course, I knew that some people were leaders and some were followers. And, having administered personality assessments, I was aware that attributes like "dominance," "boldness," "self-acceptance," and "independence" often went hand in hand with leadership.

But this was all quite theoretical, and gradually I realized something was missing in my own experience. If I was going to work with and counsel leaders or would-be leaders, it would be great to have some leadership experience of my own. But the opportunities to lead seemed limited for me as a solo practitioner.

Then in 1998, colleagues in the MCDA suggested that I run for an open seat on the board. It sounded intriguing, so I jumped at the chance. During my second year, I was encouraged to run for president-elect, and I won. The following year (2000–2001), I was president, and suddenly reality set in.

Although the thought of serving as president was exciting, I was, to be quite honest, scared to death. I had never led a professional group before and had no idea what I was doing. During the first three to four months, I scrambled to learn all I could. As someone who thrives on detail, I quickly studied as much as possible, talked to all the other board members, came up with agendas and initiatives, and hung on for dear life! Those early months passed by in a blur. I felt I was constantly running and, at times, on the verge of a panic attack.

And then, somehow, things just seemed to fall into place. I had a great board to assist me, I achieved consensus on most of my ideas, and best of all, key initiatives—events, programs, writing—were actually getting done. Not only did it turn out to be a great year for the MCDA, it was also one of the most eye-opening, and inspiring, experiences of my career. I had more confidence in my abilities than ever before, a deeper understanding of my strengths and weaknesses, and a bigger, more effective professional network.

In the past I hadn't been intentional in building a network. But through my MCDA presidency, it happened naturally, and I soon had new referrals and much greater visibility than I'd had in the past.

I tell you this story for a couple of reasons. First, if you're currently feeling less than confident about your own professional abilities or offerings, know that this feeling will pass. But you must move out of your comfort zone. As the late, great Dr. Susan Jeffers taught us, we must "feel the fear and do it anyway." Second, we're more credible to clients when we teach by example. We routinely urge our clients to get out there and try new things. But showing how you've done this yourself—especially if you've overcome fear and grown in the process—provides much greater value and also enhances your own self-confidence as a professional. Never underestimate the power of being a role model.

MASTERMIND GROUPS

It's easy to go to meetings or networking events and make only superficial contact, briefly catching up with the regulars or exchanging business cards, perhaps connecting on LinkedIn. Consider engaging more substantially, especially with people you know and respect and with whom you have interests in common. Meet regularly with your key allies and partners for both social outlet and to exchange new ideas and resources. Ask them directly if you can be a resource for them and they for you. Establish peer coaching groups, like a mastermind group—a group formed by colleagues to provide advice and mutual support to members on matters of business and professional development.

My own mastermind group got started in 2007 with two initial members, me and my colleague George. He and I had been part of an earlier mastermind group of five people formed as part of the Minnesota branch of the National Speakers Association. After that group disbanded—not all of the members were committed to give as much as they took away—we decided to start our own group, with George spearheading the effort. Eventually our group grew to eight people, and we've been meeting now for over fourteen years.

Participating in a mastermind group has a number of benefits: a consistent schedule and structure that keeps meetings productive, regular opportunities to receive and offer advice on business problems and challenges, and mutual support through professional and personal crises.

For two hours each month, typically on a Wednesday, we meet at a centrally located restaurant. (During the COVID-19 pandemic, we continue to meet monthly via Zoom and still have rich, enjoyable discussions and new learning.)

We share responsibility for planning and leading discussions on a wide range of topics, including new techniques we've learned about, a book we're reading as a group, or a product or speech someone's developing they'd like feedback on. Sometimes we invite speakers to present on a topic of interest. In addition to our monthly meetings, we hold potlucks twice a year to both socialize and engage in some long-term planning. The group has been a great way to maximize our resources and have fun doing it.

Because we all have independent practices, many of our meetings are focused on our businesses. We've used the group to better identify our ideal clients, make referrals to one another, and challenge ourselves with new ideas and initiatives. Looking back at my notes for the group, I see that a couple of our early meetings were devoted to formal assessments. We asked the group what formal assessments they were using in their practice. This survey helped us determine which members we could refer clients to if we weren't using a particular assessment ourselves, and what new assessments we might want to learn. For example, I first learned about the Hogan assessments, which measure work performance, personality, and leadership, at one of these meetings and later pursued training in their use.

Our group goes beyond business matters to attend to members' personal and emotional needs. At every meeting, there's time for socializing before we get down to business, and that's when we catch up with what's going on in our lives. If someone is going through a personal or professional challenge, we serve as sounding boards and offer support. Over the years, there have been many personal and professional crises among our members: starting a new business; coping with difficult clients; accidents and illnesses; the deaths of parents and siblings; breakups and marriages. We're always there to support one another, and that's invaluable.

Everyone in my mastermind group is involved in career counseling and coaching in some way. Three do primarily executive coaching and development, four work with a range of clients, including executives, and I work mostly with nonexecutives. Three of us are licensed psychologists and have a strong interest in career assessment. We all own businesses, and some of us also partner with other consulting firms.

One great thing about belonging to a group like this is that we get to know each other and our unique strengths well. This both enriches the group and results in referrals.

After years of working with me, my colleagues know I'm a detailed-oriented guy who appreciates data and structure. They know I'm task-focused and like to get things done. They also know that while I've worked with all kind of clients, I especially enjoy working with folks in technical fields like IT, engineering, finance, and health care.

The three of us who are licensed psychologists often compare notes on test interpretations and other assessment matters. One of the psychologists, Tamara, tutored me early on in my career when I was first learning how to do formal assessments. Because others in the group are trained in assessment but prefer to focus their work in other areas, we can sometimes be a resource for them, and they a source of referrals for us.

With the majority of the group doing at least some leadership coaching and development, there's plenty of collective knowledge to draw from in that area. And some members have interesting specialties related to leadership. For example, Molly follows Brené Brown (research professor and author of *Dare to Lead*) and incorporates some of Brown's principles into her work. Carmen is an expert in personal branding and is Reach-certified.

When it comes to type, our group tends to mirror career counseling and coaching in general. According to the Myers-Briggs Type Indicator (MBTI) assessment, I'm an ISTJ (Introverted, Sensing, Thinking, Judging), a rare bird in a field dominated by intuitives. The majority of our group members are ENFs (Extraverted, Intuitive, Feeling). I like to think that given my type, I bring a kind of quiet, common-sense, bottom-line approach my colleagues appreciate. For their part, my more extraverted colleagues are gregarious, fun, caring, and full of great ideas. Belonging to the group is one of the best things I've done for my business and my career.

REFLECTING ON CHAPTER 3:
BUILDING YOUR NETWORK

In your career so far, what times can you remember when you took a chance by reaching out to someone—especially someone you didn't know—for help with career issues you were encountering or to discuss something of mutual interest, as I did with Rich? Were you nervous or apprehensive before connecting? What good things resulted from your willingness to connect?

My presentation "Fear Busters: From Apprehension to Connection" is all about reducing fear by connecting with others instead of remaining isolated. If you are feeling fearful or apprehensive about your current career situation or prospects, know that reaching out to others will help.

Some professional associations can serve you well for a while but then become less relevant as your career develops. In my own career, ASTD (now the Association for Talent Development) was a key resource for many years. Later, however, as I moved further into career counseling and coaching and specializing in assessment, it became less relevant to my needs. What's your current strategy for joining and participating in professional associations?

In your participation in professional associations so far, to what extent do you get involved in association events and initiatives? Have you ever taken on a leadership position? Taking on the presidency of the MCDA was a major step out of my comfort zone. But it paid off in multiple ways. Consider how you might take a more active role in your local association. It doesn't have to be a classic leadership role—just something that will help you grow.

As influential as association memberships can be in your professional development, forming a mastermind group can take things further by providing an extra level of commitment and support. One caveat, though: mastermind groups tend to work best when members have developed a certain level of expertise they can share with the group, so everyone benefits equally. If you are just starting out, consider focusing first on finding mentors and building your network and expertise.

Part 2

ASSESSING YOUR CLIENTS

Chapter 4

· · · · · · · · · · ·

THE CAREER ASSESSMENT PROCESS

Trying to do career counseling or coaching without a process in place is like trying to fight your way through the jungle with a machete—you expend a lot of effort but don't really know where things will end up. That's essentially how I was operating when I first started out. I used to dive right into whatever the client's issues or needs might be. We'd generate a few quick goals on the fly, and then launch straight into the work. While well-intentioned, this approach was hit or miss. Often clients weren't clear on where we were going, what to expect, and what the likely outcomes would be for our work together. And more often than not, I was as lost as they were!

As career counselors and coaches, we naturally want to make things better for our clients as quickly as possible. Because of that, we can get so involved in the presenting issue that we easily miss other issues or needs. Having a clear process allows you to systematically identify issues on several fronts, as well as gather multiple sources of information, some of which can confirm what the client is saying. It's not that we don't believe our clients, but we need more information in order to make an intelligent assessment of their needs. We need a plan, not a machete!

If you're interested in building your own assessment process, this chapter will give you a solid foundation and a complete methodology to follow, should that be your goal. Then in the chapters that follow, we'll delve deeper into each of the core assessment components and how they come together. If there's a specific assessment issue that's troubling you—perhaps your clients aren't pulling their weight, for example—consider Section 1 of "The Quick-Reference Toolkit," which offers a quick-reference, problem/solution approach to the assessment process.

KEY ASSESSMENT TASKS

So what does an effective assessment process look like? That will, of course, ultimately depend on a number of factors, including your work environment and role, the particular clients you serve, and your unique interests as a career development professional. So rather than dictate a one-size-fits-all process that might not fit your particular situation, I will instead offer three tasks I believe are essential when assessing clients:

1. Get to know your clients well—beyond the immediate problem they're presenting. To do that, it helps to take a step back and ask some thoughtful questions. How do they feel about their career so far? What makes them happy? Are there other issues that are impacting their journey? Who are their role models? Taking the time to do this can get clients thinking more positively and can pay off throughout the engagement.

2. Extend that information with more objective data, the kind that's best obtained through formal assessments like the Myers-Briggs Type Indicator (MBTI) assessment, 16PF Questionnaire, and other instruments. One of the most interesting and gratifying aspects of assessment for me is seeing the patterns that emerge when I compare my clients' responses to initial questions with their formal assessment results. The combination of qualitative data (from the interview) and quantitative data (from the assessments) provides a richer, more reliable view.

3. Take steps to ensure your hard work with assessment doesn't just get filed away but instead gets directed into a concrete, actionable plan. This doesn't happen automatically, which is why I've developed some simple tools to capture, process, and organize assessment results into actionable form.

A good way to look at assessment is to think about structure. Consider a bicycle. When you go somewhere on your bicycle, you determine where you're going, but it's the bicycle that supplies the means to get there. When we guide clients in their careers, we provide them with "vehicles" (concrete tools and strategies) for getting where they need to go. When we try to work with clients without these tools and strategies, we end up winging it, which can result in awkward silences, lack of meaningful activity, and a general sense of going nowhere—not the kind of impression we want to establish with clients. Structure provides a greater sense of direction and control and lets clients know there's a purpose behind the steps we're taking.

MY ASSESSMENT PROCESS

First, I start to get to know my clients using a structured interview. Second, I use a battery of formal assessments to extend that information further. And third, I use worksheets to help clients sort through their assessment results, which they ultimately craft into a game plan. I also draw on research I've conducted in two key areas: (1) work values and job satisfaction and (2) work-place bullying. For the first area of research, I developed an online assessment product, the Career Compatibility Scale (CCS), which measures the extent to which clients' needs are being met on the job in nine key areas. I cover the CCS and workplace bullying in detail in Part 3, "Assessing the Work Environment."

Think of the assessment process as a large filter or funnel through which you pour different buckets of data—client answers to interview questions, results of assessment instruments, notes from discussions, and so on. The filtering or narrowing happens when clients begin to process this information and get their thoughts on paper. I also like to think of this process as getting rid of the "impurities" in the data and getting to the good stuff: the careers, roles, and tasks that make the most of clients' strengths and that they're most motivated to do. The good stuff becomes part of a game plan clients can use as they move forward in their careers. (For examples of completed game plans, see chapter 8.)

ASSESSMENT PROCESS BENEFITS

Structuring assessment this way—starting with a structured interview, utilizing a variety of formal assessments, and having clients complete the worksheets—allows you to amass a lot of information quickly and systematically. It can also reveal a lot more about clients than you would get from a less structured process with fewer sources of information. To get a sense of how this works, see the sidebar "The Power of Assessment: Don's Story."

Another major benefit of having a structured process is that it gives you something clear and concrete to communicate to clients about what you'll be doing during your sessions. Clients always come with questions, some articulated, some not. How long will we be working together? Will this help get me a job? How will I know if I'm making progress?

Having a process means you have a clear plan for clients that you can articulate, thereby answering many of their questions and putting their minds at ease. Think of track and field runners jumping hurdles. Each hurdle represents a stage or phase in their run, from beginning to end. In a similar way, the various elements of my process, from the structured interview to the game plan, signal clear phases of assessment, assuring clients that progress is being made.

Finally, when you utilize a consistent, repeatable process across multiple clients over an extended period, you gain useful information that you can share with individual clients. For example, over time I've observed that many of my clients want to know if what they're experiencing or discovering during assessment is "normal." One of my structured interview questions is about how people came to be in their current jobs or careers. Several years ago I analyzed over three hundred responses to this question and discovered that fully 58 percent of my clients had arrived at their careers by happenstance rather than design. So if my client is beating herself up over a lack of career planning, I simply cite that statistic, and she immediately feels better.

THE POWER OF ASSESSMENT: DON'S STORY

Don, now an internal software consultant for a digital marketing firm, is a great example of how things get revealed during assessment that aren't always apparent at the beginning of an engagement. On paper—he had sent me his résumé prior to our first session—Don looked like your standard IT professional, with all the usual technical skills highlighted and software packages checked off. Nothing stood out that would differentiate him from his peers. And while his résumé did state that he was "entrepreneurial" and had leadership skills, he had not backed up these points effectively with any real proof or detail.

The problem Don approached me with is an increasingly common one these days: he'd been working as a software developer in a series of temporary gigs and was now looking for something more permanent and stable. Unfortunately, all he could seem to get was temporary work. Part of the problem was his résumé: While it was serviceable enough to get temporary projects—agencies tend to be big on technical skills, and Don had plenty of those to highlight—it wasn't enough for the kind of permanent position he was looking for now. For that, we needed to dig deeper into who Don was and what he could bring to the table.

In his late fifties, Don really wanted to do a thorough exploration. He saw his next career chapter as perhaps his last. As it turned out, Don had a much more interesting background than what was reflected on his résumé.

The Structured Interview

In interviewing Don, I learned that he came from a family of writers and farmers who loved to learn and take on new challenges. His own career background was diverse: after working on his uncle's farm in his youth, he decided to attend college for computer training, something his parents had suggested and a few of his cousins were doing. Unfortunately, his grades were poor, so he dropped out of college and found work as a handyman, putting practical skills he had learned on the farm to good use for several years. Eventually tiring of that, he returned to his earlier goal of studying computers, this time pursuing a degree in computer science with a focus on software development.

Don had a strong sense of accomplishment and gained a great deal of satisfaction from seeing the results of his efforts. When I asked him to name three words to describe himself, he answered "builder," "servant," and "peacemaker." An intriguing mix!

Results from Formal Assessments

When I administered the MBTI assessment, Don tested as an ENFP (Extraverted, Intuitive, Feeling, Perceiving), not at all a common type for IT folks. (Interestingly, ENFPs do occur in relatively large numbers among career counselors and coaches, as well as in other helping professions and creative fields.) Don was strongly motivated toward social interaction and helping others, as well as information systems and sales. Another assessment, the 16PF Questionnaire, revealed that Don could easily become bored if he wasn't challenged but also had the tendency to be overly accommodating to the needs of others. He tended to trust other people implicitly and could be taken advantage of if he wasn't careful—often a double-edged sword for folks who enjoy caring for other people.

Information Processing Worksheets and Exercises

I had Don fill out my Career Ingredients Summary Sheet, a tool I use with clients after testing. He wanted a work environment that was "creative," "challenging," and yet "relaxed." He described himself as "trusting" and "adaptable." And he wrote that "purpose" and "meaning" were important in his work. Occupations he would be open to included teacher, computer programmer, or coach and trainer. When I had him do a special exercise as homework—I asked him to state the purpose of his career and envision a perfect role for himself—he wrote several pages, which became the basis for his game plan.

Don's Game Plan

In his game plan, Don revealed that he wanted to work in an environment that would allow for work-life balance and also give him the chance to build deeper bonds with coworkers outside of work. He wanted to be in an environment where he could be productive and relevant for years, not just weeks or months. He wanted a role in which he could both do the work himself (that is, be a strong individual contributor) and develop others. He wanted to collaborate with a team in a culture that embraced growth and problem-solving. And on a purely practical note, he wanted the office to be within biking distance of home.

Once Don's game plan was in place, there were two key tasks to complete: (1) determine what companies were out there that would fit his needs and allow him to thrive, and (2) write a powerful résumé that would make him attractive to those companies. Although Don's résumé was lackluster and needed work, he had previously written a powerful cover letter that had landed him gigs and with a few tweaks would land him work again. (Don had inherited the family flair for writing; he just hadn't yet applied it to his résumé.) While we ended our work together with the game plan, I'm happy to say that not long afterward, Don was hired as a software consultant, with a commitment by the hiring company that he would be hired full-time if the role was a fit. It was, and Don was hired on permanently.

Don's story illustrates the beauty of an integrated assessment process. Every layer of the process seemed to reveal a new element of who he was. Over the course of the engagement he went from being a nondescript IT guy to a more complex individual with surprising attributes and dreams. Three important themes present from the beginning were reaffirmed during assessment: his entrepreneurial spirit, his need to serve others, and his desire for continuous learning and growth. Happily, his new role embraces all three.

For more client examples, see chapter 12, "Client Case Studies."

GETTING CLIENT BUY-IN

A major benefit of having a clearly articulated process is that clients know what to expect from your sessions, thereby having more confidence in what's to come. When clients first inquire about meeting with me, I provide a brief, nontechnical overview of my process. I tell them that I can help them better understand what's most important and meaningful to them through an interview, taking a battery of tests, and developing a game plan. As we begin to meet, I reiterate those points and introduce the idea that there will likely be some homework or worksheets that can assist them in drilling deeper into particular areas.

If my process seems unclear to them for any reason, I try to clarify and connect how the pieces all work together. I explain to them that the more they discover and understand, the better equipped they'll be to make career and life decisions. Of course, I also check in regularly with clients about their needs, their expectations, and what they most want out of the process.

A key document I use to orient clients is my Client-Coach Expectations Agreement, shown on the next page. I generally have clients sign the agreement at the beginning of our first session together. This agreement sets the tone for our sessions, which I want to be based on an equal partnership—one in which clients play an active role and don't just passively receive information. It also reveals whether clients are seeing other coaches, consultants, or therapists for help. Finally, it gives clients a sense of my approach—that I'll be open and honest in my communications with them, even if the information may be hard to take at times.

The agreement also addresses a few housekeeping details, such as being on time for sessions and paying promptly. While some of us would rather leave these things unsaid—and hope for the best—I have found it's better to make this clear from the outset. It's all part of establishing a tone of trust and mutual respect, something you'll find pays off throughout the engagement.

I generally have clients sign the agreement at the beginning of our first session, right before the structured interview. By this time clients have committed to working with me, at least for a session, so they're in the right frame of mind to consider the agreement. While clients tend to vary in the amount of information they provide on the form, all sign without protest, and most seem to appreciate the straightforward and businesslike approach. Again, it's a good way to set the tone for the relationship and the work ahead.

ASSIGNING HOMEWORK

Homework is anything that gets clients moving toward their goals, and therefore it's an integral part of my process. It can consist of any number of assignments, like conducting an informational interview, reading a book or journal article, signing up for a course, gathering feedback from friends or colleagues, and seeing a therapist for additional help. Homework also includes completing various assessment components, such as taking a formal assessment or completing a worksheet after testing.

Some clients are eager to set their own assignments; others need more prodding. In any event, getting clients moving forward is all about helping them

CLIENT-COACH EXPECTATIONS AGREEMENT

I greatly appreciate the opportunity to work with you and hope to address as many of your career needs as possible. To help us get started on the right foot, please read this document, answer any questions, and acknowledge by signing and dating below.

A few things I need to know about you:

Are you seeing other counseling/coaching professionals? If so, I need to know so that the help I provide you complements, and doesn't undermine or duplicate, these other services. Please answer briefly here. Example: "I'm seeing another coach for job interview coaching" or "I'm seeing a therapist to deal with anxiety issues."

_____

_____

Will you be responsible for owning your own career progress? That is, are you able and willing to try new things, complete any homework I assign, and take any necessary steps toward meeting your goals? I can assist and encourage you but I can't make you take action; only you can do that. *Please say a few words here about how you plan to assume ownership for your career progress.*

_____

_____

A few things you need to know about me:

I will be open and honest in working with you. I am a strong believer of sharing feedback, some of which will be positive and some of which may be negative, difficult to hear, or perhaps unflattering. Important: I will not reveal confidential information to others in the course of our work together, unless you provide written consent.

I will provide as much support as possible, but you need to communicate your needs and take ownership of the process. We will work together as a team.

I expect courtesy and respect from the people I work with. For example, I expect timely payment when service is delivered and advanced notification of cancellations or the need to reschedule (24 hours is preferred).

By signing this document, I acknowledge that I have read it carefully, answered any questions honestly, and understand our mutual obligations.

_____   _____   _____   _____
Client/Candidate Signature   Date   Dean R. DeGroot, MS, LP   Date

help themselves. Here are three strategies I have found helpful for doing just that in my practice:

1. Match homework to your clients' learning style.
2. Leverage your clients' bias for action.
3. Use additional exercises when needed.

By the time I've completed my structured interview and formal assessments, I feel I really know whom I'm working with. I often have a good idea how a client learns best, whether it's from information they've volunteered or clues that have emerged from the interview or testing process. If a client has mentioned reading as a favorite pastime, for example, an appropriate reading assignment may be an effective activity. If a client has demonstrated a high degree of sociability or clearly values others' opinions, I might suggest they seek feedback from friends or colleagues.

Many clients want to run with the ball, so you just need to hand it off. They're eager to dig right in and don't just want to talk about or intellectualize the situation. In fact, they're often disappointed or frustrated when too much time is spent discussing or theorizing. For those clients, a homework assignment (or perhaps several) gives them an immediate sense that they're getting something done. Just find out what they're most eager to tackle first; that's your clue for what to assign. Or let the client set the assignment themselves, and simply offer feedback.

While many clients are eager and ready for immediate homework, others benefit from further reflection. Some may be struggling from negativity or lack of self-confidence. Others may be fixated on something bad that happened to them at work. In Section 2 of "The Quick-Reference Toolkit," you'll find several activities you can try with clients, including a set of exercises for thinking more positively. Sometimes the simplest exercises can make the difference between a client wallowing in self-pity and getting unstuck.

When Clients Fail to Do Their Homework

It's my experience that when clients aren't clear on what's expected of them—when they don't understand their vital role in committing to a process and completing the work—homework is more likely to be blown off. I've also learned that I can't assume that just because clients have come to me for help, they're willing to work! They may well have the naïve notion that everything will magically come together. So I always gauge their readiness to work and make sure they know what to expect.

The Client-Coach Expectations Agreement helps set the stage for what's to come—letting clients know I expect them to show some effort. In addition to having them sign the agreement, I also ask them directly if they are willing and ready to work hard.

But once expectations are set, I try to be as flexible as possible. For example, if there are different possibilities for homework, I'll ask clients which assignments they're more likely to complete or which they find more useful. If the homework is something I usually assign anyway, such as the Career Ingredients Summary Sheet I ask clients to complete after testing, I always try to connect the homework with a benefit. For example, if a client has expressed interest in completing a game plan, I explain how the summary sheet feeds into that process by allowing them to start identifying important criteria.

If clients fail to complete their homework, I'll ask what got in the way and if they're still willing to complete at least part of it. Sometimes they're unclear as to what they should do or what an assignment is getting at, so all that's needed is some clarification. And often it's these clarifying discussions that get things moving in interesting new directions. Sometimes clients don't want to carry out the homework assignment alone and feel more comfortable having someone help them. In that case, I might get them started on the task, or we might identify a friend, significant other, or family member who's willing to work with them. Once I understand the roadblock a client is facing in doing their homework, I can usually help them through it.

REFLECTING ON CHAPTER 4:
THE CAREER ASSESSMENT PROCESS

Have you ever gotten sidetracked by a client's presenting issue, causing you to lose control of the initial session? If so, how might a clearer process have helped? Based on your experience so far, whether you're a student or a working career counselor or coach, what have you learned about the importance of having a process when working with clients?

If you're a student, what have you learned about the career assessment process and its various components in your studies? Are the components you've learned about similar to mine (structured interview, formal assessments, worksheets, game plan)? If not, how do they differ? If you're a working career counselor or coach—even if you don't currently offer formal assessments—you likely have some kind of assessment process in place. What's involved, and how does it compare to the process I describe in this chapter? I've learned a lot about my own process by comparing it to what colleagues are doing.

When clients first contact you, how do you describe your process to them? Or, if you're a student, how is the assessment process described in your textbooks? As I've stressed, having a structured process you can clearly articulate to clients has major benefits. Most importantly, it makes it clear that you have a plan for working with them, which tends to increase their confidence in your services.

In my work, I have found that setting expectations results in more effective engagements and actually puts clients at ease, because they know what's expected of them. When you first start working with a client, do you set expectations for working together? If yes, do you do so formally (using a signed agreement) or informally? If no, how might setting expectations help things go more smoothly? If you're a student, what have you learned about the importance of setting expectations in your study of career counseling and assessment?

It's important to me that clients start taking action early in the process, and we do that through homework, whether that involves reading a book, taking a career assessment test, or doing some other activity. If you're a working counselor or coach, what's your approach to homework? If you're currently a student, what have you learned in your studies about assigning homework?

Chapter 5

• • • • • • • • • •

THE STRUCTURED INTERVIEW

Today I feel confident about my interview process. But in the early days, getting the information I needed could be a struggle. There were many unproductive interviews, including times when I had to send emails or make follow-up calls to get information I knew I should have gotten during the interview. And there were times when I wasn't sure how to proceed with the client, because I just hadn't laid sufficient groundwork. This resulted in some confused moments and awkward silences, the kind we all dread.

For me, the solution was to inject more structure into the interview process. Frankly, I'm just not the kind of person who does well with unstructured, meandering conversations, the "let's see where this takes us" or "tell me what you're feeling right now" type of interview. Yet I knew I needed to ask the kind of thoughtful, open-ended questions that drew clients out and yielded solid information. So I developed an interview that allows me to engage clients effectively while getting the information I need. In this chapter, we'll start by looking at what the interview entails and how it's intended to get clients thinking positively about their future. Next we'll look at strategies for leading and managing the interview effectively. We'll wrap up with tips on how to counter any nervousness you may have when meeting clients for the first time.

The structured interview is the foundation of my assessment process. It's an opportunity to get a first glimpse into who my clients are and what's motivating them. For a sense of just how powerful a good structured interview can be in setting the stage for further work with a client, see the sidebar "Important Clues from the Structured Interview: Frank's Story."

ABOUT THE STRUCTURED INTERVIEW

You may be familiar with the structured interview used in hiring, especially if you come from an HR or recruiting background. With this kind of interview, all candidates get asked the same questions, the purpose being to have a fair and consistent process and to ensure that questioning stays focused on key aspects of the position. I also ask common questions of each client in my structure interviews, but otherwise the goals are quite different.

One goal is to have clients open up and tell their stories—something I achieve by having a range of questions to ask them on a number of topics. Although it took me a while to compile a list of questions I was happy with, the questions in my current list have been in place for about fifteen years.

I've developed twenty-one questions in two categories: job-related and personal (see page 43 for the full list). While most of these questions are straightforward on the surface, the information they reveal is as varied and complex as the clients I serve. Some questions are purposely designed to surprise clients and get them thinking. For example, when I ask clients what value they add to the world—and what value they *want* to add to the world—many have never really thought in those terms. But most welcome this question.

Having clients answer questions that are both work-related and personal gets at today's reality that people are demanding, and are expected by employers to have, balance in their lives. So to get the big picture, I want to know not only what they most enjoy about their work but also how important and meaningful work is in their lives.

During the course of an interview, I typically try to ask about fourteen to fifteen of the questions from the list. Naturally, though, I will ask those questions that are most germane to the client's needs and concerns, which will differ with each client. Depending on the client, sometimes questions from the work-related list will resonate more than those on the personal list, or vice versa.

Although I like to complete the interview during the first session, it's not uncommon for a few questions to spill over to the next session. The main thing is to get the information I need so the next steps make sense.

When I ask my structured interview questions, I'm also looking to answer underlying questions like these: What is it that's most motivating the client? What seems to interest them most: people, things, ideas? How do they define success? To what extent are they influenced or controlled by other people? Do they plan carefully or tend to just let things happen? How much control do they feel they have over their lives or careers? What are their dreams and how capable do they feel of fulfilling them? How willing are they to change?

Through the structured interview, I learn how self-aware clients are and what additional information they might need to enhance that self-aware-ness—information we can often get from career assessment instruments like the Strong Interest Inventory assessment, Myers-Briggs Type Indicator (MBTI) assessment, or the 16PF Questionnaire. As you'll see in the case studies and other client stories in the book, career and life themes that emerge during the interview invariably reemerge when clients take formal assessments and later complete worksheets to process the data we've gathered.

In addition to forming the foundation of your assessment process, client responses to interview questions can be used for further analysis and even product development. In chapter 9 I describe how I used responses to struc-tured interview questions to develop the Career Compatibility Scale (CCS), a work values and job satisfaction assessment. The interview may also lead to the realization that a client has been bullied on the job. That's another special area of interest for me, which I cover in chapter 10.

STRUCTURED INTERVIEW QUESTIONS

The questions listed below are ones I've found yield particu-larly helpful information about clients. For the interviews you conduct, you should feel free to add or substitute questions you have found useful.

Job-Related Questions

What were your most recent positions? What positions or roles
were you most effective at?

What is it you have gained in your current/last position?

How did you find out about the field you're in and decide to
follow this route?

What kind of supervisor do you work best for? Worst for?

Tell me about a work experience that has been memorable for
you. Why was it memorable?

Is your work meaningful to you? How important is work in your life?

What job responsibilities or duties were/are most interesting to you? Least favorite?

If you could have any job you wanted, what would it be?

What are your sources of job satisfaction?

Describe someone you have admired, appreciated, or respected in your life.

Personal Questions

What are your thoughts about transition/change/loss?

When you think about your background and history, who have been the people or what have been the events that have most shaped your life and allowed you to grow?

What are your hobbies/interests/leisure activities?

What are some things that make you happy about life? Upset?

Tell me about three accomplishments/experiences from your earliest history (childhood to age twenty-two)—those that you were particularly proud of.

Give me an example of how you go about making decisions for yourself.

What value do you bring to the world? Want to bring?

What messages did you receive about work while you were growing up?

What are three words that would best describe you as a person?

What was the best piece of feedback you have ever received?

What has been a great movie or book that has impacted you? Why?

IMPORTANT CLUES FROM THE STRUCTURED INTERVIEW: FRANK'S STORY

"Life-changing and confidence-building." That's how my client Frank described his feelings about our work together at the end of our fifth session. By then we had done formal assessments, and Frank had completed some worksheets, so we had a lot of material to work with. But when I look at my notes and think about how my sessions with Frank transpired, the foundation we laid during the structured interview really paid off.

Frank cooked for a living and had been at it for about ten years. He came to me because he was frustrated with the long hours, marginal pay, and not having much of a life outside of work. He wanted something better for himself, something more professional and creative, but he wasn't sure what.

Looking at Frank's responses from the structured interview, I found the following:

Memorable work experiences: times he had overcome fear and doubt in his professional life

Most interesting job responsibilities: creating dishes and training others

Sources of job satisfaction: creating, learning, positive feedback, and overcoming challenges

People he admires: chefs with new ideas, new approaches, and curiosity about food production

Hobbies and leisure activities: fishing, reading (especially on biology), and nature

Early accomplishment he was proud of: being voted best artist in high school

A favorite book: *In Defense of Food*, by Michael Pollan

Frank, an INTJ (Introverted, Intuitive, Thinking, Judging), was clearly someone who was driven and creative. But self-doubt was also a common theme that kept emerging in our discussions. As you can see in two of his interview responses—one on memorable work experiences and another on sources of job satisfaction—overcoming doubt and challenges in his life was important to him. When I asked him about his tendency toward self-doubt and what he was doing about it, he reminded me that he was seeing a therapist for that purpose. Clients like Frank who are determined to improve will do whatever they need to achieve that goal.

When I last met with Frank, he was looking into several possibilities for expanding his horizons—the environment, arts, or sciences (all with an emphasis on food or food science). Having purpose in his work is important to Frank, and he believed that a scientific role dealing with food would have greater societal benefit, make more impact on people's lives, and be more consistent with his values.

At each of the subsequent sessions I have with clients, I keep my structured interview notes close by, to remind both them and me what we're working toward and what's most important. I find these notes keep paying dividends as we revisit themes—like Frank's quest to overcome self-doubt and his clear interest in the food industry. And any time my work can help change lives and build self-confidence, as it did with Frank, is highly gratifying.

To see how other clients' responses to structured interview questions provided important clues, see the case studies in chapter 12.

DRAWING ON POSITIVE PSYCHOLOGY

As career development professionals, we witness a lot of uncertainty and even suffering in our work. I've seen older clients who've been cast aside or ignored, clients who've been bullied at work, and clients who've been laid off repeatedly or had other major career setbacks. Many suffer from loss of identity and purpose, doubts about their skills and capabilities, confusion and disorganization, and worries about what's next for them.

In the late 1980s, before I got into career coaching via outplacement, I worked as a psychologist in a human services context, which was all about observing and measuring behavior, diagnosing problems, and identifying conditions. But once I got into career coaching, I discovered I was much happier unmasking opportunity than problems. At some point I asked myself: Do I really want to focus on my clients' losses and misery, or would I rather tap into something that could propel them? And wouldn't this be a more positive experience for the client as well?

That's why I've purposely included questions designed to elicit a positive response, such as:

What value do you bring to the world?
What was the best piece of feedback you ever received?
What's one of the most memorable projects you've been involved with?
What job responsibilities most interest you?
What makes you happy about life?

In my work as a whole, and particularly in my approach to interviewing, I've long been inspired by the work of Martin Seligman, considered by many to be the founder of positive psychology. Seligman urges people to reframe negative thoughts into more constructive ones. This includes looking at bad things that happen as temporary versus permanent and situational versus pervasive. Although I believe it's important to allow your clients to share their concerns and frustrations, I want to have most of the first session deal primarily with strengths, interests, what has worked in the past, and passions.

Clients come to me for assistance and support, and creating a great deal of negative energy in the first session is not the best way to begin a relationship. I want them to leave our first meeting feeling hopeful and knowing they have a process that will propel them into a positive future. I want them to focus less on their career woes and more on what makes them happy, as well as think about what's most meaningful to them.

Another question that gets clients to open up in interesting ways is to ask them what books or movies have had an impact on their lives. For some books and movies clients have cited, and some thoughts on what you can glean from their answers, see the sidebar "A Great Question to Ask Your Clients."

If you're finding that you and your clients are getting bogged down in the negative, and especially if you're not making the progress you'd like together, consider injecting some positive thinking into your interview process. In addition, take a look at who's in charge of the interview. I have found that when clients dominate the interview process—especially when I allow them to vent at length about their situation—the information gathered suffers along with the overall effectiveness of our sessions. And since clients are paying us for our expertise (whether directly or through tax dollars or student fees), we owe it to them to give them their money's worth by leading the interview effectively.

A GREAT QUESTION TO ASK YOUR CLIENTS

In my list of structured interview questions on page 43, the last question you'll find in the "Personal" category is "What has been a great movie or book that has impacted you? Why?" This is one of my favorite questions to ask my clients, because it can tell me so much about them: their outlook on life, crises they've been through, how they view themselves, and even how they learn best.

Here is a small sampling of books and movies clients have identified:

Atlas Shrugged
the Bible
Man's Search for Meaning
The 7 Habits of Highly Effective People
American Beauty
The Lord of the Rings
Saving Private Ryan
The Shawshank Redemption
Star Wars (original, 1977)

Man's Search for Meaning, a book by Holocaust survivor Viktor Frankl, stresses resilience of the human spirit under adversity. It can help clients overcome their own obstacles. Discussing it sheds light on their values, philosophy, and spirituality.

American Beauty, a movie which explores midlife crises, resonated with one client in particular, a man in his fifties suffering his own midlife crisis and helping a friend through his. I might not have learned about this had I not asked the question.

Movies like *The Shawshank Redemption* bring hope. And discussion of them can yield crucial insights about how clients see themselves and others and bring to light a client's experience of injustice.

Finally, clients' reaction to the question about how a book has impacted them can tell you if reading is important to them as part of their learning process. That can help when deciding what to assign for homework.

LEADING THE INTERVIEW

As I've noted, before I started using a structured interview, my initial session with clients lacked the kind of structure and direction I needed to gather good information. This resulted in another problem: because there was no real plan or structure in place, clients frequently ended up dominating the discussion, which was often all about their confusion, low self-esteem, or other frustrations. Before I knew it, an hour had passed, and I still really didn't know much about them—what could really help them or provide clues for direction, that is. Yet clients rightly expected results from our work together.

Most clients simply don't have the luxury of unlimited time and money. They want and need assistance but can't spend hours paying an hourly rate that's generally much higher than what they earn themselves. Given that reality, it's up to me to guide the process to ensure that they get what they need from the experience. The structured interview process I've developed respects my clients' time and budget by quickly yielding useful, positive, and actionable information. And, most importantly, it allows me to manage the discussion in a way that gets results.

In the interview I don't want clients to dwell too much on their problems, nor do I want to spend time going over minute details of their job history or other mundane details about their work. We're trying to shape a future, not reminisce about the past. Besides, good interview questions yield background information naturally as clients look back at favorite projects, explain why different jobs they held either suited them or didn't, and open up on other topics that get them thinking and expanding their horizons.

I do want to stress something here: When clients bring up issues and problems, I don't ignore them. I listen to them, write down any relevant points, and follow up with questions as needed. But I also try to get back to my structured interview questions as soon as possible to ensure that I get the information I need and that my clients' investment in me is money well spent.

Developing an effective interview process took time. So, too, did developing my skill in leading that process effectively and without guilt. But the results are worth it when I see clients' reactions to the questions I ask and the insights they gain from answering them, as well as their satisfaction with our work together as a whole.

TIPS FOR CONDUCTING AN EFFECTIVE INTERVIEW

Plan to ask the questions early in your first session with clients, and make sure they're aware that you'll be interviewing them. (For more on preparing clients for working with you, see "Getting Client Buy-In" in chapter 4.)

On your question sheet, add as much space as you need between questions to record your answers. I have found that writing answers directly on the sheet is the best way to ensure I won't lose track of them. For me, the act of writing also keeps me focused and shows the client that I'm engaged and actively listening.

Consider starting the interview with job-related questions, which for many clients can be less intrusive than personal questions when you're first getting to know them.

To ensure you get your questions answered, be firm in directing the interview. (See "Leading the Interview," above, for some insights.) Some questions may need to wait for the next session, but always strive to ask as many as possible in the first session.

As you meet with clients in later sessions, keep your notes close by to compare them with formal assessment results, completed client worksheets, and so on. You will be amazed at some of the patterns you will see in the data.

OVERCOMING FIRST-SESSION JITTERS

A bit of anxiety before the first session with a client is natural, especially if you're an introvert like me. That's something that's eased over the years as I've developed strategies for coping, but if you're new to career counseling and coaching, you may be overwhelmed with nerves and a feeling of self-conscious-ness—the feeling that all eyes are on you and the client is judging you. Well, they are, of course, but not nearly as much as you think. Here are three of my best suggestions and strategies for coping with first-session anxiety:

1. Focus on assessing the client, which will take your mind off your own nerves.
2. Ensure that the client feels at ease. This will make both of you more comfortable.
3. Take advantage of structure to help eliminate much of the uncertainty.

Your first session with clients, even before the interview starts, is full of opportunities for preliminary observation and assessment. Was the client run-ning late? Were they breathless from rushing to make it on time? Did they bring the materials (test results, portfolio, résumé) you asked them to bring? Focus on your curiosity about the client and their state of mind and demeanor, and you'll be much less self-conscious and worried about your own performance. And remember to write down your initial observations about the client at your earliest opportunity.

Practicing little rituals to make the client feel more comfortable—greeting them with a smile, asking mundane questions such as whether they had any trouble finding your office, offering them a beverage, making sure they're seated comfortably—can put both you and the client more at ease and go a long way to establishing a positive relationship.

If, once the interview starts, my client seems unhappy or their body language suggests they're nervous or uncomfortable—it doesn't happen often, but when it does, it needs to be dealt with—I'll stop and ask them if anything is wrong and if we need to discuss it before proceeding with the interview. The fact that I need to intervene this way tells me something else, that the client may lack assertiveness. In cases like that, I make a note for my files.

Take advantage of structure in your process to help lessen uncertainty. For example, having an agreement for clients to sign (see either chapter 4 or "The Quick-Reference Toolkit" for a copy of my Client-Coach Expectations Agree-ment) gets both you and your client busy and engaged in an activity, and it can naturally trigger discussion that helps break the ice. The structured interview itself provides a natural way to step back from the immediate situation. By the time you're three or four questions into the interview, both you and your client will be more at ease and enjoying the conversation.

When you're new to counseling or coaching, there's a tendency to think that everything the client is doing or saying, all of the emotions they're displaying, are attributable to you and you alone. If they become tearful when answering a question, you may feel it was you who made them cry, not the question. Here's what's really happening: you've provided the client with an opportunity to share what's meaningful to them, and they are honoring you by revealing something important about themselves. If you lack confidence, you may think you've messed up somehow. But that's usually not the case, especially if you're asking thoughtful questions designed to get the client to open up.

REFLECTING ON CHAPTER 5:
THE STRUCTURED INTERVIEW

My interview process is structured, which means there's a series of questions I ask of most of my clients. If you're a student, did you learn about this type of interview in your studies or practice sessions? If you're a working career counselor or coach, is the interview process you use planned and scripted ahead of time (structured), or is it more spontaneous?

When you interview clients, what kind of information do you gather, and why? Do you distinguish between work-related and personal questions? If not, how might doing this help? I have found that starting with work-related questions and then moving to more personal questions generally works better, because most clients are more at ease discussing work than their personal life, at least at first.

Clients I work with typically have limited budgets, and therefore it's critical that they view our first session together as time well spent. For me, that means I need to manage the interview in such a way that I get the information I need to start helping my client right away. So while I listen to client concerns, my main focus is on moving them toward a more hopeful future by focusing on the positive. What interview strategies have you learned about if you're a student or employed as a working counselor or coach? In what ways might they differ from my approach?

A simple way to ensure a more successful interview is to make sure clients are aware that you'll be interviewing them in the first place, which is something I communicate to clients before our first session. Otherwise, if they're not expecting an interview, they may begin to question your approach. This goes back to setting expectations and getting buy-in from clients, which we talked about in chapter 4. If you're a working counselor and coach, do you tell your clients to expect an interview? If you're a student, what have you learned about preparing a client for the first session?

Does the idea of meeting a client for the first time make you nervous? Remember to focus on the client, not on your own performance. If this is an area of concern for you, review the tips in the last section of the chapter, "Overcoming First-Session Jitters." And keep in mind that it will become easier as you gain experience.

Chapter 6

• • • • • • • • • • •

FORMAL ASSESSMENTS

Don, the consultant you met in chapter 4, described himself in the interview as a builder, servant, and peacemaker. When I learned he was an ENFP (Extra-verted, Intuitive, Feeling, Perceiving), these self-described attributes made sense, particularly when you consider the "feeling" part of the equation. And his 16PF Questionnaire results showed, as they often do for clients, a potential downside of his personality—the tendency to be taken advantage of by those he cares for.

Formal assessments help me and my clients build on the insights and opportunities unearthed during the interview. They're an essential part of my process, whether clients bring in previous assessments they've taken or we undertake new ones (usually a combination). But of all the assessment components, formal assessments may be the most challenging to get a handle on. This chapter should help you get a grasp on some of the bigger challenges, including putting together a battery of assessments that works for you, assigning assessments to individual clients, and sharing test results. You'll also find tips for learning formal assessments, and a Q&A with answers to questions you may have when first starting out.

If you want to learn how to work with test publishers to purchase and administer assessments, make sure to see Section 3 of "The Quick-Reference Toolkit."

While formal assessments are often what people think of when they think of career assessment—and they do provide essential information you can't get elsewhere—they are just part of the larger integrated process described in this book. Knowing their limitations is an important part of learning about assessment in general.

PUTTING TOGETHER A BATTERY OF ASSESSMENTS

The core battery of assessments I use with clients provides me with an excellent cross-section of information on interests, personality, interpersonal style, and values. These assessments also meet criteria that are important to me as an independent practitioner: they're affordable (for both me and my clients); relevant to my client base (all are career-related assessments developed for use with clients of different ages); based on recent data (most are updated regularly); and easy to administer online. Having assessments that complement each other is also important. One other consideration is whether the test publisher provides collateral resources, such as handouts, which can be useful during the test results phase. (See Section 3 of "The Quick-Reference Toolkit" for more.)

The table below lists the formal assessments I use most often with clients (in alphabetical order), the particular report I use for that assessment (for most assessments, multiple reports or profiles are available), and a brief discussion on what the assessment does and why I find it useful.

Assessment Instrument	Report I Use	What It Does and Why It's Useful
California Psychological Inventory (CPI 434) assessment	Narrative	This report provides an overall picture of one's personality across four dimensions: social and interpersonal tendencies; maturity and responsibility; intellectual functioning and achievement potential; and style. It helps you gauge leadership potential and also identify clients' potential based on "highs" and "lows" in their personality profile across these four dimensions. I like the Narrative report for the level of detail it provides, including definitions clients find helpful.

(table continued on next page)

Assessment Instrument	Report I Use	What It Does and Why It's Useful
Fundamental Interpersonal Relations Orientation-Behavior (FIRO-B) assessment	Interpretive Report for Organizations	Organized into three dimensions—Inclusion, Control, and Affection—this report helps explain what clients need interpersonally from those they live and work with and to what extent they are expressing these interpersonal needs (taking the initiative themselves or waiting for others to take the initiative).
Myers-Briggs Type Indicator (MBTI) assessment	Step I and II profiles	As people mature, they want to understand how they operate in relation to others around them. The MBTI offers insights into how clients gain energy, process information, make decisions, and operate with or without structure, and also encourages greater awareness and tolerance of people with different styles. I generally use Step I for clients new to the MBTI. Step II is appropriate for those who have taken the MBTI before in some form and want an updated or more detailed profile.
16PF Questionnaire (Sixteen Personality Factors)	Career Development Profile	Which careers tend to correlate with a client's personality? The Career Development Profile helps answer this question through a comprehensive narrative that explores clients' career interests, preferred work and organization roles, problem-solving approach, and interpersonal style. The report also examines how people cope with stress and can reveal if the level of stress a client is undergoing warrants additional counseling and support beyond career counseling and coaching.

Assessment Instrument	Report I Use	What It Does and Why It's Useful
Strong Interest Inventory assessment (Strong)	Basic Profile	Some kind of interest inventory is a must in assessment, and the Strong is considered one of the best in highlighting occupations that correlate with clients' interest patterns. The occupations used for comparison are well researched and cross-referenced with popular tools such as the O*Net and Occupational Outlook Handbook. A not-so-obvious use of the Strong: it can help explain clients' difficulty in making decisions, which can be a result of having too many interests or too few.
A values assessment instrument (I used Values Scale, which is now out of print, but see the case studies for results.)	Original Values Scale report	For many clients, awareness of values is deeply important. With the Values Scale no longer available, I suggest you try other tools for measuring client values. One to consider is the Values Preference Indicator, an online assessment offered by CRG (crgleader.com), which measures twenty-one values (accomplishment, creativity, friendship, security, wealth, etc.).

In settling on a battery of assessments, I wanted tests that could provide similar shades but were distinctly different, rather than using ones that were very similar or had nothing in common with one another. For example, the Strong Interest Inventory assessment and the 16PF Questionnaire both compare people to occupations, so the results can reveal interesting patterns. But because the Strong is an interest inventory while the 16PF is a personality assessment, the 16PF can reveal emotional and behavioral clues not available in the Strong. So the two assessments complement each other effectively.

Given all of the assessments available out there, I'm occasionally tempted to add more. In practical terms, however, there's only so much effort I'm willing to exert, and money I'm willing to spend, to expand my assessment offerings. I have found that offering additional tests that aren't significantly different from what I already offer results in diminishing returns. Most of my clients are on limited budgets anyway, so making the most of their time and money is important. As with all businesses, you need to be aware of costs of inventory and upgrades. That said, I do keep an eye out for new developments and would not hesitate to add a test if it significantly enhanced my offerings.

One of my favorite assessments in the battery is the California Psychological Inventory (CPI 434) assessment. It's excellent for assessing clients' leadership potential and effectiveness, and it's also useful for identifying any psychological, emotional, or behavioral tendencies that may be holding them back. It can also help explain why someone might be a poor fit for a job. See "The Versatile CPI" for more.

THE VERSATILE CPI

Of the formal assessments in my go-to battery of tests, the California Psychological Inventory (CPI 434) assessment is perhaps the most similar to the 16PF Questionnaire in terms of the ground it covers. Both, for example, draw on the Big Five personality traits—openness to experience, conscientiousness, extraversion, agreeableness, and neuroticism—for some of their questions. And both provide glimpses into the state of one's psychological health and well-being. The CPI 434, which bases several of its questions on the Minnesota Multiphasic Personality Inventory (MMPI-2), a clinical instrument, goes the furthest in this area.

A unique and interesting feature of the CPI 434 is its use of "profile patterns"—a way of classifying results according to the test taker's potential for various professional positions, including executives, middle managers, salespeople, law enforcement officers, and other categories. Because of this and other features, the CPI 434 is one of my favorite instruments. I've used it for many applications, including assessing potential for various roles (management, sales, law enforcement); assertiveness training (assessing bold versus passive personality); and identifying clinical and mental health issues, such as alcoholism and depression. (For serious concerns, I might have the client take the MMPI-2, either through me or another clinician.)

The CPI 434 is particularly useful for analyzing how one's personality and working environment can be a match or mismatch. I remember one client who was working for her father's company and was miserable. In her CPI assessment results, my client scored well above average for what the CPI classifies as Creative Temperament. She was very artistic and an independent thinker—a major mismatch given the buttoned-down environment of her father's firm, which valued tradition and conformity. In three of the case studies in this book (Kevin, Jim, and Sue), my clients were also mismatched in their jobs, and the CPI 434, along with other formal assessments, helped shed some light on why.

The CPI has been around since 1956, when it was first created by Harrison G. Gough, whose name still appears on the title page of CPI profiles. Sometime in the early 1990s, when I was still coming up to speed on the CPI assessments, I sent some questions via email to CPP (now the Myers-Briggs Company), the test publisher. To my astonishment and delight, I received a detailed, typewritten response from Gough himself. That speaks volumes about the thought that went into this fascinating and useful assessment.

ASSIGNING ASSESSMENTS TO CLIENTS

Once you've assembled a battery of tests to draw on, the question then becomes: Which clients get assigned which assessments and why? Just as putting together my core battery of tests required some time, it took me a while to figure out why and when to assign assessments to individual clients. It's a complicated question, because every client is different, and the reasons for assigning assessments are also varied.

Here are five top considerations when thinking about assigning formal assessments:

1. What does the client want to learn through assessment? This is a question I generally ask when clients first contact me or, more often, during our first session. Asking this question also helps me understand what they already know about assessments, whether they've taken them previously or will be taking them for the first time with me.

2. If the client is asking for a specific formal assessment, which clients occasionally do, do they understand what the assessment entails and what it can (and cannot) do for them? An important part of my job as their career counselor and coach is to explain what particular assessments do and how my client will benefit. Sometimes a different test may be in order, given the client's need.

3. What testing has the client had previously, either through another counselor or coach or through the client's own efforts? (I make a point of asking clients to bring in any assessment results—formal or informal—that they feel have given them some insights.) Whatever the case, I need to evaluate what they've done. Does the client agree with the findings? Are the findings themselves reliable? What questions remain?

4. How motivated is the client to take assessments? Some clients, often those who haven't had assessments done before, are reluctant to take assessments at all, or might agree to only a test or two. For other clients, formal assessments represent an exciting process of discovery that they enjoy immensely. Many of these same clients also enjoy confirming previous test results, which can boost their self-confidence and ability to move forward.

5. What do I, as their counselor or coach, need to learn? This is an important question that relates to several factors: what I picked up during the structured interview, the quality and usefulness of any previous assessment work the client has done, and, perhaps most importantly, the client's own level of self-awareness. Will I be able to help them now based on what I know, or is more assessment necessary?

This last point is worth stressing: I believe that we as career counselors and coaches must exert leadership and self-advocacy when it comes to getting the information we need. If the information I need is best obtained through a particular formal assessment, I will advocate for doing that assessment. If the client is unwilling for any reason, I will either explain the benefits of the assessment further or suggest an alternative. What's important is that I stand behind my assessment process. If I vacillate or seem uncertain, my client will pick up on that and may lose confidence in what we're doing.

SHARING TEST RESULTS WITH CLIENTS

Does the idea of giving test feedback make you nervous? When I first started giving test results to my clients, I was often, to be frank, a nervous wreck. Did I really know what I was talking about? Would I lose my train of thought or get lost while going through the results? Would the client notice I didn't quite have my act together? So in 1991 I hired a fellow psychologist to tutor me in interpreting test results and giving feedback to clients. As a master evaluator and test-feedback professional, Tamara taught me key nuances of providing test feedback, spotting themes, and interpreting data.

What most impressed me about Tamara was her approach to communicating results. She had a gentle way of providing feedback, a way of nudging the client in a certain direction that was flattering without being phony or condescending. She would highlight the positives in the results, but she also made sure the client was aware of any negatives or areas for development. She was great at soliciting feedback from the client: "How does that sound?" "Does that make sense?" "Could you see some of that playing out in your work?" "What seems realistic about the results to you?" "What doesn't make sense?" "Let's talk about possible contradictions." In other words, she engaged the client in the analysis.

Not only did Tamara share her expertise, but she provided the insights and sensitivities of an ENFP (Extraverted, Intuitive, Feeling, Perceiving), which was very helpful to me, her polar opposite as an ISTJ (Introverted, Sensing, Thinking, Judging).

MY TEST FEEDBACK PROCESS

Tamara's tutoring helped a lot, as did repeated practice and experience working with actual clients. I've also found that preparing thoroughly before a session is essential.

Above all, I do my homework. Before meeting with the client, I analyze the results, highlighting or underlining key words and phrases and noting any questions that come to mind. I also look for similarities and differences between assessments, if there's more than one, and between my structured interview findings and the assessments.

If I'm unclear about something or want a broader understanding, I'll revisit the appropriate test manuals or guides. If the patterns or combinations are unique or puzzling, I might consult with a colleague to get some additional insights.

In sharing results, I draw on Tamara's model of engaging the client with questions. What do they think of the strengths and positives? What do they think of the concerns or potential weaknesses mentioned? How do they feel about the information in general?

As I go through results with the client, I notice what "pops" or resonates for them and write down key words or themes. In that and subsequent meetings, I'll often bring up those points again to see if they still resonate and how important and meaningful they are to the client.

Finally, when all of the results have been discussed, I usually ask clients about what they most learned or got out of the test feedback. How much of this information was new or known to them? What, if anything, is confusing or unsettling for them?

If you get nervous at the very thought of giving test results to clients, as I once did, taking time to prepare can take the edge off your anxiety. Also, actively engaging the client in the process, rather than seeing the whole thing as a performance on your part, can go a long way toward making the process more pleasant and productive. And finally, don't hesitate to seek out mentoring or tutoring, as I did.

Before we move on, I want to point out an important by-product of doing formal assessments that may surprise you. As a cognitive behavioral psychologist by training, I've always been particularly attuned to clients' attitudes toward assessment and what I can learn from them. How enthused are they about taking assessments? How are they reacting to the results? How might their attitudes be related to problems they're encountering at work or in their career? Although discussing these issues with clients can be sensitive, our willingness to do so can mean better results in the long run.

Assessment and Client Attitudes

As counselors and coaches, we know that assessment results yield an array of useful data on clients' personalities, preferences, values, and other factors, and that these are essential for career development and job searching. After all, the better clients know themselves, the better equipped they are to explore a career, write an effective résumé, and search for and evaluate job opportunities.

But less obvious are the more subtle psychological and behavioral factors assessment reveals: clients' overall attitude and flexibility, the presence of career-impeding traits such as stubbornness or arrogance, and openness to feedback and willingness to learn. It's these factors, rather than degrees earned or jobs worked, that tend to spell success or failure. Here are four key factors to consider:

1. When you ask clients to take an assessment, you've essentially assigned them *work*. Are they eager to get to work or resistant? Dig deeper with the client to learn what this means in terms of attitude and flexibility.

2. Assessment results may reveal stubbornness, arrogance, or other negative factors. A deeper understanding can pave the way for development and also help the client frame these traits appropriately as strengths or weaknesses. Perhaps the client is simply in the wrong job, and a current "weakness" is actually a strength waiting to be utilized.

3. Consider how receptive your client is to the assessment results. While tests are not 100 percent accurate, there's almost always some degree of validity. So if a client rejects the results out of hand, this could indicate defensiveness or difficulty with receiving feedback, neither of which play well on the job or in the business world in general.

4. Assessment should be viewed, above all, as a learning experience. So your clients' reactions to assessment provide major clues about their willingness to learn, a make-or-break factor in today's competitive marketplace.

If we as career professionals can play a role in identifying behavioral issues that may affect our clients' prospects, we offer them a special dividend. In fact, for some clients, the feedback we offer may be the most objective and open feedback they've ever received. I've had clients thank me for shedding light on issues they either were unaware of or had underestimated.

We all know that performance reviews at work can put people on the defensive. The feedback we offer during career assessment, on the other hand, can be a gift, often strengthening clients' resolve to make improvements or modifications in their behavior. But even when clients seem to resist our efforts, it's an opportunity for us to support their development and honor their investment in our services.

LEARNING FORMAL ASSESSMENTS: FIVE KEY STRATEGIES

If you decide to take on formal assessments as a specialty, or even if you only use them in a limited fashion, there's a lot to learn. Fortunately, you have many resources at your disposal. Here are five strategies I've found to be effective.

1. Learn the fundamentals of career assessment.
2. Hire a mentor to help you learn the ropes.
3. Obtain your materials, training, and certifications from trusted publishers.
4. Tap your network for business partnerships.
5. Never stop learning!

While I'm a great believer that you learn best through doing, I also believe you need a foundation in basic principles. In Appendix B, you'll find information on several key texts on career assessment, including a comprehensive guide published by the National Career Development Association. Other, more specialized texts are focused on the use of assessments in the workplace or as part of organizational and management consulting. One book, *Do What You Are*, a best seller targeted at general readers, is one of the most thorough, engaging, and practical books you'll find on the MBTI assessment.

One of the best investments I ever made was to hire my colleague Tamara to tutor me in interpreting test results and communicating them to clients (see "Sharing Test Results with Clients" earlier in this chapter). I've learned a lot from other colleagues as well, particularly those in my mastermind group. When looking for a tutor or mentor, find someone who has been in the trenches so you learn practical methods based on real-world issues and experienced by actual clients. And don't feel guilty about asking for help. Just remember that no practitioner starts off being perfect at their craft.

When it comes to obtaining your assessment materials, look for reputable publishers offering official versions of assessment tests and recognized certifications. The web is awash with assessment materials, many of them of questionable value, so knowing which providers you can trust is important. In Section 3 of "The Quick-Reference Toolkit," I list the test publishers I obtain my assessments from, along with tips for working with them. These are reputable publishers that maintain high standards and invest in ongoing research.

Once you've developed some expertise in formal assessments, look for opportunities to partner with colleagues. As I mentioned in chapter 1 on specializing in assessments, I have found that some counselors and coaches would rather focus on their specialties and *not* do formal assessments. They appreciate someone with a solid grasp of assessments to whom they can refer clients or outsource work. These partnerships can also help you focus your practice as you compare your strengths and offerings with those of your colleagues.

Finally, keep on learning. There are many opportunities to learn formal assessments—courses offered through university programs, training offered by the leading test publishers, professional association events and conferences, and much more. The training doesn't have to be directly related to assessment to be beneficial. For example, at a recent Minnesota Career Development Association conference, I picked up some new job-search and decision-making techniques that complement my assessment process.

A QUICK Q&A ON FORMAL ASSESSMENTS

As I stress in chapter 14 ("A Career Q&A with Dean"), interviewing others to gather information—something we encourage our clients to do—is an excellent way to learn about the field. The questions and answers that follow are based on my personal experience and views on formal assessments. For additional insights and perspectives, I recommend that you identify others with expertise using formal assessments and ask them these or any other questions you may have.

Q: Are formal assessments always necessary as part of assessment?

A: If my clients have been recently tested or are very self-aware (or both), I might not need to assign them any formal assessments, but I will always ask about any previous testing they've had and ask them to bring in their results. Formal assessments provide objective information you just can't get in any other form.

Q: How do I know which tests to offer? There are so many of them!

A: It took me about ten years before I had a battery of tests I was happy with. But you can accelerate the process. First, read the first section in this chapter in which I explain the battery of tests I use and why I use them. Also, write down criteria for what you need. Here are six criteria to get you started. You want tests that are (1) affordable; (2) recent (that is, the research behind them is reasonably current); (3) relevant in terms of the population you're serving; (4) career-related rather than strictly about personality or aptitude; (5) complementary (each test provides something the other doesn't); and (6) easy to administer. Want more in-depth information? See Appendix B for some key texts and reference books on assessment.

Q: What if the client doesn't want to take assessments, or can't afford them?

A: As I noted above, I would ask them to bring in copies of any previous tests. I would also try to impress upon them the importance of testing to the overall assessment process. In the past, I have occasionally lowered my testing fees or even done testing for free in order to get the information I needed, but that's not something I would do today or recommend in general. (Asking for lower fees when you're just starting out is different. See the question "What if I don't have much experience with assessment? How can I charge reasonable fees?" below.) Also, consider what a client's refusal to do testing might say about their attitude in general. See the section "Assessment and Client Attitudes" in this chapter.

Q: The idea of going over test results with clients makes me nervous. Any tips?

A: Do whatever's necessary for you to absorb the information so that it's clear in your mind. That way you won't find yourself just reading the results to the client, or worse, losing your place in the text or train of thought. In the early days of my practice—the first three or four years or so—I would write down key points from the assessment reports, things like the highest and lowest scores, unusual trends or patterns, and any questions I wanted to ask the client. I did this for each test I gave the client.

Q: What do I do when test results don't make sense or deliver mixed messages?

A: In cases like that, you just need to step up your analysis. One of my clients, a financial analyst, was unhappy at work. On paper, the work Brad was doing looked like a perfect fit. For example, his results on the Strong Interest Inventory assessment showed him to be very similar to accountants, financial managers, investment managers, and buyers. However, there was a softer, less analytical, side to Brad, and that showed up in his MBTI assessment results. Brad was an ISFJ (Introverted, Sensing, Feeling, Judging). On the 16PF Questionnaire, his highest score was "helping," and he had similarities to many helping professions. His FIRO-B assessment results showed a high need for affection and inclusion—not exactly typical results for a financial analyst. These results helped explain his strong interest in community service, such as working for Meals on Wheels and Habitat for Humanity. Brad eventually left his job to do work that allowed him to interact more closely with people and serve them more directly.

Q: I'm just starting out, and all this assessment information seems overwhelming. Any advice?

A: First, remember that you're a facilitator who can only gain experience by practicing your craft. Find some students or other people who just want to share their situation, provide them with a few insights and assessment tools, and see what happens. If you think your lack of experience may be perceived as a liability, perhaps some clients may be willing to work with you at a reduced fee, knowing that you're fairly new in the field. Everything is negotiable. Remember, too, that even though you're just starting out, you likely know more than your clients about the assessment process. Go easy on yourself, and allow yourself to learn.

Q: What if I don't have much experience with assessment? How can I charge reasonable fees?

A: Again, you can only gain experience by practicing your craft. Be patient, and you'll get there. You'll need to seek out opportunities to practice—perhaps even volunteer—and you probably won't be able to charge as much as you'd like at first. In the early 1990s, just so I could get the experience, I charged clients a meager $40 an hour—definitely at the low end for a licensed psychologist. But I considered this a "training wage." The people I served were happy with the reasonable rates, and I learned a lot from working with them. As I gained experience and confidence, I gradually raised my rates. Today my hourly fee is still reasonable—I don't like to gouge my clients—but definitely more in line with what I'm worth.

Q: Should I go after certifications? Special credentials? Is it worth the time?

A: To administer many of the assessments I mention in this book, you'll likely need to go through a certification process provided by the test manufacturer, or through some other training provider with expertise in the specific assessment. Certainly, being certified in the most popular assessment tools, such as the MBTI assessment and Strong Interest Inventory assessment, can be an advantage. Beyond that, factors like your individual career goals, educational background, and clientele will determine just how far you need to go—or will want to go—to add to your training and credentials. With regard to formal credentials, the NCDA has several programs you might want to check out. To learn more, go to ncda.org, select Professional Development, then Credentialing. Also, see "Qualifying to Administer Assessments" in Section 3 of "The Quick-Reference Toolkit."

When it comes to learning formal assessments, what's most important by far is hands-on experience. The more exposure you can get to them, the better you'll be able to determine if they're something you want to work with and invest in. And the more you work with them, the more comfortable you'll be.

Q: I want to get myself tested as a way to train myself in assessment and also decide what assessments I want to offer clients. Is that something you would recommend?

A: Definitely. When I first got into career counseling, I got tested in all the assessments I was administering as a consultant. Sometimes I was able to take a test for free from the consulting company I worked with. In other cases, I attended training seminars in which testing was part of the training fee.

I also recommend getting tested through a counselor or coach with expertise in assessment. You'll benefit in three ways: you'll learn more about yourself and how you want to focus your role or practice; you'll see career counseling and coaching modeled for you, including how to communicate test results effectively; and you'll build your knowledge of specific assessments in a way that's comfortable and nonthreatening.

REFLECTING ON CHAPTER 6:
FORMAL ASSESSMENTS

In deciding what formal assessments you will offer in your practice, there are several things to think about, including affordability, making sure the tests you use complement each other, and making sure your materials come from reputable publishers who keep their materials regularly updated. Using the various criteria and tips for learning about formal assessments I've offered in this chapter, start making a list of what you might want to cover in the formal assessments you'll offer your clients.

When deciding which formal assessments I'm going to assign to individual clients, a key question is whether I've learned enough about the client to start helping them take their next steps. Always keep your own information needs in mind when ordering tests for your client. Think about clients you've worked with, either in practice sessions as a student or in your work as a career counselor or coach. Have you taken your own information needs into account, not just the client's?

One of our most challenging tasks as career counselors and coaches is delivering test results to clients. Doing this effectively requires a thorough grasp of test findings, which you can only achieve if you do your homework. I also learned a great deal from being tutored in this skill by a colleague—someone with a different (in fact, opposite) personality type than mine who helped me to more effectively engage clients when delivering results. Start thinking about how you might build your skills in this area.

There are many different ways to bolster your knowledge of formal assessments: reading, practice, finding a mentor, forming partnerships with colleagues, continuing education. (See also Section 3 in "The Quick-Reference Toolkit" on taking advantage of the resources offered by test publishers.) Think about where you are right now in the process of learning about formal assessments, and set some goals for yourself.

We can be incredibly hard on ourselves when we're still in the learning process. But it's always helpful to remember that, even when we're just starting out, we likely know a lot more about assessment than our clients do. Finding opportunities to practice doing assessment in a low-key, nonthreatening way—I gave assessments to family and friends when first starting out—will help build your confidence. Before you know it, you'll be working with paying clients who value, and benefit from, the expertise you offer.

Chapter 7

PROCESSING ASSESSMENT INFORMATION

Earlier in the book you met Don, a contract software developer looking for a permanent position, and Frank, a cook looking to explore new, more promising possibilities in the food industry. What both had in common, and what they share with other clients you'll meet throughout the book and in the case studies, is a willingness to dig in and *think* about what they were learning through assessment. Part of that was the clients themselves: both Don and Frank are intelligent, creative, serious about their goals, and willing to work hard. But they also benefited from my assessment approach, in which I ask that clients own what they're learning in assessment and then focus it on a plan of action.

The real work begins when the client starts to sort through and internalize what they're learning from assessment. This chapter will explore how to help clients manage the assessment information they're taking in. I'll discuss the need for information processing, how I use worksheets, and how I prepare clients for the next step of creating a game plan.

If you want your clients to come out of assessment more enlightened than before and ready to move forward, they need to take an active role, not just be passive receivers of information. More specifically, they need to take what they've learned and make it their own by writing things down, thinking things through, and discussing it afterward. And as their counselor or coach, you need evidence that they've learned something from the experience and are ready to put it to work. Having them complete the worksheets in this chapter, or something similar that you adapt to your own process, is a good way to gauge what they've learned and get them moving toward a plan for the future.

UNDERSTANDING THE NEED FOR INFORMATION PROCESSING

Have you ever worked with a client over several sessions only to have them say, either directly or indirectly, "Now what? What should I do next?" After years of working with clients, I gradually put my finger on the problem. Most clients who are stuck haven't yet *processed* the information coming out of assessment. They haven't yet made it their own or applied it to themselves specifically. To help resolve this problem and encourage clients to focus more intently, I developed a simple worksheet I call the Career Ingredients Summary Sheet (shown on page 72). The summary sheet reminds clients of key areas we addressed during assessment; helps them sort, prioritize, and simplify by eliminating less desirable options; and prepares them for writing the game plan.

A lot gets discussed during the interview and in going over formal assessments—strengths, weaknesses, key personality traits, career goals, and so on. Clients learn about strengths they can now put to use and industries that might welcome someone with their attributes and skill set. Often their career goals change when they discover new information and gain new insights.

Clients also learn what they *don't* want in their work. A distiller will tell you that distillation makes a product purer by separating impurities from the quality substance. The "impurities" might be results from assessment that don't appeal or aren't important to the client. On the Strong, for example, my client might look very similar to a paralegal but find legal work unappealing. So she would leave that off the sheet. Filling out the sheet also addresses the problem of information overload: clients don't have to attend to *everything* in their assessment reports—only what's most salient.

Finally, I encourage my clients to write a game plan, which outlines criteria they need to thrive in their work. (I discuss the game plan in detail in chapter 8.) The ingredients from the summary sheet are often a starting point for the plan. When clients write down the same thing in both places, it's much more likely to be something that's meaningful to them and something they'll act on.

Another tool I often use with clients is the Career and Job Compatibility Matrix, shown on page 73. With this worksheet, clients select from options arranged in different categories—industries, occupations, work environments, and so on; it gives them another way to sort and prioritize. I've found that the

CAREER INGREDIENTS SUMMARY SHEET

Use this sheet to record anything that stood out for you during our initial interview and when reviewing your test results. Feel free to add any additional thoughts that come to mind.

Strengths	Weaknesses	Insights
		What have I learned about myself?
Environment/Culture	**Personality Traits**	**People**
		Whom do I like hanging out with, especially at work?
Possible Industries	**Possible Occupations**	**Areas of Meaning**
		What's my purpose? What's worthwhile for me?
Career Goals	**Personal Goals**	**Outcomes**
		What results do I want right now?

CAREER AND JOB COMPATIBILITY MATRIX

Complete this form by checking or circling items in each category that are most appealing. If you don't see an item listed that comes to mind, add it to the list.

Preferred Industries	Preferred Role	Would Rather Avoid
Financial services Health care Life sciences Communications Media Retail Government Automotive Manufacturing Military Technical/IT Other:	Individual contributor Manager Negotiator Collaborator Decision maker Assistant Partner Strategist Sponsor Planner Implementer Other:	Politics Conflict Decision-making Standing out Risk taking Other:
Preferred Sector	**Preferred Company Size/Group**	
Corporate/Entrepreneurial Nonprofit Government	Small Medium Large	
Preferred Environment	**Preferred People Attributes/ Relationships**	**Other Considerations**

Artistic/aesthetically
  appealing
Modern
Rustic/older
Competitive
Cooperative
Nurturing/warm
Learning/growth
Challenge/results
Team-oriented
Encourages autonomy/
  independence
Quality conscious
Clearly defined/structured
Respectful
Mission-driven
Strong brand identity
Other:
	Professional
	Highly educated
	Customers
	Mechanical/hands-on
	Artistic/creative
	Social
	Quiet/reserved
	Productive
	Male
	Female
	Helpful/caring
	International
	Local
	Humorous
	Inclusive
	Independent
	Appreciative
	Competent
	Other:	

ideal time to have clients complete either the summary sheet or the matrix is after they've completed formal assessments. In fact, I've now made it standard practice to offer clients the Career Ingredients Summary Sheet after testing.

Note that the assessment components we've discussed in the book so far—the structured interview, formal assessments, and now the information-processing worksheets—can go a long way to increasing clients' self-awareness, as well as their comfort with change. Occasionally, though, clients need an additional boost of self-confidence or help with something that's troubling them. In Section 2 of "The Quick-Reference Toolkit," you'll find several exercises I use to boost my clients' self-esteem, encourage them to think more positively, and help them achieve better work-life balance.

COMPLETING AND DISCUSSING THE WORKSHEETS

Once clients' self-assessment sheets are completed, I'll make copies for myself, and we'll sit down and discuss what they've written or highlighted on the sheets. If I notice words or themes repeated from prior sessions—I always keep my structured interview notes and clients' test results close by for comparison—I'll mention that and ask clients why they wrote what they did.

My client David, an introvert, noted the following on the "Insights" section of his Career Ingredients Summary Sheet: "My results on 'inclusion' from FIRO-B: have to reach out to others more." The FIRO-B assessment is an instrument that looks at clients' needs and behaviors when interacting with others in terms of three basic factors: Affection, Inclusion, and Control. It measures to what degree clients *want* these factors in their lives and *express* this desire to others. For Inclusion, David tested average on "wanted" but lower than average on "expressed," meaning he needed to be more assertive in expressing his needs and wants to others.

While David and I had discussed this finding briefly when going over his test results, the fact that he noted it himself as a key insight led us to discuss it further and think about steps he could take to reach out to others and be more open to them about his needs.

Discovering and Rediscovering Strengths and Goals

When completing the worksheets, clients will sometimes note possibilities they hadn't considered before but are now considering based on what they've learned through assessment. When that happens, we'll talk about ways they might begin to explore the new possibility. In some cases, they decide to revisit a role in which they had previously been successful. My client Kevin is a good example of the latter scenario. Before being lured into a job as production manager, Kevin had done well as a technical consultant. In the "Possible Occupations" section of his summary sheet, Kevin wrote "technical consultant or engineer," with a view to revisiting or considering both possibilities.

Using the worksheets to process information is all about creating further *saliency* for your client. That is, what may have been a mere possibility or idea grows into something more real for them when they write it down. If you find that your clients are drawing a blank or asking, "Now what?," even after you've worked hard at assessment, consider that they may just need to process things further. Again, writing things down is key, as is discussing what it means and linking it to earlier assessment results. All of this reinforces what's most important for the client.

(To see worksheets Liz completed, see chapter 13. For more on Kevin and David, see their case studies in chapter 12.)

MOVING TOWARD THE GAME PLAN

If you think back to chapter 4, and also to the discussion earlier in this chapter, you'll recall that the goal of doing the worksheets is to be able to write a game plan, something we'll discuss in detail in the next chapter. Here I just want to outline some of what happens between the worksheets and the game plan, and the importance of keeping the client's eye on the prize. I also want to be clear on the realities of this process: as much as I would like them to, not every client fills in every part of the Career Ingredients Summary Sheet.

When I have clients complete the information worksheets, I will often remind them that the goal is to have a game plan highlighting what they need and want in their next job or career opportunity. In other words, the worksheets aren't ends in themselves but part of a deliberate process that, ideally, culminates in a game plan and forward movement for the client. It's not just busywork. Clients appreciate that their time is being used wisely and in a way they'll ultimately benefit from.

To help them clearly see the connection between the worksheets and the game plan, I will often hand them the game plan template at the same time I do the information-processing worksheets, with the understanding that they should complete the worksheets first. The goal is both reinforcement and increased clarity: If a client writes "web designer" under "Possible Occupations" on the Career Ingredients Summary Sheet and later in the "What" section of their game plan, you have evidence that web design is a serious possibility for the client.

Clients vary in the amount of information they provide on their Career Ingredients Summary Sheet, with some completing it in full, others completing two-thirds to three-quarters, and others struggling to fill in anything at all. If the client is struggling, I'll remind them of their previous assessment results, and often a little brainstorming is all that's needed to get the ball rolling. With the Career and Job Compatibility Matrix, sometimes clients select too many items, which is less helpful than if they differentiate between the choices and prioritize. In cases like that, I might suggest that they keep their choices to between three and five items per category.

Ideally, I have the luxury of assigning the Career Ingredients Summary Sheet (and, optionally, the Career and Job Compatibility Matrix) as homework, and then meet clients in the next session to discuss their work. We then move on to the game plan, which can also be assigned as homework. For clients who can only afford a session or two, I may provide them with copies of both the worksheets and the game plan anyway, and invite them to follow up later if they're interested. Sometimes they just need more time and will email me something in a month or two. But if clients don't end up following up—some do, and some don't—that's fine. It's natural for clients to move on, and many are quite self-sufficient to begin with. What's important is that I've offered them something practical—a set of tools they can use to focus their career needs and plan for the future.

REFLECTING ON CHAPTER 7:
PROCESSING ASSESSMENT INFORMATION

After conducting a structured interview with clients, and following that up with formal assessments, you'll have a lot of good information to work with. But at this point in the process, clients need to take stock. What have they learned about themselves, and what will they do with that knowledge going forward? In your work or study so far, what tools have you discovered or created for gathering this type of information?

The Career Ingredients Summary Sheet and Career and Job Compatibility Matrix are simple, convenient tools for capturing information from clients that can gauge their level of self-awareness. Notice how the summary sheet in particular captures some of those basic questions clients need to have answers to—what they believe are their essential strengths and weaknesses, particular insights they've gained from assessment, career goals they're looking at, and so on. Think about what you want clients to gain from assessment and how you will capture it.

When you analyze what clients write on their worksheets, keep in mind what you learned from their formal assessment results. Look for patterns, as well as for client insights that strike you. An important takeaway for David was that he needed to reach out to others more if he wanted to be included in their activities, something he learned from his results on the FIRO-B assessment. I was very pleased to learn that he had taken this finding to heart and was determined to work on it.

Clients need to see the point of completing the worksheets—that it's not just busywork. I want clients to be able to write a game plan as a result of the processing they've done, and the information processing worksheets I use are intermediate steps toward that goal. That's why I'll often provide clients with a game plan template ahead of time, so they know what they're working toward. Picture your clients at the end of an engagement. Do they have a plan for the future, and how will they get there?

If at all possible, assign worksheets as homework, so you can go over them in a follow-up session. Again, these worksheets are a way of tracking clients' self-awareness and learning as a result of the assessment you've been through together. What you ultimately want to see is consistency and continuity between what was learned in assessment and what clients are recording on the worksheets. When that happens, they're much more likely to be able to complete an effective game plan.

Chapter 8

. . . .

THE GAME PLAN

I sometimes work with organizations on what's called "selection assessment"—assessment that helps companies hire and develop the right candidates. As part of this process, I typically interview the candidate, administer job-related skills tests and a personality inventory, and report my findings to HR or the hiring manager or both. In doing this work, I've observed that candidates who get hired have clearly thought through what they want and need in a job. They're able to provide compelling arguments about their strengths, and they know their weaknesses and how to fix them or mitigate their impact. They've done their homework on the products, people, and culture of the organization. And they can clearly state how they can add value to a role.

It's a fact that self-confident clients like these get hired more frequently than uncertain ones. They're also more effective decision makers because they know what they're looking for and whether the next opportunity will meet their needs. That's exactly what I want for my own clients, and it's a big reason why I have them complete a game plan near the end of the engagement.

In the previous chapter I explained how I use some simple information-processing tools—the Career Ingredients Summary Sheet and Career and Job Compatibility Matrix—to help clients sort through information from assessment. The game plan takes this process a step further by funneling that information into a more focused and actionable form. This chapter will walk you through the game plan process and show you how to help clients complete a plan. It also includes three sample game plans reflecting a range of individuals and situations.

The game plan is a foundation for planning and decision-making. It's based on simple logic: once you've determined what you want and need in your career and your work, you can start taking steps to achieve it.

WRITING THE GAME PLAN

The game plan template (shown on page 80 and also in Section 1 of "The Quick-Reference Toolkit") is organized into two basic parts: criteria and action steps. Criteria are factors clients have determined they need in order to be happy and thrive in their current role or next opportunity. On the worksheet, they are divided according to three categories: What, Where, and Who. Action steps are any steps clients take toward their goals, based on the criteria they've set.

Examples of Criteria

Let's say that a client wants to work as a full-time web designer. An entry under What might be "build websites using WordPress." Under Where, they might record "medium to large companies," and under Who, they might have "working with a strong, cohesive team." To flesh the plan out further, the client might add "creative, customized design" in the What category, "opportunities for advancement" in the Where category, and "boss who understands web technology" in the Who category. And so on. As a plan gets fleshed out, you start to get a more comprehensive picture, one that's consistent with what you know about the client.

And by recording criteria they need in these basic and easy to visualize categories—What, Where, and Who—clients are in an excellent position to start taking steps to move forward.

Examples of Action Steps

For action steps, our web designer might want to "take a course or read some books on customizing WordPress themes," "explore job ads for web designers working in medium to large companies, and "look up potential employers, supervisors, and colleagues on LinkedIn."

While using a template like the one on page 80 is ideal, just using a blank sheet of paper or even the back of an envelope is fine, too. It's the *idea* behind the game plan—the What, Where, and Who criteria—that's most important. The point is that your client's thoughts are focused, not scattered, and that the work you've done in assessment has some kind of tangible, actionable result.

THE GAME PLAN WORKSHEET

Record your criteria and action steps below. If you need extra space, make another copy, or add pages as needed.

Game Plan Factor	Criteria
WHAT: What should I be when I grow up (occupation, role, etc.)?	• • • • •
WHERE: The environment, culture, size, pace, etc., of the place I work at.	• • • • •
WHO: The people I want to work with—ideal coworkers, clients, colleagues, etc.	• • • • •

Action Steps

Write down at least five things you can do now to move your job search or business forward.

1.
2.
3.
4.
5.

HELPING CLIENTS TO COMPLETE A PLAN

A game plan can be a powerful tool for helping clients consolidate what they've learned from assessment and take steps to move ahead. Although creating a game plan is pretty straightforward, sometimes clients need some extra assistance in creating a plan that's effective.

After assessment, most of my clients are ready to write a solid game plan. But for those who struggle or need more help, we may decide to do some additional work together. With some clients, the insights are there and just need drawing out through further discussion. If clients are feeling stuck or negative, sometimes an exercise can help. (See Section 2 of "The Quick-Reference Toolkit" for motivational exercises you can use with clients.)

Here's a strategy I've used to motivate clients to write a game plan: I let them know that I'll show them my own version of what I think their game plan might look like after they complete their own draft. We then compare versions, and in many cases, most of the criteria and themes are similar. For the client, this can feel quite affirming and validating. If there are major differences, it opens the door for more discussion and analysis.

It's important that clients complete all three parts of the plan: the What, Where, and Who. I'm particularly interested in the Where and Who, because these factors are often downplayed or neglected in assessment. If my client is an introvert, for example, she may not be happy in a company where employees are expected to be highly visible and sociable. So finding the right "where" is critical.

When it comes to the Action Steps portion of the plan, sometimes clients need to take some preliminary steps to position themselves to meet their criteria. For example, my client Kevin (see his game plan on page 83) was interested in finding a position in health care or a related field. But first he needed to do some networking to scope out possibilities. And because networking was a challenge for him, I recommended he read a book on the subject and start making some connections.

Finally, I'm a believer in crafting experiments to see what works and what doesn't, and the game plan supports that by suggesting new things to try. When clients do try something new—perhaps something out of their comfort zone—they see a new side of themselves that can enhance their experience going forward. Or they may realize that although actions they took got them out of their comfort zone for a while, the experiment did not yield the positive gains or learning they were hoping for. In this case, they can always try a new experiment.

When clients contact me again weeks or months after the initial engagement, their game plans serve as a great starting point for discussion. I've also found that criteria tend to hold up very well, so in discussing their situation and looking at next steps, we're usually fine-tuning rather than starting from scratch. Think of the game plan as a prize for doing assessment well. If you do it well and pay attention to what you find—if you and your clients discuss the findings thoughtfully and get the specifics down in writing—you'll have a strong foundation from which to move forward.

SAMPLE GAME PLANS

The best way to appreciate the game plan is to see it in action, so I'm including three sample game plans in this chapter—one for my client Kevin (page 83); one for my former client and collaborator on this book, Liz (page 85); and one for myself (page 86). The game plan is a versatile document that can be used as part of the overall assessment process, as it was for Kevin, or written up to take stock of your current situation and career goals.

When assessing a client's game plan, look for consistency across the criteria. For example, in Kevin's plan, for his What criteria, he wants to play an individual contributor (or expert) role, and he doesn't want to supervise people. For his Where criteria, he notes that he wants to work at a medium-sized or larger firm. And for his Who criteria, he says he wants to work with people who are engaged and adept at their work. There's consistency here: Kevin is more likely to find an individual contributor role in a larger company where specialized roles are part of the organizational structure. And people who are engaged and adept at their work are people who may be less in need of supervision, something Kevin wants to avoid.

With the game plan, the goal is for clients to be able to articulate what they need and want based on their renewed self-awareness after assessment. In Kevin's case, for example, his supervisor had been difficult and didn't show Kevin the respect he felt he deserved. So within the Where and Who sections of his plan, Kevin includes criteria that he hopes will help him avoid that in future jobs. In his Where criteria, for example, he indicates that he wants to work in a culture in which coworkers are "respectful." And for his Who criteria, he wants to work with people who are "principled, considerate, and professional." (You can learn more about Kevin's situation in his case study in chapter 12.)

Interestingly, the style in which the game plan is written can reflect personality type. For example, notice that Kevin and Liz, both INTJs (Introverted, Intuitive, Thinking, Judging), have written their plans in more general, abstract terms ("challenges intellect," "consultant and individual contributor," "tangible results"). Looking at my own game plan, you will see more detail ("counseling/coaching individuals in transition or those who are experiencing a loss"; "Provide practical and tactical advice to people who are willing to try things out, follow through, and take ownership"). As an ISTJ (Introverted, Sensing, Thinking, Judging), I'm more comfortable when things are more detailed and specific. But either style works, so long as it's meaningful to the individual writing the plan.

After the sample game plans, we'll look briefly at what happened in the months after we wrote our plans. In each case, you'll see that writing the plans helped: Kevin landed a job that better suited his strengths, and Liz and I confirmed that what we're doing in our careers is on track. That's the beauty of having a game plan: it keeps you focused on what you need to thrive in your work.

Kevin's Game Plan

Kevin had held some production manager jobs in manufacturing that he later struggled with. After assessment, he decided that he would be happier in more of an individual contributor role, and his game plan presents some criteria for such a role.

Game Plan Factor	Criteria
WHAT: What should I be when I grow up (occupation, role, etc.)?	• Learn new things/challenges intellect • Engineer, physician, chemist, biologist, actuary, math/science teacher, medical research, statistician • Individual contributor; expert • Not supervising or leading people • Medical industry • Something that fits with my values • Solving problems • Hands-on/goal-oriented work/projects • Tangible results
WHERE: The environment, culture, size, pace, etc., of the place I work at.	• Environment: more order and less ambiguity • Culture: professional, coworkers respectful • Size: medium size and up • Pace: fairly busy, not frantic, excessive work hours not expected (greater than 50 hours per week average) • Cooperative vs. Competitive • Nonpolitical
WHO: The people I want to work with—ideal coworkers, clients, colleagues, etc.	• People are friendly • Principled, considerate, professional • People who can be trusted and are dependable • People who are engaged and adept at their work • Appreciation for team efforts more than Individual • Believe in the work they do • Enjoy challenges and learning

Action Steps

1. Create elevator pitch—need to work on this!
2. To-do list for every day—have been using a planner for this.
3. Expand network—working on this, joining Minnesota Manufacturing Association and Medical Alley.
4. Read *The 20-Minute Networking Meeting* (Ballinger, Perez).
5. Explore my marketing materials—résumés and cover letters.

Liz's Game Plan

Liz, my collaborator on this book, has always wanted to make the most of her talents as a writer and editor. For her, creating a game plan was all about defining who she is. While her game plan started out as an exercise—she wanted to see how it worked so she could help write about it for the book—she loves the finished product because it truly captures what she's learned about herself over time.

Game Plan Factor	Criteria
WHAT: What should I be when I grow up (occupation, role, etc.)?	• Thinker, writer, editor, analyst • Creator of original content requiring research, thinking, creativity (e.g., own website) • Focus on ability to persuade and inform • Consultant and individual contributor • Author, co-author, self-publisher, content owner • Books, web content, white papers, sales letters, articles, landing pages, blog posts, affiliate marketing
WHERE: The environment, culture, size, pace, etc., of the place I work at.	• Must foster autonomy, creativity • Home office or other venue (shared office space) • Quiet essential for concentration when writing • Livelier venues (coffee shops, etc.) for meetings • Structure and deadlines (primarily self-imposed)
WHO: The people I want to work with—ideal coworkers, clients, colleagues, etc.	• Creative people who love ideas and understand the skill needed to communicate them • Professionals like Dean with complementary skills who want to communicate their expertise • Small-business owners needing help with marketing materials or other content • Editors needing ideas or content • Other writers (nonfiction primarily)

Action Steps

1. Continue developing my writing skills (especially copywriting).
2. Revise website from the ground up (more emphasis on writing/original content).
3. Look for more opportunities to collaborate on writing projects.
4. Explore coworking spaces (many new ones popping up).
5. Study content needs of consultants and small businesses.

Dean's Game Plan

My own game plan reflects how I like to work after more than thirty years in the field, and writing it helped affirm that I'm on track. You'll notice that many of my action steps relate to ongoing professional development: networking, meeting with my mastermind group, staying up to date on my reading. All of these activities keep me engaged and continuing to learn.

Game Plan Factor	Criteria
WHAT: What should I be when I grow up (occupation, role, etc.)?	• Implementing, analyzing, debriefing test/assessment data • Counseling/coaching individuals in transition or those who are experiencing a loss • Presenting, facilitating, or instructing groups in life/career topics • Consulting with organizations on various employee issues such as selection, downsizing, career, performance improvement, communication, bullying/respect, or "fit" considerations • Assignments are clearly articulated in terms of scope. • Work allows for variety of functions and clientele.

Game Plan Factor	Criteria
WHERE: The environment, culture, size, pace, etc., of the place I work at.	• Private practice so I can control my schedule, variety, clientele, and type of work • Steady pace most of the time, but able to take on "crunch" projects at times • Environment can vary depending on the work situation: company site, university, client site. • Culture is open, respectful, with clear communication; nonpolitical in nature.
WHO: The people I want to work with—ideal coworkers, clients, colleagues, etc.	• People on the front lines, operations folks; individual contributors; some managers but few if any executives. Strong interest in manufacturing and health care environments. • Provide practical and tactical advice to people who are willing to try things out, follow through, and take ownership of issues that impact them. • Both individuals and organizations; can work with any size of organization, but likely more comfortable with smaller or midsize places.

Action Steps

1. Attend networking/professional organizations at least monthly.
2. Find new speaking opportunities (aim for three a year), particularly related to career or bullying topics.
3. Meet with Mastermind group each month for new/fresh perspectives.
4. Read at least three career-related books each year and several articles.
5. Continue working on the book.

Post–Game Plan: What Happened Next?

Creating a game plan is an exciting process in which you set out what you're going to need to thrive in the future. At this writing, I'm happy to say that all three of our game plans are holding up, and we're all making progress toward our goals. Is everything perfect? No. But the groundwork we laid in our plans is solid and continues to reap benefits.

Kevin

Five months after we began work together, Kevin landed a position as a technical consultant for a food manufacturer and has worked with that same company for three years at this writing. (His previous background had been in the food and medical industries, so although his first preference was to work in the medical field, he was fine with returning to the food sector again.) In general, Kevin feels he's making a difference at the company and that there are many projects he can influence. Most people at the company are friendly and relate well to each other, an important part of his Who criteria.

However, although he had a great boss for the first two years, his current boss is a micromanager. He was hired from outside the company and has been a disruptive presence. Soon after he was hired, he fired a key person on the team, another key person left, and another was forced out after only three months on the job. He expects Kevin to answer questions and work on projects after hours instead of during regular hours, and told Kevin he was lucky to have a job. Sensing his boss may eventually try to undermine him, Kevin is quietly seeking a new opportunity, something again related to project management or engineering in a food or medical environment. I have urged Kevin to document his boss's disrespectful and bullying behavior as he looks for a new opportunity.

There's an addition he'd like to add to his game plan, and that's work that doesn't require a lot of travel. In his initial work with his current company, he was required to travel frequently for various projects. That has since eased somewhat (even before the COVID-19 pandemic), and as a family man and father of three, Kevin finds he likes staying close to his home base. It's ultimately the "boss" issue—a Who factor that's not being met and that is critical to job satisfaction—that has forced him to return to search mode.

For more on Kevin, see his case study in chapter 12.

Liz

Liz's vision of her future is starting to come into reality: for example, she was able to collaborate on writing this book. For her What criteria, Liz envisions herself as a "creator of original content requiring research, thinking, and creativity." Her work on this book and her new blog certainly meet those criteria. She's also looking forward to future collaborations with other authors, particularly those working in career development, small business and entrepreneurship, and independent writing and editing.

A key goal Liz has now is to reestablish and market herself as a freelance editor—work that she has largely ignored as she has put her focus on writing. While her dream has always been to be a writer, editing is something she also does well, and having editing work can help pay the bills. So a goal she's working on right now is to add an editing services page to her website to market her capabilities in that area. She also plans to rejoin one or more professional associations that serve writers and editors. Marketing her blog and her editing services are top priorities.

For her game plan, one of Liz's action steps reads "Revise website from the ground up (more emphasis on writing/original content)." In January 2020, Liz shut down her old website and launched a brand-new website that includes a blog (lizwillis.com). Liz is using the blog to offer insights for others like herself who are older but still dream of making the most of themselves, particularly when it comes to writing.

For more on Liz, see her story and assessment analysis in chapter 13.

Dean

I continue to enjoy a variety of assignments, including career, clinical, and selection assessments, as well as doing counseling and coaching on specific issues with clients. I love the variety, which is important to me and keeps me engaged in the work. Most of my career and transition clients continue to be frontline operations types, and many are individual contributors. So I am staying consistent with my criteria in this regard. Over the past five years, my work has trended toward more work with individual clients than with organizations. I enjoy working with individual clients, so I'm quite okay with this trend. The pace of work continues to be steady, but not fast, which I like.

One area that's dropped off a bit in the last couple of years or so is public speaking. Part of that is due to my own schedule—ongoing client work, outplacement projects, work on this book, and personal travel and recreation have kept me busy, so I haven't been pursuing opportunities as aggressively as I might have in the past. But the COVID-19 pandemic has also been a major factor. Local meetings are all online, so the idea of presenting is not quite as appealing. I've also been conducting most of my client work by phone, Zoom, or Skype. While I've always done that to a certain extent for clients who were out of town or couldn't manage an in-person meeting for some reason, this is a "new normal" I'm not entirely happy with.

Until COVID-19, I hadn't fully realized just how important it was for me to go out and meet people in a variety of locations, as opposed to spending most of my work time at home. Although I'm an introvert, I do like to socialize, and I also dislike being sedentary. As for working with clients, meeting remotely is okay, but technical glitches are common, and you just can't beat the inter-action, energy, and clarity you get from in-person meetings. On the plus side, my current pace and schedule have allowed me to maintain a good work/life balance. I can do a workout, take a bike ride, or schedule a two- to three-day getaway with my wife with little problem. I have lots of flexibility while still being able to meet my obligations.

For more on my career, see the Q&A in chapter 14.

REFLECTING ON CHAPTER 8:
THE GAME PLAN

There's no point in gathering a lot of assessment information if you can't put what you've discovered into action. Having clients write a game plan—that is, determining criteria they need for the What, Where, and Who of their work— is a solution that works for me. In your work with clients, or in your studies as a student, what strategies have you discovered for turning assessment results into action?

The game plan is based on the reality that *where* you work and *who* you work with is critical to your success, and that you might not get to realize your "what" (what you want to be or do when you grow up) if you don't attend closely to the where and the who. In the assessment strategies that you've learned about in your studies or used in your work, how much emphasis is placed on these external factors? (In Part 3 of the book, "Assessing the Work Environment," I delve deeper into some of these issues.)

In my assessment process, the game plan represents something tangible cli-ents can take with them at the end of an engagement to help them focus their efforts and keep moving forward. Are you aware of similar tools or worksheets for consolidating assessment information and determining next steps? How do they compare with the game plan? (One of the benefits of the game plan is its simplicity.) For an optional cover sheet you can use with the game plan to introduce it to clients, see Section 1 of the "Quick-Reference Toolkit."

The game plan is a versatile tool that can be used during a client engagement or simply as a "taking stock" exercise. If you are in the process of planning your future as a career developmental professional—whether you're a student or currently working—try writing a game plan today, and see what you discover and what might need further thinking through. Also, if you haven't already, make sure to read Part 1, "Assessing Yourself and Your Career," for more ideas.

One of the benefits of having a game plan is that it becomes a point of reference when clients return for additional coaching later on. With Kevin, for example, we knew from our original assessment that an individual contributor role, and not a supervisory one, would best suit his strengths and be in his best interests. So, some months later, when Kevin spoke of moving on after a new boss took over at his work, we kept his game plan close by when discussing his options. In assessing clients, look for ways to capture key facts you can quickly revisit should clients contact you again.

Part 3

ASSESSING THE WORK ENVIRONMENT

Chapter 9
. . . .

WORK VALUES ASSESSMENT
AND JOB SATISFACTION

To be successful, our clients must find a match between what they have to offer and what employers or business clients are looking for. And that can be a daunting task. The fit between employer and worker is often not adequately addressed in assessment, where the focus tends to be on client considerations rather than external factors like work environments, corporate cultures, and worker-boss relationships. To explore this territory, my colleague Rich Bents and I developed the Career Compatibility Scale (CCS), a work values and job satisfaction assessment tool.

In previous chapters we looked at my overall assessment process, leading up to the game plan. Over the course of an engagement with selected clients, I usually employ the CCS sometime during the formal assessments phase, after the structured interview and before information processing. I find the CCS particularly useful for clients who are experiencing some kind of conflict or mismatch between their work and what's most important to them.

This chapter will discuss how the CCS was developed and the key features of the tool, along with highlights from a report produced for my client Ed.

If you're not currently focusing on work values and job satisfaction as part of your assessment process, exploring these factors could open up a new dimension. For example, how many of your clients are unhappy with their working relationship with their boss or the degree of influence they have at work? I'm guessing a good percentage of them. ("Boss" and "Influence" are two of the nine CCS themes.) Again, most assessments focus on the individual and not on others they work with or the specific environments or conditions they work in.

For an example of a work environment that wasn't working for one of my clients, see "Right Work, Wrong Place: Denise's Story" on page 97.

A BRIEF INTRODUCTION TO THE CCS

About ten years ago, after interviewing hundreds of clients and recording their responses over the years, I had amassed a treasure trove of comments on underutilized skills, dysfunctional teams, toxic bosses, and other woes affecting clients' happiness and their ability to thrive at work. Some of the interview questions that had elicited these responses included:

- What kind of supervisor do you work best for? Worst for?
- Is your work meaningful to you? How important is work in your life?
- What are your sources of job satisfaction?
- Describe someone you have admired, appreciated, or respected in your life.
- What makes you happy about life? Upset about life?

Fortunately, these same interview questions yielded plenty of positive responses as well. I learned what had made clients' work meaningful, tasks they had found particularly satisfying, role models they had looked up to, and things that had made them happy, both at work and at home. My files were overflowing with information on my clients' job and life satisfaction—or lack thereof.

Then I had an insight: Instead of just storing this data in my files, why not use it to help my clients assess how well their current job was meeting their needs? So I started analyzing client responses by topic. I ultimately identified nine facets or themes of work that could be measured and explored: Boss, Environment, Influence, Organization, People, Purpose, Recognition, Task/Challenge, and Team.

These nine themes became the basis of the CCS, which I began developing in 2010 and piloted in 2012 in partnership with Rich. I make the CCS available to my clients and client groups, and it's also featured on Rich's website, ShareOn Corporate Leader Resources, which provides an extensive library of assessments and other tools for consultants, psychologists, educators, and business professionals. (See Appendix C for an invitation to try the CCS.)

The CCS measures how important certain workplace factors are to a client and to what extent these factors are being met in their current or recent job. For each theme, test takers answer four to five question sets, or pairs, based on a Likert scale. Upon completion, each test taker receives a detailed personalized report explaining which themes are most important to them, where gaps exist between what they report as important and what they're experiencing at work, and ways they can begin addressing areas with the largest gaps.

RIGHT WORK, WRONG PLACE: DENISE'S STORY

Denise worked as an occupational therapist (OT) in a nursing home. She found the place deeply depressing, and when she came to me, she was seriously thinking about changing careers. On the Values Scale, a key scale for measuring work values I've often used with clients, Denise scored highest on altruism, achievement, and social interaction, all positive values for someone in OT. Other tests, including the Strong Interest Inventory assessment and 16PF Questionnaire, also suggested OT work would be a good fit.

But none of these assessments looked at *where* Denise was currently working or *whom* she was working with. The Values Scale, for example, ranks values according to importance, but it has nothing to say about where or with whom Denise might best realize her values of altruism, achievement, and social interaction. As it turns out, it was the environment in which Denise was working—not OT work itself—that was not a good fit.

While she loved being of service to others (altruism), her needs for achievement and social interaction weren't being met in the nursing home environment. First, with an older clientele, many of whom were frail, there was only so much she could do to improve their situation, which she found frustrating and depressing. Second, as the sole OT at the nursing home, she had no higher position to advance to and no peers to talk to or bounce ideas off of. So not only did she feel that her professional growth and achievement opportunities were limited, she was also lonely.

Denise eventually found a summer program that allowed her to apply her OT skills with children. Suddenly she felt alive again—she loved her new OT role and the work she did. The organization was large enough that she now had peers she could count on for friendship, support, and feedback. And because she was doing OT with kids instead of elderly clients, she was able to see more results from her work. When she told me about her new job, I wasn't surprised that it fit her so well. When I first interviewed her, she had said she wanted to get married and have children someday, and so I think there was something about the vitality of children that inspired and motivated her.

Although I actually worked with Denise before I developed the CCS, it's stories like hers that inspire me to continue working on it, to help clients understand that their work environment—the company, culture, people, pace, tasks, and so on that they experience on a day-to-day basis—can have a huge impact on their prospects, effectiveness, and happiness. Yet these external aspects of assessment are not always explored to the extent they should be.

While there are many tools out there that measure work values, to the best of my knowledge, none of these tools measures whether those values are actually being met in a client's current work situation. Most values instruments do not connect values directly to current conditions but instead look at them in isolation. By measuring the gap between what clients value and what they're experiencing at work, the CCS links work values and job satisfaction in a meaningful way.

CCS THEMES AND WHAT THEY MEASURE

When it comes to job fit and satisfaction, what counts is the importance of a particular facet of work to the client. For example, if it's important to my client that his efforts at work be acknowledged and that doesn't happen, this lack of recognition—one of the nine themes—may have a negative impact on his job satisfaction. For another client, exerting influence (another theme) might be more important than receiving recognition or rewards. Below are the nine themes in more detail.

1. **Boss.** Having a manager, supervisor, or other leader to report to and receive guidance from; what level of interaction, feedback, information, and support you need from your boss in order to thrive in your job.

2. **Environment.** Feeling comfortable in your work environment, including liking the people you work with; feeling both physically and emotionally safe and free from harassment; and feeling that the pace of work and culture of the organization are a good fit given your needs and values.

3. **Influence.** Taking responsibility for your own or others' work and making an impact on that work; what level of authority and involvement you prefer to have in the decision-making process.

4. **Organization.** The organization's size, rate of growth, reputation, and prominence in the community, and whether opportunities for advancement are available; structure—the degree to which hierarchy, roles, and tasks are clearly defined—is also important.

5. **People.** Interacting regularly and positively with other people in the organization, as well as the extent to which other people's cultural background, social status, values, educational level, and behavior affect your ability to work successfully at your job.

6. **Purpose.** Having a purpose beyond material gain and working for an organization whose mission goes beyond making a profit; helping such an organization fulfill its mission is more important to you than a high salary or other tangible rewards.

7. **Recognition.** Receiving praise and/or tangible rewards (good pay, raises, bonuses) for the work you do; need for warmth, affection, and respect from others.

8. **Task/Challenge.** The relationship of your work role, assigned tasks, and required skills to your overall job satisfaction; how important it is to have tasks and projects that challenge you, that require continuous improvement and education, and that involve high performance standards.

9. **Team.** Working on a team versus working independently; what size the team should be, how often the team should meet, and how the team should interact, including cooperating with one another, sharing responsibility, and communicating project information.

Again, the CCS measures how important each of these themes are, as well as the gap between what clients want in their work and what they're actually experiencing. Both are explained in detail in the report clients receive upon completion of the CCS.

THE CCS PERSONALIZED REPORT

After clients complete the CCS, they receive a comprehensive, eighteen-page personalized report organized into four sections: "CCS Gap Overview," "CCS Importance Overview," "Themes in Detail," and "Recommendations for Development."

Our goal for the CCS report is to create greater clarity as to why a particular role or job is or isn't working. There's a certain power to seeing something on paper that screams, "Make a change!" or, conversely, affirms, "You're in a good place."

Report Section	What It Does
CCS Gap Overview	Lists the nine themes in order, from the theme with the largest gap to the theme with the smallest, with the top three gaps highlighted. Again, the gap is the difference between your ideal and your current situation based on answers to the question pairs.
CCS Importance Overview	Lists the nine themes in order of importance, from most important to least important. While determining the gap between the ideal and current situation is the central function of the CCS, "importance" is a significant factor that clients can put to good use in assessment. For example, they can use it in prioritizing criteria in their game plan or in making decisions.
Themes in Detail	Each of the nine themes is described in detail, with results broken down on the basis of theme-based questions asked during the assessment.
Recommendations for Development	For the three themes with the largest gaps, test takers are invited to engage in some brief developmental activities, including answering questions and taking steps for further exploration. For example, for the Environment theme, one question posed is "What is it that makes you feel uncomfortable about the work environment?" A follow-up activity is to find two people and/or resources to help you improve the situation.

When my client Ed was first hired as an art instructor at a private college, he was thrilled. But once he realized that the college was more focused on the bottom line than helping students—at least that's how it seemed to Ed—he became disenchanted and quit.

When Ed took the CCS, his results showed a very high importance score (ninety-second percentile) for Purpose—the importance of having a purpose beyond material gain and working for an organization whose mission goes beyond making a profit. This need to find purpose had come up repeatedly in my discussions with Ed over the years.

According to the "CCS Importance Overview" in Ed's report, Purpose, the theme most important to him, is followed by Environment and then Task/Challenge.

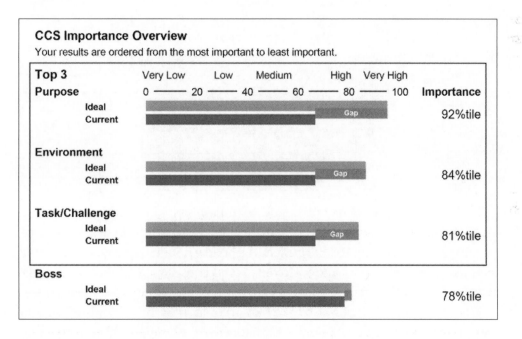

Interestingly, while Purpose was Ed's highest-scoring theme in terms of importance, it wasn't the highest gap. His gap for Purpose was only moderate.

However, on the specific issue of the company's mission, the gap was significant. According to the Purpose page of the "Themes in Detail" section of Ed's report, based on his response to the statement "The mission of the organization is an important ingredient in choosing a job," he scored a whopping 70 percent gap between what was important to him and what he had experienced at work (see the graph on the next page).

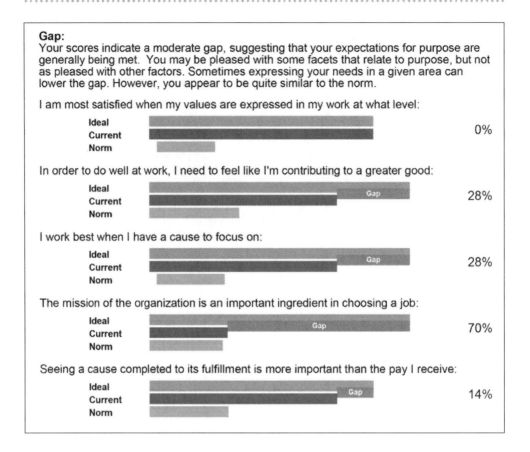

This graph illustrates one of the most useful aspects of the CCS: the ability to analyze aspects of a theme at a detailed level. So again, even if Ed was experiencing only a moderate gap for Purpose in the aggregate, the large gap concerning the mission of the organization is telling—and consistent with his disenchantment with the college and its focus on the bottom line instead of students.

When assessing clients, I also take into account how their CCS results mesh with other findings. For example, Ed happens to be an ENFP (Extraverted, Intuitive, Feeling, Perceiving). In *Do What You Are*, a book that applies the Myers-Briggs Type Indicator (MBTI) assessment to career choices, the authors explain that ENFPs crave work that's "consistent with [their] personal beliefs and values and lets [them] create opportunities that benefit others." When I last connected with Ed, he was volunteering for a food bank and exploring ways he could use his art to help others in need.

To see Ed's full case study, see chapter 12. For more on the book *Do What You Are*, see Appendix B.

The CCS Report and Group Assessment

As of this writing, the CCS personalized report is available only for individuals, not groups. However, if teams or other groups take the CCS for the purpose of team assessment or development, results can be analyzed to highlight any gaps common to the team, as well as identify themes the team overall believes are important. Also, because the "Themes in Detail" portion of the report breaks down a theme according to answers to specific questions, it allows for a detailed analysis of what's happening with regard to that theme. For example, the Purpose theme can be analyzed in terms of the importance of:

- having one's values achieved through work
- contributing to the greater good
- having a specific cause to focus on at work
- the company's mission (as a reason for choosing that employer)
- fulfilling a cause versus achieving monetary gains.

Similarly, the "Recommendations for Development" pages create a structure for engaging team members to address any themes with significant gaps and to lower the gaps to more manageable levels. For example, if a majority of team members believe in the company's mission but many of them are having difficulty achieving those values through work, this gap can be explored at both an individual and a team level.

If you're interested in organizational development and performance theory, see "Classics on Motivation and Performance" for a short list of classic theorists and books that relate to the CCS. While, as I've explained, the roots of the CCS are very practical—it began as an analysis of responses to interview questions—CCS themes do happen to correlate well with some of the classic theory.

CLASSICS ON MOTIVATION AND PERFORMANCE

When clients are dissatisfied with work, it's often tied to lack of motivation, as well as confusion about what they need to perform at their best. Below are three classic sources on motivation and performance that I've studied and benefited from in my practice.

In his Two-Factor Theory, first developed in the 1950s, Frederick Herzberg differentiated between motivators—challenging work, responsibility, recognition, and other positive factors—and hygiene factors, things that don't motivate per se but can cause dissatisfaction if not present. For many people, things like salary, status, working conditions, and the like fall into this category. In 1993, Herzberg, along with Bernard Mausner and Barbara Bloch Snyderman, wrote the highly acclaimed *The Motivation to Work*, in which they use worker accounts in their research.

In the CCS, Task/Challenge, Recognition, and Influence all represent motivators. Hygiene factors are Boss, People, Organization, and Environment.

In their book *First, Break All the Rules*, Marcus Buckingham and Curt Coffman identify twelve questions that provide a framework for determining high-performing individuals and organizations. These questions correlate strongly with Herzberg's motivators, but not with the hygiene factors, which the authors feel have little connection to high performance. Yet because hygiene factors are related to job satisfaction—if they're absent, employees may be dissatisfied—they're still important. The authors emphasize the key role of managers and bosses, contending that people don't leave companies, they leave bosses. Many of my clients either praised their bosses or cited them as a reason for leaving their jobs.

In the CCS, Boss, Environment, Influence, People, Task/Challenge, Purpose, and Recognition all relate to the ideas Buckingham and Coffman put forward in their book.

David McClelland, who wrote *The Achievement Motive* (1953) and *Human Motivation* (1987), studied work performance in managers and other employees to determine what led to work success. He and his colleagues established "achievement motivation" as an interaction between the individual's personality and their environment. The three key conditions needed for achievement were (1) a work environment where they could assume responsibility for solving problems, (2) a willingness to take some risk and establish goals, and (3) a need for regular recognition, feedback, and other information in order to know how they were doing.

In the CCS, these conditions correlate with the Influence, Task/Challenge, and Recognition themes, respectively.

REFLECTING ON CHAPTER 9: WORK VALUES ASSESSMENT AND JOB SATISFACTION

I created the Career Compatibility Scale (CCS) because I realized that, based on clients' answers to interview questions, a lot of factors relating to job satisfaction might not be addressed in more traditional assessment and testing. In your studies, or in the work you've done with clients, to what extent have work values and job satisfaction factored into the equation? What assessment tools are you currently aware of that measure these factors?

Clients contemplating a career change need to think carefully about what's prompting the change—their chosen career or the environment they're working in. My client Denise, featured in the sidebar, chose the right career but the wrong work environment. Once she discovered the right environment, which was working with children rather than with the elderly, she was much happier. What strategies have you used, or studied about, for clients changing careers?

Think about the nine themes the CCS covers: Boss, Environment, Influence, Organization, People, Purpose, Recognition, Task/Challenge, and Team. Just off the top of your head, what client issues do these themes suggest for you? Do you currently have a way of capturing this information? Feel free to use these theme descriptions to develop your own interview questions or other assessment tools.

How important is each theme to you in your work? In taking the CCS myself, I discovered that "Boss" is an important theme for me. Although I enjoy being an independent coach and consultant, I also appreciate receiving direction and insights from knowledgeable authorities. That's why having mentors has always been important to me in my own career development.

The CCS was created by compiling and analyzing responses from my structured interview. Have you ever thought of utilizing data you're gathering through assessment to create your own assessment product? Even if you don't create an actual product, analyzing assessment data at a more detailed level can deepen your knowledge of assessment and its uses.

Chapter 10

· · · · · · · · · · · ·

ASSESSING AND HELPING
BULLIED CLIENTS

Sometime around the early 2000s, I began to notice a disturbing trend in my business. Instead of focusing on career development issues and job search, some of my clients seemed to be fixated on one thing and one thing only: *survival*. More specifically, clients were being bullied at work and wondering what to do about it. Should they stay, or should they leave? Should they fight, or should they give in? Should they contact HR or keep quiet? Was it really the bully's fault, or was there something wrong with them?

When you think about career assessment, workplace bullying probably isn't the first thing that comes to mind. But in assessing clients today, I believe we need to consider how they've been treated at work, and whether that treatment has had a negative effect that may be impacting their self-esteem or limiting their potential. Mistreatment that's more subtle than outright bullying, perhaps in the form of neglect or indifference, can also have a major impact on clients' well-being and career prospects. We want to do all we can to help clients avoid getting bullied again.

This chapter will discuss what research has found about workplace bullying and how to use assessment to help bullied clients. Adding a greater awareness of this topic to your repertoire can enhance your assessment capabilities overall. If workplace bullying is of particular interest to you and you want to further your research in this area, see Appendix D, where you'll find several resources on bullying to explore. I believe that the more aware we are of this important subject as career development professionals, the better we can serve our clients.

Before we get further into the chapter, I want to briefly explain how I define bullying. Workplace bullying is any kind of ongoing, disrespectful behavior that's intended to minimize, marginalize, intimidate, or control an individual.

Bullying includes a complex of behaviors that occur along a continuum, from gossip to physical aggression. Repeated disrespectful or hurtful behaviors—bullying is rarely a one-time event or action—can lead to health risks such as anxiety, sleep disruptions, depression, high blood pressure, and rashes. The target of bullying often feels unsafe or insecure, resulting in being less effective at work. Bullying in the workplace must be addressed.

UNDERSTANDING THE SCOPE OF THE PROBLEM

When you look at the statistics on workplace bullying, they're pretty sobering. Here are some highlights from a 2014 survey conducted by the Workplace Bullying Institute (WBI) and from my own research conducted on clients I surveyed from 2011 through 2013.

Research	Findings
WBI (2014)	According to the WBI survey, it's estimated that in the US: • 37 million people are bullied annually in the workplace (and more than 1 out of 4 will experience workplace bullying at some point in their career). • 61% of bullied people leave their jobs because of it, while only 15% of bullies do. • 72% of employers deny, discount, rationalize, encourage, or defend workplace bullying.
DeGroot (2011–2013)	When I interviewed 33 targets of bullying (27 women, 6 men), I found that: • 59% had been bullied or abused when they were a child or teen. • 73% of targets were between the ages of 41 to 61 (mean average of 45.6 years) and had a mean average of 5.7 years tenure with the organization. • The vast majority of bullies (61%) were immediate supervisors; if other levels of management were included, the percentage rose to 77%. • HR and Employee Assistance Programs (EAPs) were able to help in only 13% of cases, and 74% of respondents believed HR was not helpful or actually made their situation worse.

The WBI has conducted additional surveys since 2014; see WBI.org. I also discuss the WBI briefly in Appendix D.

USING ASSESSMENT TO HELP BULLIED CLIENTS

Whether clients approach me directly about bullying or it comes out gradually during the engagement, assessment helps me better understand and manage the situation. Each component, from the structured interview to formal assessments to homework, has a role to play.

The Structured Interview

In the interview, I almost always ask clients to describe the type of boss they work well for, or, conversely, bosses they don't work so well for. When watching clients answer this question, I pay particular attention to their body language. If a client is feeling harmed in some way, it often shows up in their nonverbal behavior. When this nonverbal behavior is accompanied by answers that suggest abuse might be happening, I'll come right out and ask them if they've been bullied at work.

Another question I like to ask clients is what they've gained in their current or most recent position. While you would think this question would prompt someone to describe a positive experience—and that is in fact my goal in asking it—I've found that it can be an opportunity for clients who've been "kicked around" to open up about their situation. When clients talk about "headaches" or "getting the runaround" or mention other woes, it's often a sign that something's amiss at work. When that happens, I'll ask some follow-up questions to learn more.

Of course, discussing bullying with clients can be sensitive. Most adults feel a certain amount of embarrassment, or even shame, about the treatment they've experienced at the hands of a toxic boss or colleague. Who wants to admit that they were bullied? Isn't that something *kids* go through? (According to my survey, 59% of respondents were, in fact, bullied or abused as children. And the effects of childhood bullying can linger for years and make the target more susceptible in adulthood.) Talking openly and honestly about the bullying is essential.

Formal Assessments

In my experience, tests almost always reveal vulnerabilities that bullies tend to take advantage of. While this in no way justifies bullying, it does help us understand how it can take place. Assessment instruments such as the FIRO-B assessment, 16PF Questionnaire, and CPI 434 assessment are especially useful for revealing important clues on the target-bully dynamic, as shown in the table below. I've also included a brief discussion of my Career Compatibility Scale and key themes it addresses that are relevant to bullying.

Assessment Instrument	Clues to the Target-Bully Dynamic
Fundamental Interpersonal Relations Orientation-Behavior (FIRO-B) assessment	When a client shows a low need to assert control and a high need for affection and inclusion, the bully may see an opportunity. Because the target isn't a take-charge type, the bully may move in to fill that void, either believing that the target wants their guidance or control or merely taking advantage of the situation. To add to this dynamic, targets who value warmth and support from others are likely to be conflict averse and so may fail to report the abuse until significant damage has been done.
16PF (Personality Factors) Questionnaire	Targets can fall prey to bullies if they are too forthright and trusting (nonpolitical and too honest with their thoughts and ideas), have a high need for harmony and support, and tend not to be assertive. Also, when I see that my client's "Apprehension" score is high, that's telling me they're worried or fearful of something, and that warrants further investigation.

(table continued on next page)

Assessment Instrument	Clues to the Target-Bully Dynamic
California Psychological Inventory (CPI 434) assessment	The following score combinations suggest that clients may have been bullied: *lower* scores in dominance, self-acceptance, communality, sense of well-being, and intellectual efficiency and *higher* scores in sociability, empathy, and FM (femininity–masculinity). (FM has to do with how expressive you are emotionally and how you make decisions. Femininity is associated with being more in touch with your feelings and the tendency to seek input from others when making decisions, while masculinity is associated with less emotional expression and more objective decision-making.) The following pattern reflects someone who's potentially difficult or narcissistic (a potential bully): *higher* scores in dominance, capacity for status, and social presence, along with *lower* scores in empathy, self-control, tolerance, and flexibility.
Career Compatibility Scale (CCS)	If a client's CCS report shows large gaps between "ideal" and "current" on the Boss, Influence, and Environment themes in particular, this could indicate that stress, and possibly bullying, is taking place. Because these themes measure key relationships (Boss), opportunities to impact one's situation (Influence), and whether one feels safe (Environment), they are relevant to the target-bully dynamic and may provide important clues when discussed with the client.

Formal assessments may also have misleading results if a client is being bullied or abused. For example, let's say the client's results on the Strong Interest Inventory assessment are flat, showing very little interest across the board. That could be a function of depression or anxiety the client is experiencing due to bullying or other abuse happening in their lives—*not* a true reflection of their interests. So whenever I see anything that looks like stress, fear, or depression in a client's 16PF or CPI assessment results, I watch for other, more subtle clues as well.

Homework and Information Processing

At this stage of the process, we start to address issues like the client's physical and psychological well-being, how to manage their current situation, and recognizing and taking steps to lessen their vulnerability. Every case is different, but in my work I've identified common themes and some effective approaches.

First and foremost, bullying requires a team approach involving me and the client, so that my client feels fully supported. While this is true for any of my client engagements, it's vital when a client has been bullied. Feelings of vulnerability, loss of self-esteem, anger, fear, and resentment require special attention and understanding from me as a counselor and coach.

With regard to my client's state of mind and physical health, we tackle that early on so the situation doesn't get worse. I often encourage social contact, exercise, and working on self-esteem. I might have them write down positive self-affirmations, identify their strengths, or think about options for what they could do next. Achieving work-life balance is particularly important, so clients don't remain fixated on issues at work and feel they have greater control over their lives.

In any bullying situation, there are options to explore and decisions to be made. So there's a lot of discussion around the pros and cons of staying or leaving, determining what alternatives exist, thinking about ways my client can survive in the short term while job searching in off-work times, and so on. Having a game plan (see chapter 8) is useful for gauging options. I try to avoid having clients jump from the frying pan into the fire because they don't have a clear sense of their needs. Sometimes the client is desperate to escape, so they take a job without having done their due diligence.

Again, it's important that clients understand why bullying happened and how best to avoid it in the future. Sharing findings from formal assessments is a good first step. In addition, I aim to educate clients on things like body language, office politics, and when and how to share information related to the bullying. Although it's tempting for clients to vent, I don't want them to further jeopardize their position at work or burn out their social network with constant "woe is me" stories. No matter how worthy bullied clients may be of understanding from others, no one wants to be around or hire "damaged goods."

Finally, although I'm a licensed psychologist who has made bullying a focus, there are limits to what I can do myself. In some cases, clients may benefit from seeing a therapist or joining a support group. And I always encourage clients to seek support from friends and family. For example, my client Jessica (see her case study in chapter 12) reached out to both her husband and her father and got help from her physician and a therapist. The bottom line: clients need to know they're not alone.

Assessment helps me better understand and advise my clients who've been bullied. I'm able to gain insights on certain vulnerabilities that may not readily be evident. Another important step is to help "bully proof" clients, so they don't walk into the same situation again.

A PERSONAL PERSPECTIVE ON BULLYING

In his book *Callings*, Gregg Levoy refers to something he calls "boomerangs"—themes that recur throughout our lives and send us important messages about who we are and what we're called to do. My decision to include bullying in this book stems in part from that idea. I didn't reach out to find bullied clients; they came to me. And yet, when I consider my personal history, I almost feel I've been called to do something about it.

For me, bullying started when I was young, an awkward farm kid who loved to learn but found the social aspects of school, especially dealing with bullies, more challenging. Unfortunately, I had to live with that reality from grade school to high school—and beyond.

It wasn't so much getting teased by some tougher boys on the school bus, although that hurt. At least it was just words. But at school it got more serious when the "townies" would gang up on us rural kids. And being passive, unathletic, studious, and socially naïve, I was fair game. In fourth and fifth grades, I can remember being pushed around and even punched on the school playground. In tenth grade I had to walk down a dimly lit hallway to get to my shop class, and on a couple of occasions, two or three guys came out from a side hallway and jumped me. One time a guy had a stick and hit me with it. I had to go to shop every day for a quarter, terrified it would happen again.

Fast-forward to 1984, and I found myself in an awkward situation: the hapless employee of a female boss having an affair with a male staff member I was supervising. She was a female version of a bully—they are statistically rarer, but they do exist—constantly nitpicking my work, challenging my performance, and attempting to sabotage me. My supervisee, knowing he had the advantage, didn't respect my authority, which further eroded my performance. He left before I did, but I left shortly thereafter, dismayed with how I'd been treated and the sick, incestuous environment I'd had to work in.

Taking on the Bullying Challenge

These personal experiences with bullying, along with an unexpected influx of bullied clients in the early 2000s, got me thinking seriously about workplace bullying, and I've made it into something of a specialty. In 2010, I developed a presentation, "Navigating the Minefield: Bully-Proofing Your Workplace," which I delivered to the Minnesota Career Development Association. Since then I've conducted further research and continued to fine-tune the presentation, which I've delivered to different groups, including the National Career Development Association's annual convention in Chicago in 2016. In 2017 I developed a webinar for career counselors and coaches based on the presentation. For more information and a link, see Appendix D.

In "Navigating the Minefield," I ask questions like these:

- What, exactly, is bullying, and what constitutes bullying or disrespectful behavior? (In the presentation, I show a continuum of disrespectful behavior, from body language to fault finding to physical violence.)
- What does bullying look like from the target's perspective (isolation, humiliation, fear, lack of credit for work)?
- What kind of damage does bullying do, to both targets and organizations?
- Why is bullying allowed to happen, and what can be done about it?
- What can organizations do?
- How can targets best help themselves and avoid getting into similar situations?
- What can counselors and coaches do?

For both the 2010 and the 2016 presentations of "Navigating," there was a great turnout of career counselors, coaches, and other career development professionals. Many were hungry for ideas and interventions, either because they were also working with bullied clients, or because they had at some point been targets of bullying themselves. They found the topic validating and in some cases cathartic: here, finally, was an opportunity to tell their stories and share their experiences with others. As with so many forms of abuse, targets can feel as if they're alone or different, when in reality these situations happen to many. I love doing this presentation because of the lively discussions and fresh ideas it generates.

Why We Should Care About Bullying

Work is supposed to be about development, growth, productivity, and building a better world. To achieve that kind of growth, we need to use our brains—specifically, our cerebral cortex, the part of the brain that allows for learning, critical thinking, and other higher-order functions.

But guess what happens when people are bullied? The amygdala (the "primitive" or "lizard" brain, as it's sometimes called) kicks in. The impulse to freeze, fight, or flee—none of which is conducive to productivity or growth—takes priority over everything else. When she was being bullied, my client Jessica, normally a highly capable and productive software developer and trainer, was in a constant state of anxiety. Her productivity plummeted. Multiply what happened to Jessica by the estimated 37 million people who are bullied in the US each year, and you can see we have a problem.

When a Client Is a Bully

I once had a client who became a real problem in our sessions. When I asked Bob at our first meeting what other counseling he'd had, he admitted that he had just terminated his relationship with another counselor and had in fact run through *six or seven* counselors before coming to me. When I asked him why he had seen so many, his response—"Perhaps I'm difficult to work with"—should have registered as the huge red flag it was and sent me running from the room. But Bob, like many folks who have been abused, had learned how to manipulate others, and he convinced me that he really wanted to work with me. He was downright flattering, in fact.

However, once we started to work together, Bob began to thwart my efforts at every turn. He seemed incapable of or unwilling to stick to the topic, refused to take the assessments I suggested, and questioned and criticized my approach. When I finally convinced him to take the 16PF Questionnaire—an assessment designed to reveal not only strengths but trouble spots as well—the results affirmed what I was seeing in our sessions. According to the 16PF profile, Bob had "difficulty coping," found it "hard to be constructive or optimistic," and tended to "challenge those who differ with him." When I pointed out some areas for development mentioned in the profile, Bob was quick to dismiss them.

As it turned out, Bob had been bullied on the job and abused and neglected as a child, and he had some mental health challenges. But rather than learning from assessment and talking through the issues, he seemed passive-aggressive and resistant, fully embracing his victim role and using it to manipulate those he pretended to seek help from.

Once Bullied, a Lifetime of Vigilance

In retrospect, I should have trusted my instincts and ended the engagement much earlier in the game—we had about six or seven sessions together before finally terminating it—but strangely, I put up with what can only be described as abusive behavior by a client. When I think back to those sessions, I came away not feeling energized and uplifted as I normally do when working with clients, but instead beat up, confused, negative, emotional, and thwarted in my efforts. Once again, I was allowing myself to be bullied, this time not by a schoolyard bully or boss but by an emotionally unstable client.

Working with Bob stands out not only as an object lesson in how to better manage client relationships, but also a reminder that once we become the target of bullying, we continue to be vulnerable and need to remain vigilant. Targets of bullying often learn to please others and seek harmony in order to cope. In sticking with someone as troublesome as Bob for as many sessions as I did, I may have in some way been seeking harmony and not wanting to rock the boat. I may have even considered myself at fault to some extent.

Today I'm much firmer about setting boundaries and would never accept abusive behavior from a client, even those who've been bullied. But I'll gladly help bullied clients who are willing to help themselves.

BULLY-PROOFING CLIENTS FOR THE FUTURE

To avoid situations in which they risk being bullied, clients need to equip themselves with three kinds of information when looking for work: information about the companies they're thinking of approaching, information about the position itself and the people they'll potentially be reporting to and working with, and information about themselves and their needs. I try to train clients to be detectives at some level, armed with ways of gathering the intelligence they need and asking key questions.

At the company level, clients should consider the company's reputation, turnover, culture and philosophy, hiring practices, history of downsizing, and so on. They should ask whether the company has respectful workplace guidelines, an employee assistance program (EAP), and a policy on nepotism. (My files are full of horror stories involving family members working in the same company!) In addition to conducting the usual research, such as reading business articles, checking out key pages on the company's website, and so on, clients should look to websites like LinkedIn or Glassdoor.com to see who's worked with the company and can shed light on its culture.

At the position level, clients should ask why the position is open (they should trust their gut on this one), who their boss will be, and whether they (the boss) will be involved in the hiring decision. Another key question to ask is whether any major changes have happened with the team and why. As with research at the company level, LinkedIn or Glassdoor.com can be invaluable tools for getting the "inside scoop" on what's really happening when it comes to the position itself.

On a personal level, clients need to consider whether they'd be a good fit for the job. For example, they should ask themselves what kind of people they're likely to work best with. My client Kevin (see his game plan in chapter 8 and case study in chapter 12) had worked under a boss who, while perhaps not an outright bully, was often difficult and failed to treat Kevin with the respect he felt he deserved. In the Where section of his game plan, Kevin wrote that he wanted to work in a professional culture with coworkers who were "respect-ful." And in the Who section, he indicated he wanted to work with people who are "friendly, principled, considerate, and professional." In other words, Kevin did not want to work with inconsiderate bullies!

It's important to note that bullying is not always intentional or the result of psychological problems. Often it happens when poorly trained managers encounter subordinates who aren't meeting their expectations and then take it out on the subordinate rather than managing them more effectively. For their part, employees need to ensure that they're managing their own careers and experiences at work, and that includes developing positive relationships with their boss and teammates. In today's fast-paced environment, where you're often only as good as your last project, employees need to prove themselves early and often. They need to take the lead in finding out what their boss and team most need from them and how they can best contribute. If they fail to do this, they may be shown the door. In cases like that, it's not bullying that's going on; it's just the reality of the workplace.

REFLECTING ON CHAPTER 10:
ASSESSING AND HELPING BULLIED CLIENTS

In your studies or reading about assessment, how often have you encountered material about workplace bullying and working with bullied clients? If you've worked with clients who've been bullied, do you have any strategies in place for working with them?

If you've worked with bullied clients, do you find that they usually report the bullying directly? Or does the fact that they've been bullied come out more gradually as the engagement proceeds? In my experience, relatively few clients come out with this directly, but it becomes apparent as you work with them. They tend to be distracted from doing career work and need to resolve their situation first.

Consider the interview questions you typically ask your clients, or interview questions you have learned about in your studies. Do these questions encourage clients to open up about their work situation, including negative aspects like bullying? In this chapter, I cited two examples where questions not focused directly on bullying nevertheless tend to yield important clues.

In the chapter, we looked at three ways to help clients find a good fit and avoid a toxic workplace, including researching the company, researching the position, boss, and team, and taking the time to know their own needs for a good fit. Based on your studies in career counseling, or your experience as a career counselor or coach, what might you add to this list? (See also chapter 11, "Assessment and Job Fit.")

Given statistics on workplace bullying, it's highly likely that you or a client will be a target of bullying at some point during your working lives. See Appendix D for resources on understanding and coping with workplace bullying.

Chapter 11

. . . .

ASSESSMENT AND JOB FIT

When it comes to communicating who they are and what they bring to the table, many clients have no clear idea of their larger context or story, or what others might value. This makes it difficult to justify or sell themselves to others. When asked the question, "Why do you want to work here?," for example, they may not have much more to offer than, "it seems like a great opportunity," or "it meets my salary requirements," or "it's close to where I live." Employers need more than this kind of response, of course. Fortunately, when done properly, assessment unearths a huge amount of information that can be channeled into effective communication with employers and other interested parties. This chapter discusses mining assessment for insights, understanding what employers need, and harvesting the products of assessment.

Before we get into the specifics, I want to stress the value and usefulness of what we're talking about here, regardless of your role or particular niche as a career development professional. While some of my colleagues, especially those working with executives, specialize in helping clients with communication (branding statements, résumés, LinkedIn, speaking), you don't need to be a writing or branding expert to benefit. The ideas in this chapter are relevant to anyone who wants to fully leverage assessment to help clients better represent themselves to others. Let's face it: today we must all be good communicators in order to sell our strengths and assets to employers, colleagues, and business partners. And that starts by having the right information at our fingertips.

MINING ASSESSMENT FOR INSIGHTS

One of the things I love about having an integrated assessment process is the wealth of information—and different *kinds* of information—it yields during the various phases of assessment. All of this becomes useful raw material for communication.

The structured interview is designed to draw clients out and get them to focus on the positive people and events in their lives. As clients answer these open-ended and often surprising questions, they become more self-aware and articulate about who they are and what they want, which ultimately helps them communicate better with potential audiences. As a bonus, listening to clients answer questions helps me identify—early on—communication challenges that may trip them up later, such as difficulty answering questions clearly or succinctly.

Formal assessment instruments such as the Myers-Briggs Type Indicator (MBTI) assessment, 16PF Questionnaire, and other instruments bring objective information to compare with insights gained during the interview. In working with clients, a key role I play here is *translator*. When interpreting MBTI assessment results for clients, for example, I help them understand how to communicate—in plain language—what the report is saying about their preferences and what this might mean to employers. In addition, I ask my clients to read the report and highlight anything that resonates. Together we identify what's most salient in the results and how best to communicate it to employers and others.

Worksheets bring even more information into play as clients sort through what they've learned during assessment and start to focus more clearly on where they might best fit given their strengths and weaknesses. This helps communicate a richer picture to others, including answering those tricky "Tell me about yourself" and "Why should we hire you?" questions that often trip clients up.

Finally, a great way for clients to further capture the thoughts and language coming out of assessment is to record them in a game plan. Recording criteria for what they need in their work—the What, Where, and Who—helps clients better assess opportunities that arise and communicate with prospective employers, in written form and in interviews.

UNDERSTANDING WHAT EMPLOYERS NEED

As someone who's consulted with organizations on their selection processes, I believe the two most critical factors clients need to communicate to prospective employers are *value* and *fit*. Employers hire people who can draw connections between their experience, skills, and talents and the job to be filled. For clients who may be nonreflective by nature or lack a realistic sense of what employers are looking for, assessment can draw them out and also help them better identify and communicate their value.

Fit can be more complicated to communicate, because employers often view it from a different perspective than applicants. I remember interviewing an engineer who was a candidate for a job in manufacturing. He thought he was a great fit since he seemed to have the right skill set and had worked in a number of manufacturing environments. But the employer wanted someone with stronger interpersonal and social connection skills, which were "must haves" in that particular organization.

When it comes to communicating value and fit, each component of my assessment process—the responses in the structured interview, the formal assessment reports and profiles, the completed worksheets, and the game plan—helps unearth words, phrases, and ideas that can be used for that purpose.

Often when I'm reviewing a client's structured interview responses, I'll point out certain words or themes in their answers, and we discuss what they might mean for them. With my client Kevin, for example, the words "projects" and "results" came up repeatedly in his answers. Kevin later landed a job as a technical consultant, in which he got to advise on several projects.

Formal assessment reports and profiles, such as the MBTI Step II Profile and 16PF Career Development Profile, are full of useful language and terminology. I will look for the language in a client's test results that most resonates with them. For example, intuitive types may identify with words like "abstract," "theoretical," and "original" and be able to translate this into research or writing skills they can offer a business or client.

The Career Ingredients Summary Sheet is another place I watch for language clients can use to communicate fit. If my client writes "nurturing and supportive" in the "Strengths" box, for example, I encourage her to communicate these strengths in an interview, especially when they're consistent with what we learned earlier in the assessment process.

When completed, a game plan offers a wealth of relevant information—all in the writer's own words—that can be put to good use in communicating to others. Drawing from my own game plan, for example, I can say that "I enjoy providing tactical advice to people who are willing to try things out, follow through, and take ownership of issues that impact them" (from the "Who" section of my plan). The purpose of the worksheets and game plan is to capture the client's self-understanding, and use it to communicate authentically who they are, how they add value, and what they enjoy.

When clients discover their strengths through assessment, they become more articulate salespeople on their own behalf. They're better positioned to research prospective organizations, ask good questions, and communicate both their value and fit.

HARVESTING THE PRODUCT OF ASSESSMENT

In my spare time I love to garden—composting, tilling the earth, smelling the earth, planting young seedlings or seeds, and seeing them grow, blossom, and provide produce. I can work in my garden during the summertime for hours at a time, pulling weeds, plucking the dead leaves and produce, placing them in the compost, stirring the compost, and seeing richer, blacker soil emerge. I share the harvest with friends, family, and neighbors, happy that I have treasures to offer them.

As I work with clients and we bring to the surface ideas and language they can use to communicate their strengths and their value, I feel a similar sense of satisfaction. Assessment, like gardening, needs a plan—and often some hard work—before anything comes to fruition, but when it does, it's highly rewarding. And just as I love to share fresh produce with friends, I love to share ideas and insights with clients. Even more, I enjoy hearing what they've learned about themselves through their homework and information processing work, especially since it represents the fruits of their own labor.

Just as it takes time for produce to develop in the ground before it's ready for picking, clients often need time to arrive at their brand or identity—the point where they feel authentic and are ready to present themselves in the marketplace. And they do that by sorting through what's important, and what's not, in the assessment data we gather. Clients flourish when they know what criteria they most need to be successful.

I started this chapter by pointing out that many clients have difficulty articulating their value to others. The key is to pay attention to what comes out of assessment and utilize it to its fullest. When it comes to produce from my garden, I hate to waste it and would much rather give it way than throw it away. I feel exactly the same way about assessment. We've done the work. Now let's share it with the world!

REFLECTING ON CHAPTER 11:
ASSESSMENT AND JOB FIT

I use a variety of techniques to capture language or have my clients capture it for discussion and later communication in résumés, interviews, and so on. For example, I always bring my notes from the structured interview to later sessions, when we go over test results or self-assessment work, and we note any common themes that emerge. What similar techniques do you have in place? If you're a student, what have you learned about capturing assessment language for communication purposes?

It's a well-known fact that writing things down can help you absorb and retain information more easily, as well as make it more likely you'll achieve any goals you record. In your work with clients, or in your studies of career counseling and assessment, how much focus has been given to writing things down (for example, completing assessment worksheets) relative to discussion? How might more writing help?

Formal assessment reports and profiles are rich with language for communication and branding, especially those containing longer narrative text, like the 16PF Career Development report. Fortunately, you don't need to have taken or given assessments to start to get an appreciation for this. As I explain in Section 3 of "The Quick-Reference Toolkit," many test publishers provide sample reports and profiles for downloading from their websites. Also, if you're interested in the MBTI assessment, I recommend the book *Do What You Are*, discussed in Appendix B. It's a gold mine of ideas and language for communicating personality type.

Employers want to know how well a candidate might fit their environment and what value they'll bring to their organization. Using information from the various assessment tools discussed in this book (interview notes, test results, worksheets, game plan, etc.), write down your thoughts on how these can be utilized in career and job search communications.

As a former farm kid who still loves to garden, I've come to view career assessment data as a kind of harvest from the hard work of assessment. Think about the value that can come out of assessment and how you can best take advantage of it in helping your clients communicate more effectively. Also, think about how you'll communicate this value to your clients.

Part 4

CAREER STORIES AND TRANSFORMATIONS

Chapter 12

. . . .

CLIENT CASE STUDIES

Over the thirty-plus years I've been practicing as a counselor and coach, I've worked with a wide variety of clients in career transition or experiencing crises in their lives—accountants, lawyers, interior decorators, designers, managers, executives, carpenters, actuaries, IT professionals, sales representatives at various levels, engineers, HR professionals, clerks, students, business and financial analysts, bankers, truck drivers, medical professionals, self-employed people, unemployed individuals, and others.

I've chosen to highlight seven clients in this chapter for three reasons. First, they represent typical clients for me in that they're mostly nonexecutive, degreed professionals trying to make a change or get refocused. None are rookies (such as college students with no work experience); all have some experience in the work world. Second, their stories illustrate that most people who come to us for career work have other things going on in their lives they need to deal with— bad or bullying bosses, family or mental health issues, or other factors that complicate the picture. Third, all seven clients worked with me over several sessions and underwent comprehensive testing, so I was able to learn a great deal from working with them. Note that all names and some facts have been changed to maintain confidentiality.

I love hearing my clients' stories. I want to learn about proud moments, shaping experiences, and how they've approached adversity. I want to know what grounds them and what their outlook is for their future. I also love giving them permission to redefine and remake themselves. But to do that successfully they also need to be aware of their past, of patterns in their lives—roles, attitudes, mistakes—that will likely continue to influence their future in some way. When done well, assessment combines hope for the future with a realistic respect for the past and what it means.

A key takeaway from these cases is that assessment, when done thoroughly and well, bridges the gap between confusion and self-awareness, and between despair and hope. Each of these clients came to me in considerable distress, and in each case, they came away with a richer understanding of themselves and of the possibilities for their future. In assessing clients, we're in many ways also assessing ourselves and realizing our own unique strengths. Sometimes this is a function of having things in common with the client; other times working with clients who are our polar opposites can bring out the best in us.

KEVIN

Having been let go from two management jobs in the space of only three years, Kevin, age forty-nine, was determined to do better. His most recent position, production manager for a manufacturing firm, had seemed promising at first, but things quickly deteriorated. He struggled with the role, which required him to lead a team of technical and engineering staff as well as interact with customers on a regular basis.

Kevin had also had some serious problems with his boss. Impossible to please, his boss never seemed to recognize Kevin for what he did well and only pointed out the negative. This left Kevin feeling vulnerable and incompetent. The situation was further complicated by the fact that Kevin had been hired for the position by another boss who was no longer working at that branch of the company.

Kevin had been recruited to the production manager position through a well-regarded technical services agency that sought him out. He was flattered by the attention—enough to ignore any misgivings he may have had.

Clues from the Structured Interview

At our first session, when I asked Kevin about his favorite activities over his career, he immediately identified troubleshooting and engineering work. He also mentioned "projects" and "results" frequently throughout the interview. His least favorite activities were supervising others and dealing with "people stuff."

"I'm not much of a schmoozer," he admitted.

Still, having been tapped twice for management roles, Kevin wanted to see how he could improve as a manager. A devoted family man and father of three, he knew he could make more as a manager and wanted the financial security. Some of his peers and acquaintances had achieved the management ranks— well before he had in most cases—adding pressure for him to follow suit. If he could just further develop his leadership, communication, and political skills, Kevin felt, he might get better results.

Formal Assessments

Because Kevin seemed keen on staying in management but was clearly struggling, I was particularly interested in exploring leadership potential and leadership dynamics as part of my testing. Had his boss set Kevin up for failure? Or was there something about Kevin that made the role a poor fit for him? Did Kevin like the idea of management more than the reality? Here's what I discovered:

Assessment Instrument	Highlights
California Psychological Inventory (CPI 434) assessment	The CPI 434 showed Kevin to be reserved and unassertive but with a high achievement orientation and strong drive to keep learning. Strong leaders, in contrast, exhibit high self-confidence, assertiveness, sociability, and empathy.
Myers-Briggs Type Indicator (MBTI) assessment	Kevin had tested previously as an INTJ (Introverted, Intuitive, Thinking, Judging) and brought in his report for my review. INTJs tend to view the world logically and analytically and less in terms of people and feelings. Because they love to think and analyze and constantly improve things, they may be tapped for management roles. However, they can stumble when they're required to develop and supervise others. INTJs can be effective individual contributors.

(table continued on next page)

Assessment Instrument	Highlights
Strong Interest Inventory assessment	Kevin's Holland code was IRC (Investigative, Realistic, and Conventional), very similar to others in technical and professional roles such as dentists, engineers, veterinarians, etc. Most telling here, though, was that one of Kevin's *lowest* interest scores was on "Management." In fact, he looked quite *dissimilar* to people in supervisory, management, and directing roles, such as business and finance supervisors, public relations directors, top executives, and others in management and leadership positions.
Fundamental Interpersonal Relations Orientation-Behavior (FIRO-B) assessment	Control was Kevin's highest need, which is consistent with many technical types. Affection was his lowest, consistent with his dislike of conflict and people issues. His "expressed" behaviors were lower than his "wanted"—meaning he wants more of these behaviors (affection, inclusion, and control) from others than he's willing to display himself. This is a classic description of someone who's a follower rather than a leader.
16PF Questionnaire	Results highlighted Kevin's need for harmony and his tendency to be conflict averse. On matters relating to leadership, there were a few red flags: "He's not very comfortable taking charge of others," and "It may be difficult to easily cope with situations that call for him to be assertive and demanding." Given that managers need to be comfortable with conflict and deal with it swiftly and effectively, these findings are telling. Like the Strong, the report also revealed that Kevin's personality was similar to those in technical, rather than managerial, roles.

These assessment results clearly pointed more to an individual contributor than a leader. Kevin was receptive to these findings and even somewhat relieved. In many ways they confirmed what he had known all along—that he really liked the work, but not leading staff or the political jockeying that leaders need to be comfortable navigating. While his boss was certainly part of the problem, Kevin's lack of confidence really had more to do with the job being a poor fit—he hated putting out fires and dealing with chaos.

Homework and Information Processing

For Kevin, initial homework primarily involved taking formal assessments. Then I had him fill out the Career Ingredients Summary Sheet. The table below shows the section of the summary sheet, notes that Kevin recorded, and my analysis of his notes.

Section	Kevin's Notes	My Analysis
Strengths	Achievement, influence, and continuous learning	These are all good to have. But keep in mind that "influence" doesn't necessarily mean influencing *people*. In Kevin's case, my impression was that he liked using his expertise to make a difference, but to influence *project* results, not people directly.
Weaknesses	Perfectionistic tendencies	As it turned out, perfectionism was one of the things that got him into trouble in his production manager job. Rather than tap the expertise of his team, too often Kevin did the work or made decisions himself without consulting his team or letting them grow by making their own mistakes.
People Needs	Prefers direction	While Kevin can be quite independent and likes to achieve and bring ideas to the table, he also likes strong managers who can provide leadership and direction. While he wants to have influence on projects, he'd rather someone else ultimately be held accountable.

(table continued on next page)

Section	Kevin's Notes	My Analysis
Possible Occupations	Technical consultant or engineer	These were positions Kevin held *before* being promoted to production manager roles. This suggested that higher-level managerial roles with more supervisory responsibilities were not something he found attractive.
Career Goals	Interesting and fulfilling work	Note that there's nothing here about "helping others be the best they can be" or "leading others to meet the company's goals." This suggests that another reason Kevin may have been fired was because he was too focused on the work itself, giving little thought to the needs of his boss or team.

With the findings from self-assessment tending to confirm much of what we had discovered from the initial interview and formal assessments—that Kevin was more of a strong individual contributor than a leader—his next homework assignment was to write a game plan with criteria for what he wanted in his next position. To create his plan, Kevin thoroughly reviewed his test results, worksheet notes, and other thoughts he had recorded. His game plan reflects those findings: he wanted a hands-on role that drew on his technical skills and in which he would work with others who were cooperative rather than competitive, cared about what they were doing, appreciated challenges, and did not play political games. (Kevin's game plan is featured in full in chapter 8.)

Outcome

With his game plan as a guide, Kevin began networking and making inquiries. Although early in the process he made the mistake of focusing too heavily on recruiters and not on those who could hire him directly—a common tendency I see in introverted clients—I encouraged him to expand his efforts, and soon he was reaching out and making some good contacts.

Five months after we began our work together, Kevin landed a job as a technical consultant for a fast-growing manufacturer. Fortunately, his new role required strong technical knowledge and skills but no direct supervision of employees.

About six months after landing the technical consultant job, Kevin made another appointment to see me, this time to discuss a potential opportunity he had learned about through a friend. While he was still doing fine in his technical consultant role, he craved a bit more influence on the engineering side of things, which the new opportunity presented. We agreed he should explore the new opportunity, but not make any abrupt moves until he learned more and carefully thought things through.

At my most recent meeting with Kevin, he was thinking more seriously of moving to a new job. A new, micromanaging boss was making his life difficult and undermining his work. Unfortunately, bad bosses can thwart the best of plans.

Analysis

Kevin's case reflects a common problem in hiring—the tendency to select or promote strong performers to management positions without fully vetting their capabilities. This can happen for a number of reasons: Employers want people who can generate results, assuming, often incorrectly, that technical expertise can be translated into leadership ability. Recruiters, anxious to please their corporate clients, may be tempted to "stretch" their candidates' talents. And candidates themselves can be seduced by the larger salaries offered to managers.

However, from his initial admission that he didn't like "people stuff" or "schmoozing" to the formal assessment and other results analyzed above, it seemed clear that Kevin wasn't suited for or happy in managerial roles requiring significant supervision or leadership of others, despite his desire for a management salary. In addition, Kevin had expressed a strong desire to spend more time with his family, and managerial roles typically demand longer hours.

Kevin may not be great at leading, but he is personable and articulate. Those attributes, combined with his strong technical abilities, make him a strong individual contributor and a real asset to any company that recognizes his true capabilities. Also, his ability to recover from his situation—when he first came to see me he seemed quite desperate and shattered by the loss of two jobs in quick succession—was impressive. He knew he needed guidance and structure and fully embraced my process.

Finally, I mentioned at the beginning that Kevin had difficulties with his direct boss. While I'm confident after the assessment we did that the job was a poor fit for Kevin, and that that was the primary reason for his being fired, I'm also convinced that there was an element of bullying going on that affected his performance. That said, Kevin's situation was fundamentally different from my client Jessica's (see her case study later in this chapter), who was well suited to her role. I discuss workplace bullying in detail in chapter 10.

SHIRLEY

A promotions planner at a Fortune 500 company for nearly twenty years, Shirley, age fifty-five, found herself being systematically ignored by a series of younger bosses.

Things used to be great at work. For years she'd had supportive bosses and received excellent performance reviews. But now she was in a department where she didn't fit, with a young boss who ignored her. Any decisions she made were second-guessed. Younger members of the team were offered regular growth and learning opportunities, while Shirley was left to fend for herself.

Treated as if she didn't exist, kept out of the loop on important projects, and with her former responsibilities drastically reduced, Shirley felt desperate, unhappy, and stressed.

Clues from the Structured Interview

When I asked Shirley to recall a memorable work experience, she described a customer service position she'd held earlier in her career. Whenever she encountered irate people, she said, she was able to "immediately calm them down," a strength she used again in supervisory roles and in connecting with her team.

When asked to pick a word that described her well, she didn't hesitate: "caring."

That theme continued as she talked of returning to a former passion, helping others. Shirley had once considered nursing and had even attended nursing school. And while that hadn't worked out, one of her favorite hobbies now was volunteering at an assisted living facility.

When I asked her whom she most wanted to hang out with, she said people involved in health care in a nonprofit environment. She also wanted to spend more time with friends.

Formal Assessments

With formal assessments, my goal was to help Shirley explore what she was passionate about so she could start to repurpose and reinvent herself. For her part, Shirley loved to learn, so she embraced this part of our work with enthusiasm.

Assessment Instrument	Highlights
Myers-Briggs Type Indicator (MBTI) assessment	Shirley tested as an ENFJ (Extraverted, Intuitive, Feeling, Judging). Results showed a clear preference for judging, which was consistent with the need for planning and structure and predictability she'd mentioned in the interview. In the MBTI Step II assessment, "harmony" themes were very apparent.
Strong Interest Inventory assessment	Shirley's Holland code was ECA (Enterprising, Conventional, and Artistic), and she had common interests with social workers, HR directors, and some teaching and counselor roles, findings that were consistent with her need to help others and for social interaction. The Conventional theme seemed to relate to her need for structure and appreciation for methodical processes.
Fundamental Interpersonal Relations Orientation-Behavior (FIRO-B) assessment	Shirley's strong need for inclusion and affection highlighted her social needs, which were not being met at work.

(table continued on next page)

Assessment Instrument	Highlights
16PF Questionnaire	Helping was Shirley's highest score, in keeping with many of her stated interests: "She seems to have concern for people who might need assistance and support from her." Positive interaction with others was also emphasized: "She likes to put forth a feeling of warmth when interacting with others." "She usually does her best to promote harmony among others so as to reduce the possibility of conflicts with people." Her need for predictability was also highlighted in the report: "She likes to work within a rather structured framework where what is expected and how it will be done are fairly well spelled out." Finally, there were signs of the leadership that had led to her early success in the company: "She tends to be seen as a leader by most people."

In analyzing Shirley's test results, I noticed the following common themes: harmony, predictability, inclusion, affection and caring, and also "getting things done" (she had a high score on Enterprising on the Strong, for example). Shirley also craved structure and predictability—not surprising for someone who had spent her entire career in corporate America.

Homework and Information Processing

When I first met Shirley, she was in pretty rough shape, both emotionally and physically. In the last few months before she contacted me, she had experienced an increasing number of stress headaches, along with spiking blood pressure. So to help alleviate her stress, I encouraged her to have a conversation with her doctor about anti-anxiety medications.

Then, to make things more palatable at work, we discussed the idea of her transferring to another department. Although she did try requesting transfers a couple of times, her requests were denied. She also contacted HR and got some relief from discussing her situation with them—it was good to at least be heard, Shirley said—but they had no real solutions to offer.

To help balance the loneliness and lack of inclusion she was experiencing at work, I urged her to reach out to others. She joined a women's friendship club and began to benefit from the new friends and camaraderie. This played to her natural preferences as an extrovert.

Shirley was also interested in doing more writing, so we talked about her taking a class to enhance her skills in this area. In addition, we discussed networking strategies she could try, one related to exploring elder care and another related to cooking, which she enjoyed as a hobby.

Finally, we engaged in some on-the-fly exercises. I had her create several lists, including what she believed her positive attributes were, negative elements that were happening at work, and her career fears. I then asked her to come up with some action steps she could take to make life better for herself. Shirley craved structure and predictability in her life, so she enjoyed this process of creating and discussing her lists and thinking about what might come next.

Outcome

While all these efforts helped lighten Shirley's mood and began to improve her prospects generally, things didn't change at work. After being assigned another young boss who was nice at first but later turned out to be critical and unsupportive, she decided to resign.

When we last met, Shirley was applying for nonprofit jobs and taking a class on elder care. Much happier, less stressed, and feeling supported in her efforts, she appeared to be well on her way to a new, more meaningful career that suited this phase in her life.

Happily, too, she was able to secure two very positive recommendations from vendors she had worked with in her capacity as a promotions planner—people who appreciated her helpfulness, outgoing nature, and problem-solving abilities.

Analysis

Shirley's case represents a classic plight of aging workers today. Had she not been a highly competent worker and consistent contributor, she never would have lasted nearly two decades in the same company. Yet, despite her contributions, she was forced out by a younger boss who had no intention of rescuing her and who was, we have to assume, glad to see her go. (When Shirley left the company, there wasn't even a farewell card or party—a sign she saw as a final act of disrespect.)

While there's no excuse for the neglect that Shirley received at the hands of her younger bosses, her situation is more typical than not. Often younger managers have no idea what to do with older employees. They can sometimes feel intimidated by older workers' experience and knowledge. So instead of tapping their talents, they relegate them to inconsequential tasks and gradually force them out.

While some in our field are working to change the way older workers are perceived and treated and help them stay on the job, and I applaud their efforts, my goal with Shirley was different.

As with all my clients, I wanted Shirley to know she had other options and could make real progress once she identified her wants and needs, set some goals, and started taking charge of her priorities. The career assessment process really tapped into her motivations and values and gave her renewed energy for taking the next steps. And taking steps toward her future, however small, gave her new optimism and a new sense of control.

Early on in her work with me, when Shirley was at her most depressed, she said she felt that in some sense she was dying, as if she no longer mattered. She had spent a large chunk of her life at one company, and in many ways her self-worth was tied to that. Assessment helped her see that there was a whole new world beyond the company, a positive future was hers if she chose to embrace it, and that it was indeed time to leave her job and get on with the rest of her life.

JIM

When I first met Jim, age twenty-eight, a business development professional in the banking industry, he'd been fired from three jobs in the space of five years. He was constantly "stepping on landmines" and had just been written up for conduct on his current job.

Since graduating with a BA in business administration, Jim had worked in banking, a buttoned-down, traditional environment with strict rules, policies, and high expectations for employee conduct and excellence. Such sins as tardiness, procrastination, and impulsivity simply weren't tolerated.

Unfortunately, Jim lacked the emotional filters needed to work effectively in such an environment. He had a tendency to do or say whatever he pleased whenever he pleased. He was often late to meetings and behind in his work. He was easily distracted.

What Jim *was* keenly aware of, however, was his rejection by teammates and the fact that he didn't seem to fit in the way the others did. He felt like a failure in his work, but he wasn't sure why. The place seemed very political and unfair.

Clues from the Structured Interview

When I asked him to describe a proud moment in his life, Jim recalled coming off the bench "as a sixth man" in high school basketball. A sixth man is not a starter but a reliable performer who comes off the bench more often than other reserve players.

So I asked him, "What kind of work situation might allow you to operate as a sixth man?"

That led to a discussion of IT, where a lot of work is project-based and requires bright team players with technical expertise to make things happen. Jim also mentioned that while he enjoyed some aspects of customer service and helping others, he also needed his share of independence and downtime.

When I asked him for three words he'd use to describe himself, Jim said "emotional," "hard-working," and "funny." On that last point, while his attempts at humor in the conservative, buttoned-down banking industry may have fallen flat and even gotten him into trouble, his quirky sense of humor (Jim was a bit of a nerd) would turn out to be a much better fit later on.

Formal Assessments

In assessing Jim, I was particularly interested in issues of fit. How well did he fit—or not fit—the kinds of roles he had had in the banking industry? What might work better? Here are highlights of Jim's test results—mixed, but with some strong clues nonetheless.

Assessment Instrument	Highlights
Myers-Briggs Type Indicator (MBTI) assessment	Jim is an ISTJ (Introverted, Sensing, Thinking, and Judging). ISTJs tend to be reliable, hands-on performers who like to get things done. In terms of introversion and extraversion, Jim had a slight preference for introversion. He can be a real talker in one-to-one situations, but he also likes his downtime.

(table continued on next page)

Assessment Instrument	Highlights
Strong Interest Inventory assessment	For occupational themes, Jim tested high on Realistic, Enterprising, and Investigative. He looked similar to mechanics, engineers, military personnel, accountants, financial professionals, some business managers, and IT professionals.
16PF Questionnaire	This profile highlighted much of what I saw in interviewing Jim: worry, anxiety, difficulty being optimistic, low self-control, and a tendency to challenge anyone who differed from him. But what also emerged was a picture of someone who might be happy in an expert or technical role: Jim was intellectually curious and "enjoyed helping and influencing others through solving problems." His highest career activity themes were "investigating" and "producing"—similar to engineers, architects, designers, and other technical professionals.
California Psychological Inventory (CPI 434) assessment	Jim's results were fairly average, suggesting a low-key performer in terms of leadership. There was some evidence of influencing and social interaction, but nothing high. There were also signs of issues that had been causing him grief: inability to read nonverbal clues and nuances, rebellion against rules and structure. What was interesting here, though, was a glimpse of what might be a better role for him. According to the profile, Jim looked "more like an individual contributor than a leader."

These results shed light on why his banking roles, all of which required outstanding social skills and a strong stomach for politics, had not worked out well for him. Another factor was the family dynamic: Jim was the third of four brothers in a very traditional family. His two older brothers were in medicine and engineering, and his younger brother was an accountant. His father, a business executive, had high expectations for his sons and strong ideas about what they should and shouldn't do. Jim had studied business administration and entered banking at least in part to meet these expectations. However, the banking culture, with its need for conformity to rules, discipline, and behavior, was simply a bad fit. Jim was more of a free agent. He liked his independence and wanted the freedom to carve out his own lifestyle.

Homework and Information Processing

In addition to taking the formal assessments outlined above, homework for Jim involved exploring IT further. As it turned out, playing around with computers was a favorite hobby, and shortly after our first meeting, he enrolled in a programming course, which he did well in and thoroughly enjoyed.

Another thing we needed to address was Jim's attention-deficit/hyperactivity disorder (ADHD). After interviewing Jim and looking at his test results, particularly the 16PF and CPI, I suspected ADHD and suggested he see a specialist, who confirmed my suspicions.

To help Jim with this diagnosis, we identified an adult ADHD support group he could join, and he also started some medications to help him with both ADHD and his low-grade depression.

We also reviewed Jim's résumé and highlighted work that was computer-related. For example, Jim had created a web page for a small business, a project he enjoyed. However, it soon became apparent that to find work equal to his capabilities and ambition, he would need to return to school.

Outcome

A few months after we started working together, Jim decided to pursue a master's degree in computer science. The programming course he had taken had whet his appetite for more, as had our discussions about his test results, which all seemed to point to IT as a viable option. He was quickly on board and pursued the degree with enthusiasm, which turned out to be a good decision for him.

With a master's degree in hand, Jim landed a position as a consultant with an IT consulting firm—a much better fit than his previous jobs.

Jim loved working with his fellow geeks and began receiving above-average performance reviews. He was also able to work on multiple projects for multiple companies, which he much preferred to more traditional corporate work.

Analysis

Jim's case is a complex one: ADHD, family issues with control, mixed formal assessment results that were partly a function of his true temperament and partly a matter of socialization. But a key takeaway from his case is that we finally identified him as the consummate outsider—a techie who was more suited to a consultative role. This took a while to work out, but it was a worthwhile journey.

Understanding ADHD is also key to understanding Jim's case. People with ADHD are easily distracted by various stimuli. Something catches their eye, and they get caught up in it and attend to whatever it is—until something else distracts them. Then they're focused on that until they're distracted once again. This can result in procrastination on projects and tardiness when they lose track of time and priorities. Jim was often late to meetings at work, for example.

Both Jim's temperament and his ADHD ruled out most management positions—people with ADHD may lack the organizational skills and ability to set priorities needed to be effective managers—so we looked at other roles that might make more sense for him. Interestingly, people with ADHD often excel in individual contributor projects and roles, such as computer work. When they're able to concentrate on a single screen and a specific problem, rather than attend to myriad other activities around them, they are more focused and less distracted. Also, roles that enable independence and setting one's own schedule can work well for employees with ADHD.

In Jim's case, pressure to follow in his father's footsteps thrust him into corporate insider roles that didn't suit him, given his ADHD and his temperament. In these roles, his true strengths and personality were suppressed, while he was expected to be the high-powered, politically savvy, alpha male type his father most respected.

Jim loved meeting people's needs and solving problems—and then moving on to the next project or company. In his new role as a consultant with the tech consulting firm, he's finally able to play this outside expert role without getting caught up in internal politics. And because he's doing what he loves, he's happily utilizing his natural sales ability to engage clients. Jim is now able to step in and save the day—to really make a difference—just as he had as a sixth man for his high school basketball team.

JESSICA

Jessica, age forty-five, a soft-spoken software developer, came to me reporting trouble with her boss. Whenever something went wrong, instead of discussing the problem calmly and rationally, her boss would launch into a tirade, berating Jessica in front of her coworkers.

One day after such an incident, her boss slammed the office door so hard that pieces of sheetrock broke loose around the doorknob. After that, Jessica was hesitant to even speak with him and experienced increased anxiety, trouble sleeping, and heightened emotions that made it difficult for her to do her job effectively.

This was one of the best jobs Jessica had ever had. She was viewed as the go-to person for one of the most profitable software applications for the company, and the role made good use of her analytical abilities as well as her desire to interact with people. She sometimes got to travel and train others, which she loved. But the bullying had definitely taken its toll, and Jessica's performance had begun to suffer.

This wasn't the first time I'd worked with Jessica. I first met with her five years earlier, when she was unhappy with her work at another IT company. So before we set out to tackle the bullying issue, I got out her original file to review my notes.

Clues from the Structured Interview

When I asked Jessica five years earlier what she needed from her work and her coworkers, she said she liked fun, kind people who were helpful, people who thought of others first. It was also important to her to feel needed and included by others. That wasn't happening at the job she held at the time.

While she had once been something of a rising star there, things had changed, and she had started to feel that she was no longer respected or even wanted. One woman, an influential guru at the company who had once been friendly and supportive, had become cold and controlling.

The job also didn't seem like a good fit with Jessica's style and personality: "lots of boring, mainframe type people," in Jessica's words—introverted, "matter of fact" types. It was also a very political place, and Jessica loathed office politics.

At the time, we did a battery of tests to get a better sense of her preferences, values, and what she needed in her interactions with others. Looking back at those test results, I could see that Jessica was the type who was potentially vulnerable to bullying.

Formal Assessments

When you look at Jessica's test results, you get a clear picture of someone who craves warmth and harmony in her interactions with others. This, combined with her political naiveté, can make her both vulnerable and highly sensitive to unkind or abusive treatment by others.

Assessment Instrument	Highlights
Fundamental Interpersonal Relations Orientation-Behavior (FIRO-B) assessment	Jessica has a strong need for a social and nurturing environment and an appreciation for warmth, sensitivity, and support from others. Her fairly low scores for Control suggest that she doesn't want to be in charge but also doesn't want someone else telling her what to do.
Values Scale	Jessica places a relatively high value on social relations and social interaction as well as economic security and prestige.
Strong Interest Inventory assessment	Results show a high social orientation, with teaching, training, and social services as potential areas of career success. With regard to interests, Jessica looked quite *dissimilar* to many IT types.
16PF Questionnaire	Her report describes Jessica as a trusting, people-oriented person who likes to "put all her cards on the table," a classic sign of someone who may be politically naïve and therefore vulnerable to bullying. People like Jessica can often be too revealing and too trusting, and others may use that against them. Again, Jessica looked more similar to teachers and social workers than she did to technicians and IT types. However, Jessica did train people in software as part of her work, consistent with some of the roles mentioned in the Strong.

Although Jessica was technically good at what she did, she was somewhat of a misfit in her work environment. She needed warm, supportive coworkers and leaders who appreciated the growth and well-being of employees. She'd found that her workplace had shifted to a more bottom-line, mercenary environment, so she left that job. Now she was in a job she loved, but her boss was making things impossible for her and putting her career and well-being at risk.

Homework and Information Processing

Because I had good assessment data already from that earlier engagement, most of my work with Jessica focused on advising her on how to manage the situation with her boss. The first order of business was to help Jessica alleviate stress. We identified supports she could turn to both inside and outside the office, including friends and family. In addition, Jessica began taking anti-anxiety medication, practicing yoga, and doing some deep-breathing exercises. We also identified outlets that could feed her soul, like music, dancing, and anything else that was fun and could keep her mind off her troubles at work.

We discussed various alternatives to her current job, from transferring to another part of the company to going part-time to leaving altogether. At the time, the company was laying people off, so volunteering for layoff, which would provide severance pay and unemployment insurance, was another option. But Jessica decided to stay and fight for her job.

Since Jessica wanted to stay and deal with the situation, we discussed how she could best express her concerns to her immediate boss. Unfortunately, Jessica had tried reasoning with her boss before and wasn't optimistic. So we decided instead that she should talk to her boss's supervisor and HR and let them know what was happening.

To prepare for these discussions, we did some brainstorming and role-playing. Jessica could get quite emotional, so it was important that she prepare herself and be armed with the objective facts of the case. We role-played the conversation and key points and made some adjustments so Jessica would feel as comfortable as possible presenting the information. The script we came up with allowed her to share the emotional consequences of the bullying while doing so in as calm and businesslike a manner as possible.

Outcome

Not long after Jessica's meeting with her boss's boss and HR, HR called in Jessica's immediate boss for a meeting to discuss the situation. And not too long after that, Jessica's boss was asked to leave the company. Happily, he was replaced with someone Jessica could work with.

Freed from the menace of constant bullying, Jessica stayed on at her job, which was what she had wanted to do all along, even though she had been tempted at times to "throw in the towel." Last time I spoke with her, Jessica was thriving at her work and happy with her decision to stay.

Analysis

This case has a happy ending in that Jessica—someone who was good at her job and loved her role—was able to keep working at the company. Unfortunately, that's the exception rather than the rule. As I discussed in chapter 10, more targets (bullied people) end up leaving their jobs than do the bullies themselves, who often are protected due to their status in the company.

Which brings me to HR. In my work, I have heard many clients complain that HR doesn't always know what's happening in the trenches—that they only act if someone in management gets involved. That's what happened in Jessica's case.

While HR was generally supportive, it was ultimately Jessica's boss's boss who got HR to take action. He was well aware that Jessica's boss had issues, and the prospect of losing an excellent employee like Jessica, and possibly others as well, was something he could no longer ignore.

It's important to remember that when people are bullied, they often can't think clearly or solve problems due to the fear and anxiety they're experiencing. As a result, their work can degrade to the point where they are in danger of being fired for incompetence. It's an insidious process that costs people their jobs, which almost happened with Jessica.

So with clients like Jessica, it's critical to find ways of helping them feel supported and empowered. Because I was there to listen, brainstorm options, and recommend specific points to highlight when talking with her boss's boss and HR, Jessica felt that she was understood and that she was regaining some control over her situation. That ultimately helped her to keep her job.

SUE

Sue, age thirty-four at the time we met, is a great example of a bright, high-achieving, ambitious professional who felt stifled by life in academia. With a PhD in statistics, she had plenty to offer if she could only find the right environment. Sue craved a more challenging, results-oriented setting where people were more motivated and accountable, the opposite of what she was experiencing at her university job as a marketing analyst and researcher.

There were additional challenges. Although clearly unhappy where she was, Sue needed help in turning things around and reaching out for new opportunities. Not only was she both perfectionistic and risk averse, she was also extremely introverted, anxious, and lacking in assertiveness.

Like many people, Sue had ended up where she was by happenstance rather than design. After a college advisor had encouraged her to go to grad school, she did so happily, eventually ending up with a PhD. But she had no clue what to do with her higher education other than stay in academia. Unfortunately, staying in academia would likely mean teaching, something she had no interest in. She also lacked confidence and was quite shy in front of groups.

One thing that Sue *was* sure of was that she admired people who got results, like her father, a machine operator who built a farm with his own hands. Compared to her father and other hard-working people, her peers at the university seemed happy to coast and get away with as little work as possible. Sue found this frustrating and depressing, so despite her issues with self-confidence, she was determined to make a change.

Clues from the Structured Interview

Early in the interview, I asked Sue to talk about experiences that were memorable for her. Her most memorable experience was finishing and defending her dissertation, a major achievement and one in which she could point to clear results.

When I asked her to tell me about people she admired and respected, in addition to her father, she cited two people with PhDs, one of whom she described as "brilliant" and "at the top of her field."

Asked about what upset her in life, Sue was ready with a litany of answers, all focused on what she perceived as personal deficits—irritability, perfectionism, risk aversion, and a tendency to undershoot any opportunities that came her way. She also admitted that she tended to focus so much on results that she paid little attention to relationships or people's positive qualities.

When I asked her how she felt about change and transition in her life, Sue talked about being the first in her family to graduate from college. Despite her admiration for her father and other hardworking people in the farming community, they were in no position to guide her in matters of career and business as she sought an escape from academia. Any network she did have tended to be made up of academics rather than business people, so that wasn't helpful either. Fortunately, Sue and I had things in common that helped me relate to her and mentor her through her career-change efforts.

Formal Assessments

With formal assessments, I wanted to help Sue explore new possibilities to use her strengths, but I also wanted to see if some of her challenges with self-confidence, assertiveness, and other issues would be reflected in the tests.

Assessment Instrument	Highlights
Myers-Briggs Type Indicator (MBTI) assessment	Sue tested as an ISTJ (Introverted, Sensing, Thinking, Judging), which was generally in keeping with the high standards and tendency to keep to herself she mentioned at our initial interview. It also helped explain the hard work and attention to detail she exhibited in her homework.
Strong Interest Inventory assessment	Here Sue tested as Conventional, with interests similar to actuaries, IT professionals, accountants, and similar jobs. She needed and craved structure in her work, which is typical for people scoring high on the Conventional occupational theme. Notably, she showed little interest in the Social theme, consistent with other test results.
Values Scale	Sue's results here, particularly her respect for achievement, advancement, and economic rewards, suggested corporate life might be more of a fit than a university setting. In addition, her high scores for prestige, economic security, and authority were consistent with the need for respect, stability, and control of her life she articulated at the interview.

Assessment Instrument	Highlights
Fundamental Interpersonal Relations Orientation-Behavior (FIRO-B) assessment	Results showed very low needs for inclusion and affection, reinforcing her preference for tasks, results, and projects over relationships. She did have a high need for control, particularly when expressed, showing a strong need to be in charge and/or set the structure or tone of projects she worked on.
16PF Questionnaire	This instrument highlighted the worry and anxiety Sue was experiencing as well as her tendency to be cautious, rigid, and even unlucky or pessimistic. It showed a high need for orderliness and tendency to be distant with others. From a career perspective, Sue appeared to be someone who was dependable, hands-on, and results oriented. Computer programmer, bookkeeper, accountant, actuary, and professor were some of the occupations that she appeared similar to in personality.
California Psychological Inventory (CPI 434) assessment	Structure-oriented, dependable, self-disciplined, driven to get results—these were potential strengths for Sue. However, the profile revealed other tendencies such as being overly critical, perfectionistic, extremely shy and withdrawn, and potentially depressed. She also scored low on self-acceptance, empathy, flexibility, and sense of well-being.

Assessment results tended to bear out Sue's own observations about her lack of self-confidence, shyness, negativity, and other issues. Some tests (the FIRO-B, 16PF, and CPI 434 in particular) suggested she was actually *understating* some of these issues.

On the positive side, the results also suggested that Sue's interest in a move from academia to the business world was warranted. In her results from the Strong Interest Inventory assessment and the 16PF Questionnaire, both of which report on possible occupations, she looked similar to a number of occupations in the business sector, such as accountants, actuaries, and IT

(table continued on next page)

professionals. Also, qualities such as dependability, predictability, structure, control, and achievement—all highlighted in Sue's results—are valued in the business world. Sue was comforted by these findings and eager to get going on her transition.

Homework and Information Processing

In addition to taking the formal assessments described above, I had Sue start some quick exercises during our sessions to start building her confidence and give her a greater sense of her assets. For each exercise, Sue made a few notes in our session and then completed the exercises as homework.

First I had her list her key marketing points. I gave her an example or two to start, and from there she developed a comprehensive list that included her work experience, skills and abilities, accomplishments, personal traits, interests, and education.

Next, I had her list her "must haves" and "must not haves" on the job. As with the marketing points, she took that task seriously, going into detail and enthusiastically sharing her findings.

Finally, I showed her an example of how to do a networking script, including questions she could ask her networking contacts. Here Sue really applied herself, developing a comprehensive script for exploring actuarial work, a field she wanted to learn more about based on testing. Sue's script had three parts: (1) talking points for her first contact with the person she wanted to interview, (2) a set of questions for an informational interview with a working actuary, and (3) questions for an informational interview with a former actuary.

For both informational interview scripts (working and former actuaries), Sue purposely included questions that would help her determine if she would be comfortable doing the work. For example, one question—"Is supervision necessary for career advancement?"—would help her determine if a lot of people contact, something she *didn't* want, would be necessary.

In working together, we also did some role-playing, which helped Sue gain confidence with networking and job interviews. Her comprehensive script was put to good use as part of our role-playing sessions, which made my job easier.

Outcome

After interviewing some actuaries and doing some additional research, Sue determined that actuarial work was not for her. For one thing, she learned that she would have to take a number of exams. This would involve a lot of practice and prep time that she felt she couldn't afford as a full-time employee and involved parent.

When we met a year later, Sue had left her job in academia and had landed a job as a market research manager with a high-tech Fortune 500 company. It had everything she was looking for in a job: a fast pace, a variety of projects to tackle, lots of autonomy (with management support to back it up), and a team of smart, energetic, goal-oriented people to work with.

Sue was another person altogether—optimistic, happy, and far less stressed than the Sue I originally interviewed. Because both the work and the people were more appealing to her than with her academic job, I believe this allowed her to be more effective as a leader than she was in the previous position.

I also like to think that once Sue was able to identify her own strengths, she could start noticing the strengths of others as well. Although assessment results showed low scores in social interaction and empathy, once Sue found a job that suited her, these were "deficits" she could manage. For example, in her research manager job she had two direct reports and did just fine, even though her assessment results (CPI 434, 16PF Questionnaire, etc.) suggest that this would not be the case.

Analysis

The homework I assigned Sue—homework which she happily expanded upon and made her own—helped take her mind off her perceived inadequacies and strengthened her belief in herself and her assets. Having something in writing also helped her better remember and articulate the points during networking and interviews.

Most importantly, it was homework that suited her natural strengths. Not only did developing the networking script help her with her job search and prevent her from going down the wrong path, it was also "proof of concept" for her own abilities, which included excellent attention to detail, strong written communication, and the patience and determination needed to complete a detailed project.

In that sense, Sue's homework was more than just a means to an end; it was also an important achievement in and of itself. Her finished networking script—and the work she put into it—was a truly impressive accomplishment. It also solved a real-world research problem—finding out whether actuarial work was a fit for her. In the act of networking with others, she was forced to communicate her strengths and approach people she wasn't used to approaching. This gave her not only invaluable experience in presenting herself but also greater self-confidence. Sue, like many people, needs to actually do the behaviors before she can feel comfortable with them.

Sue's case also clearly illustrates the fact that working in the wrong environment can be detrimental to one's effectiveness, as well as one's self-esteem. Because she had viewed her university colleagues as "slackers" with little interest in achieving results, this had a negative effect on her own self-confidence, happiness, and motivation. In contrast, colleagues at her new marketing research job were "doers"—bright and driven individuals focused on goals and results. This made all the difference.

Finally, Sue and I had a few things in common that made working with her interesting and rewarding. We were both brought up on farms. Neither one of us had parents working in the professions. And, early on at least, we lacked professional networks that could help us transition into the business world. Both of us struggled. I really do believe that there's a major learning curve to "professional life"—how you act, what you say, whom you hang out with. I could relate to Sue. Helping her build self-confidence and practice interviewing and create a campaign for searching for new opportunities was very satisfying.

ED

I first met Ed, an artist, a few years after he had moved from New York City to Minneapolis. Ed, age thirty-nine, had lived briefly in New York for the excitement and promise it provided him as an artist, but ultimately he found the pace and pressure too much and started drinking heavily. So he moved to Minneapolis—a city he felt would have plenty of opportunity for artists but at a more reasonable pace.

Once here, though, Ed quickly found his prospects limited. Although he was able to find a few creative art gigs here and there, these weren't enough to pay the bills. So he started painting houses to make ends meet. Being stuck in a dead-end house-painting job was frustrating, and he also found the work lonely and isolating.

So Ed began drinking heavily again. At the time of his first session with me, Ed was anxious and depressed and looking for answers. He had also been through a painful divorce, had trouble setting boundaries with others, and, in general, was suffering from low self-esteem.

Clues from the Structured Interview

When I asked Ed to recall a memorable experience, he talked about some art pieces he had created. He loved the freedom of "making things up," as he called it. That's what had attracted him to New York City, with its rich arts scene and endless opportunities.

He also told me about helping his father through surgery and providing emotional support to a friend who was a cancer survivor. "I enjoy helping others and building relationships," said Ed.

In between house painting jobs, Ed had had a few brief stints as a daycare worker and teaching assistant at a local elementary school. While nothing solid resulted from this work, Ed found that he enjoyed teaching kids and hearing their stories.

Clearly Ed was a talented, if troubled, artist with much to offer others, if he could only focus his talents and overcome his demons. He was eager to learn more through assessment. Who was he, really, and what was his potential? Having been through so much frustration in his career, he was at a crossroads, and here was an opportunity to reinvent himself.

Formal Assessments

With all he had been through, Ed felt as if he really didn't know who he was anymore. So to help him get a better sense of who he was and what he brought to the table—strengths, weaknesses, talents, motivations—I provided him with the following assessments.

Assessment Instrument	Highlights
Myers-Briggs Type Indicator (MBTI) assessment	Ed is an ENFP (Extraverted, Intuitive, Feeling, Perceiving). ENFPs tend to be friendly, creative, and versatile, attributes Ed confirmed as we went through his results. He's a clear intuitive and can often fail to attend to details. He also tends to avoid telling people unpleasant things.

(table continued on next page)

Assessment Instrument	Highlights
Strong Interest Inventory assessment	With "very high" and "high" scores on Artistic and Social, respectively, Ed shares interests with trainers, teachers, social workers, and others whose role is helping people achieve their potential; this role also looks similar to some of the artistic professions. Although he does house painting and other hands-on projects (Realistic occupations), his results look quite dissimilar to most of these occupations.
16PF Questionnaire	Ed's report supports much of what I learned in interviewing him, as well as themes from other tests. He tends to be "quite intuitive, appreciating intellectual discussions," "quite accommodating and not comfortable taking charge," "fairly nonconforming, sometimes making spur-of-the-moment decisions," and "curious and flexible." His three top-scoring themes, Creating, Influencing, and Helping, correlate well to various artistic occupations and some helping professions as well.
Fundamental Interpersonal Relations Orientation-Behavior (FIRO-B) assessment	Ed's results showed a moderate need for Control and Affection, so having some input and having others show affection is important to him. He tends to be loyal and cooperative, and also likes to check out decisions with others before acting.

Ed's results highlight his creativity and sociability, as well as his love of learning and helping others. He tends to be a people pleaser—preferring to maintain harmony and accommodate others. Both the Strong Interest Inventory assessment and the 16PF Questionnaire confirm his artistic tendencies, suggesting his choice of work as an artist or art teacher is a good one and reflective of his strengths and interests.

Homework and Information Processing

One of the first things I worked on with Ed was work-life balance. Ed particularly resented not having enough time to spend on his art, especially when he was stuck doing house painting or other odd jobs to make ends meet. So I had him look at what percentage of time he was putting into various aspects of his life and how this varied from what he really wanted to be doing. (For an exercise on using time more effectively, see the exercise Circle of Connection in Section 2 of "The Quick-Reference Toolkit.")

I also suggested he read Martin Seligman's *Learned Optimism*, which he found very useful. An important insight for Ed was finding positive ways to describe his experience, as well as letting go of things he couldn't control. This change in mindset helped him with stress, as did deep-breathing exercises, limiting his alcohol consumption (a constant battle), and journaling.

Another goal with homework was to channel Ed's natural sociability, love of learning, and care for others into networking opportunities. With my encouragement, he volunteered to work with kids with disabilities, an experience he thoroughly enjoyed and that also strengthened his networking skills.

Outcome

Ed enjoyed our early work together and became a regular client. He likes to use my services periodically for a "checkup" or to bounce ideas around. Over the years, we've focused our efforts in two main areas: career and job search, and his overall physical and psychological well-being.

A key crisis came when Ed landed what looked to be a perfect job at a private art college. The job paid reasonably well, and he loved sharing his craft with students. However, changes in leadership at the college led to major budget reductions, and what had once felt like a stable environment suddenly felt toxic, uncertain, and austere.

At the time this was happening, I had Ed take my Career Compatibility Scale assessment. The results (highlighted in chapter 9) show a large gap between the importance Ed assigned to "Purpose" and what he was experiencing at the college.

Shortly thereafter, Ed quit his job. He could not in good conscience work for an organization that valued profits over its students. But despite that setback and others, he remains positive and uses his sessions with me to shore up his motivation, reassess and reaffirm his strengths, and set goals for the future.

Ed recently moved to another city for a fresh start. When he last emailed me, he had accepted a volunteer position with a food kitchen and had also started networking in the local arts community.

Analysis

Ed's case represents a gradual but steady improvement over time, which, given his struggles, is significant. The Ed I first met was confused and unfocused, stressed out, and pessimistic. He felt people were taking advantage of him. He was ashamed of the failure he felt his life represented. He was looking backward instead of forward. But once he gained some clarity through assessment, he was in a much better position to think more positively and sell himself to others.

The Ed I know today is more focused, confident, and optimistic. He's achieved a better work-life balance and is able to set boundaries. He has a much greater sense of his strengths and assets and how he wants to use them in the world. He's looking forward to a brighter future. This doesn't mean that he's suddenly "arrived" and that all will be well going forward. But I can say that the work we've done together has been beneficial—mutually beneficial, in fact.

When working with Ed, I could clearly see how my own strengths complement his. As an ENFP, Ed's my opposite in MBTI terms. For one thing, he's not the least bit detail oriented, which is one of my strengths. So helping him to solve problems by taking concrete steps—an everyday thing for me—seems almost like a kind of magic to Ed.

Outside of Ed's family, I believe I've been one of the few people in his network who's looked out for him and tried to empower him to make decisions in his best interests. Working with Ed over the years has been deeply gratifying, and as he continues his quest to find purpose and meaning in his work, I'm happy to offer whatever tools I can to help him move forward.

DAVID

When he first came to see me, David, age twenty-seven, had just been fired from his job as a fundraiser for an arts organization. A former supervisor who liked David and was impressed with his previous work as an intern had recommended him for the position. David enjoyed the excitement and creative collaboration of the arts world, so the new position had been an exciting prospect.

It was a classic fundraiser role: attracting new donors and keeping existing donors happy, planning and organizing fundraising events, and reaching out to and networking with corporate sponsors. The job required plenty of calls, schmoozing, constant marketing emails, follow-up, persistence, and even being pushy at times. Unfortunately, David, a professed introvert, couldn't make the revenue numbers and didn't form the kinds of relationships that were necessary for success.

The role did require certain skills that David *was* very good at and had demonstrated in his earlier work as an intern: gathering data for proposals, managing and updating the donor and volunteer files, and checking that the organization was meeting the proper regulations. But these behind-the-scenes tasks took a backseat to the core fundraising role of making money and keeping donors happy.

Clues from the Structured Interview

When I asked him what he liked least about his job, he said, "Selling and asking people for money." Not exactly what you want to hear from a fundraiser!

When I asked what earlier accomplishments he was proud of, he recalled dabbling in costume design and independent study abroad, where he met and conversed with diverse and talented people. As a theatre major from a prominent liberal arts college, David had traveled to an arts conference in the UK, where discussions about the impact of the arts on the community fascinated him and motivated him to seek employment in the arts sector.

Finally, when I asked him to describe attributes of an ideal job, he cited creativity, collaboration with others, and doing something valuable for the community. This was all positive, but we also needed to explore more practical, concrete matters, like what kind of job duties he might excel at and be happy doing on a day-to-day basis. One thing David did say he enjoyed was analyzing data, as well as conducting online research.

Formal Assessments

Given David's dislike of fundraising but enjoyment of research and data analysis, what kind of roles might he be most suited for, and what opportunities might be available to him? Exploring these questions was one of our key goals with testing.

Assessment Instrument	Highlights
Myers-Briggs Type Indicator (MBTI) assessment	David was assessed as an ISTJ (Introverted, Sensing, Thinking, Judging). However, his results show a mix of preferences. For example, while he tends to make decisions based on Thinking, as opposed to Feeling, his results showed he had a compassionate side. Also, although he's a Sensor, he showed some preferences normally associated with Intuitives, such as comfort with abstract concepts and theory.
Strong Interest Inventory assessment	Results showed that David was high in Artistic, consistent with his love of creativity and creative environments, and low in Enterprising, consistent with his dislike of sales and asking people for money. Although he did look similar to several artistic careers (e.g., graphic designer, photographer, artist), he also looked similar to technical writers, librarians, editors, management analysts, and computer systems analysts.
Fundamental Interpersonal Relations Orientation-Behavior (FIRO-B) assessment	Here David's results revealed lower expressed than wanted behaviors, indicating he was more a follower than a leader. Affection was his highest need area, which relates to his appreciating close teammates, support, and collaboration.
16PF Questionnaire	This profile highlighted David's potential as an analyst or technician, with "Analyzing" and "Producing" his two highest career themes. Mathematician, scientist, writer, computer programmer, medical researcher, technical writer, and librarian were some of the roles he looked similar to. David's introversion was also highlighted: "He tends to enjoy more time to himself than time interacting with others. He usually is not very comfortable taking charge of others. He's inclined to be drawn toward work that is self-expressive in nature."

Although David's results were a bit of a puzzle at first—he's one of those people whose preferences on the MBTI assessment tend to be mixed, for example—some distinct patterns do emerge when you look at the data as a whole. For example, his high "Analyzing" in the 16PF Questionnaire is similar to "Investigative" in the Strong Interest Inventory assessment, his second highest area in that assessment. His high score in "Producing" suggests that he's a hands-on type who likes to see results. This seemed consistent with his work experience. When he used to design costumes for plays, for example, he loved seeing the actors wearing them because it felt like a real accomplishment that showed his contribution to the artistic process.

Homework and Information Processing

For David and clients like him who've landed in roles that are a poor fit, further processing of assessment information after testing can provide greater focus and clarity. So I had David complete both the Career Ingredients Summary Sheet and the Career and Job Compatibility Matrix.

Here are some notes from his Career Ingredients Summary sheet, along with my analysis.

Section	David's Notes	My Analysis
Strengths	Curiosity and thoroughness	These are admirable, but may not be top strengths for a fundraiser. For example, in his initial interview, he highlighted an academic conference as a memorable experience (curiosity) but did not mention how he impacted or influenced others as part of that experience. Curiosity alone has value, but becomes even more valuable when it results in action.
Weaknesses	Expressing himself directly to others	For a job that requires very strong communication skills on a number of levels (reaching out to and motivating others, interpreting what donors want to hear and responding to that, selling ideas, persistence), one has to wonder: Was this area even explored by the organization prior to hiring him?

(table continued on next page)

Section	David's Notes	My Analysis
People needs	Inclusion; feedback and encourage-ment	On the face of it, there is nothing wrong with these needs; however, wanting these from others could signal that he is more of a fol-lower or pleaser than someone who takes the initiative.
Occupations	Research, grant writer, data analysis, data coordi-nator, refer-ence librarian	For the most part, these are not the kinds of fields that would attract a fundraiser.
Insights	My results on "inclu-sion" from FIRO-B: have to reach out to others more.	David wants to be included by others but sel-dom *initiates* including others. People would likely assume from his actions that he proba-bly doesn't want to be included, when in fact he does. This reinforces the idea of his being a follower rather than an initiator. He loves collaboration and connecting with others, but not with everyone. It's a balancing act for him. Initially, David hadn't seen the connec-tion between initiating contact and gaining closeness, and the FIRO-B assessment brought this home for him.

Here are some of David's selections and notes from the Career and Job Com-patibility Matrix, along with my analysis.

Matrix Section	David's Choices	My Analysis
Preferred role	Collaborator, partner, strategist, implementor	In descriptions of successful fundraisers, "collaboration" is mentioned often. In addition, partnering with others and being strategic would also be pluses, which may explain why David's former supervisor decided to hire him. "Implementor," on the other hand, could be someone who likes working behind the scenes carrying out other people's projects rather than initiating them. Fundraisers, again, are usually initiators and self-starting individuals.
Preferred environment	Cooperative, learning/growth, respectful	None of these jumps out as an environmental factor fundraisers would necessarily emphasize. What's more notable is what David *didn't* circle or check, and that's "competitive," the kind of environment a fundraiser competing for scarce dollars would likely have welcomed.
Occupations	Research, grant writer, data analysis, data coordinator, reference librarian	For the most part, with the exception of certain grant writing functions, these are not the kinds of fields that would likely attract a born fundraiser, who, again, needs to be good at sales.
Would rather avoid	Politics, conflict, risk taking	These are qualities a true fundraiser would embrace, or at least tolerate, as part of the job. The fact that David wants to avoid them is telling.

Both worksheets highlight the mismatch between the role David took on (fundraising) and roles he might be more suited for (analysis, behind-the-scenes work). David needed to explore avenues where a role fit his talents and personality, instead of the opposite—trying to fit into a role that didn't fit his strengths and talents. Through taking the FIRO-B assessment, he also discovered how he needed to initiate more interactions with others in order to meet his social needs.

At the final meeting in our initial engagement, David expressed a desire to put together a game plan, something he intended to do on his own. He later sent me his plan in progress. Here are some quick highlights on the What, Where, and Who of his plan. What: His goal was to begin to explore data analyst and data mining roles in the arts community. Where: He thought he might prefer small- to medium-sized firms that were people-oriented, that minimized red tape, and that had a steady but not frantic pace. Who: He wanted a place where people who are different and quirky, and who value independence of thought, are accepted and where everyone pulls together for a common cause.

Outcome

At my most recent meeting with David, eight months after the end of our initial engagement, I learned that he was still exploring his career options, but that his game plan was proving to be helpful in guiding him, with only some minor tweaks needed here and there.

In addition to the arts analyst role he was continuing to explore, David had also briefly considered the possibility of working as an independent consultant to the arts community. But in thinking about the criteria he needed for his work, he realized such a role wouldn't really suit him. For one thing, he reaffirmed his strong need for work-life balance, as well as the importance of being in the nonprofit world, since working for a larger cause is vitally important to him. Also, he realized that because he really needs to be part of a supportive team, being a one-person shop wouldn't work.

When I last spoke with him, David was working on Plan B: earning money so he could afford to retool in some of the technical areas that would be needed by an analyst. There is also the possibility of his attaining a research role, since he does possess some technical skills that would be useful in that area. As part of this exploration, David will need to ramp up his networking, which is often a challenge for introverts. However, David is highly motivated and focused on carrying out his plan.

Analysis

While assessment is always beneficial to transitioning clients, the process was particularly useful for David, who went from being hurt and uncertain following his termination to discovering new possibilities that could keep him in the arts world. I enjoyed providing him with the structure he needed.

Looking back at David's test results and my initial interview with him, I could see why he ended up where he had and why he'd need to be more careful going forward. David tended to be idealistic, so he needed to keep his eyes firmly on the details so he didn't land in another role that was incompatible. This idealism included his relationships with coworkers, from whom he valued loyalty and devotion, not always a reasonable expectation in a busy workplace—but especially one like fundraising, where getting results is paramount.

We discovered that, other than his interest in and passion for the arts, what he wanted and valued in his work—and what he perceived to be his strengths and weaknesses—had almost no relationship to work as a fundraiser. Again, perhaps most telling of all was his note on the matrix that he wanted to avoid politics, conflicts, and risk taking—all welcome challenges for a true fundraiser but anathema to someone like David.

On the positive side, there was much to suggest that a data analyst or similar role might be a good fit: his self-professed strengths of curiosity and thoroughness; his desire to be part an organization where learning, research, and collaboration are valued; and his interest in implementing solutions rather than leading the charge. He can still work on reaching out to others rather than expecting them to reach out to him, something he noted with regard to his results on the FIRO-B assessment. Improving in this area will make him more effective in whatever he chooses to do.

REFLECTING ON CHAPTER 12: CLIENT CASE STUDIES

No matter how a client presents initially, important clues emerge when you interview them, especially when you use a structured interview. For example, when I interviewed Kevin, I discovered he disliked supervising people and "people stuff"—potentially problematic given that he was going after management positions! When you interview clients, whether in your work or in practice sessions as a student, pay attention to the clues that emerge, which are often surprising.

For clients who are under intense emotional distress, the structured interview can be a pleasant escape into more positive territory, getting their minds off their current situation and looking back at more hopeful times. When I asked Shirley what words she would use to describe herself, her first choice was "caring." That turned our conversation to an earlier time when she was considering nursing as a career. Have you made similar positive discoveries during your interviews?

Taken together with other assessment findings, the results of a battery of formal assessments can clearly highlight why a particular job and working environment are a bad fit. With Jim, for example, his assessment results revealed someone totally unsuited to being a marketing consultant in the traditional, buttoned-down world of banking. While Jim did have ADHD, which was certainly a challenge for him to manage, both his temperament and interests pointed elsewhere. Pick a case study that resonates with you, and note how the formal assessment results helped explain what was happening with the client and the direction they took.

Matching homework to clients' strengths can achieve good results. While Sue lacked confidence in herself and was pessimistic, she was also highly intelligent, articulate, and hardworking. Her development of an elaborate script to use for informational interviewing turned out to be an excellent application of her strengths—and completing the work boosted her self-confidence considerably. Have you witnessed any similar transformations when clients complete homework that utilizes their strengths? If you haven't yet had clients but have set tasks for yourself as part of your professional development, have you thought about matching those tasks to your strengths? For example, if you enjoy and are good at research, consider focusing your efforts there.

The words clients use to describe themselves can be quite revealing and help explain why jobs they took were a bad fit. For example, when David completed the Career Ingredients Summary Sheet, he noted his strengths as "curiosity and thoroughness" and a weakness as his lack of ability to "express himself directly to others"—again, hardly a description of a top fundraiser. When assessing clients—from the structured interview to the information-processing work-sheets—I pay close attention to how they describe themselves and why, and we discuss what it all means for them. Think about assessment processes you've used in your work or been exposed to as a student. What opportunities are there for clients to describe themselves in their own words?

Chapter 13

· · · · · · · · · · ·

ASSESSMENT OF A WRITER

by Liz Willis

In 1993, while endeavoring to transition into freelance writing and editing after leaving my job as a reference librarian, I worked briefly with a career coach whom I'll call Sheila. Sheila was one of those energetic, can-do extroverts with a huge Rolodex of contacts. After analyzing my résumé and making a few suggestions for ways I could highlight my skills, she urged me to begin reaching out to her network for writing and editing projects. While this was flattering— she seemed to believe in my potential more than I did—I found her approach intimidating. I needed a different method, one that would allow me to step back and explore some fundamental questions: Who was I, exactly? What were my real strengths and weaknesses relative to others? Why hadn't being a librarian suited me, even though an interest inventory I'd taken suggested otherwise? (See the sidebar "Burnout at the Library" on that last question.)

That's not to say that Sheila's approach was wrong, just different. Dean's approach is action-oriented, too—in fact, he's much more likely to refer to himself as a career coach than a career counselor—but the difference is that it's grounded in assessment. When I first met with him in September 2000, a few months before losing my technical writing job in a company-wide layoff, I was immediately drawn to his process, especially his structured interview questions and the array of formal assessments he offered. As his collaborator on this book, I've come to have an even greater appreciation for his process and the amount of useful data that comes out of it. So in this chapter, I want to share some of what I've learned about myself through assessment, both as Dean's client and as someone who has long had an interest in career development—much of it inspired by my struggles in that area.

EXPLORING ASSESSMENT FOR THE BOOK

In preparation for writing this chapter, I decided to explore, and in many cases revisit, several components of Dean's assessment process. First, I answered all twenty-one of his structured interview questions in writing. In the previous chapter, Dean explained how these questions provide important initial clues when assessing clients. Seeing the full set of questions with my answers should give you additional insights into the value of the structured interview.

After the interview questions, you'll find my answers to "Defining an Identity," an exercise Dean developed that complements and reinforces the structured interview.

Next, I report on several formal assessments I took through Dean in the early 2000s and more recently when writing this book: the California Psychological Inventory (CPI 434) assessment, the Myers-Briggs Type Indicator (MBTI) assessment, the 16PF Questionnaire, the Strong Interest Inventory assessment, and the Values Scale.

Following that analysis you'll find completed copies of two worksheets, the Career Ingredients Summary Sheet and the Career and Job Compatibility Matrix. For a discussion of the rationale behind these worksheets, see chapter 7.

After the worksheets, I offer brief reviews of three books that have helped me in my own self-assessment and that reinforce much of what I've learned while working with Dean.

I wrap up the chapter with some observations on assessment and how it has helped me better understand myself and my strengths as a writer. If you have clients like me who dream of living the "creative" life—clients who don't fit well into the more traditional world of work—you may find the analysis interesting. We all have something to offer the world; we just need to figure out what it is and keep pursuing it, despite any challenges we encounter.

BURNOUT AT THE LIBRARY

"I'd have to be a psychic to know that." That was my answer to a young woman who had come to the reference desk in search of a book. The book was listed as "checked in" in the library catalog, but it wasn't on the shelf where it was supposed to be.

It was early in 1993, and I was on reference duty at Auraria Library in downtown Denver. Auraria is a busy, and often chaotic, library that serves three different schools along with the general public: the University of Colorado Denver, Metropolitan State College of Denver, and Community College of Denver. I had started there as a reference and instruction librarian in the fall of 1989. While I'd had some interesting projects and assignments over the years, by 1993 I was bored and frustrated and ready for a change.

My uncharacteristic answer to the woman—I'm generally friendly and approachable—was in part due to frustration with the environment. In libraries, you don't have much control over what happens. Books are taken off the shelf and not put back (likely the case in this scenario); library materials are lost or stolen; printers and copiers break down; and students and other library users think research should be easy and complain when it isn't, often taking out their frustrations out on library staff.

So was I ever suited to be a librarian in the first place?

Sometime in the mid-1980s, while studying for my undergraduate degree in English at the University of Alberta, I went to career services and was given the Strong-Campbell Interest Inventory assessment. My results showed I was "very similar" to librarians. I can't remember now what the career counselor said exactly, but I ultimately decided to enter the master's program in library science at the University of Western Ontario. I studied there from 1987 through 1988.

While at library school I don't recall being super excited by any of the courses I took, and my final grades reflected it—solid, but nothing to brag about. My entire career as a librarian lasted from 1989 through 1993. In January 1989 I started a six-month contract at the University of Nevada–Reno. We moved to Denver in July 1989, when my husband was transferred, and I started the job at Auraria in September of that year.

I did reasonably well in both positions, and shortly before I resigned from Auraria in May 1993, my contract was renewed. But my heart wasn't in the work. My rude comment to an innocent library user was a sign of growing frustration with work that wasn't rewarding or suited to my temperament. It also points to one of the limitations of interest inventories: they only show part of the picture. I may have been "similar" to other librarians in many ways, but not in the ways that counted if you wanted to love the work and serve others in an authentic way. Better to be authentic and well suited to the work than burned out and miserable.

STRUCTURED INTERVIEW QUESTIONS

I enjoyed responding to these questions in writing in 2020, and I suspect that my answers are more articulate than when I first answered them in Dean's office in 2000. I remember that one question in particular—"What makes you happy?"—had me sputtering for an answer.

Work-Related Questions

What were your most recent positions? What positions or roles were you most effective at?

I have been an independent writer, editor, and proofreader since my last permanent job (as a technical writer) ended in 2000 after a company-wide layoff. Of the projects I've taken on since then, I've been most effective at those requiring a lot of planning and analysis, such as a web-based résumé guide I wrote for a government agency providing career information to the public.

What is it you have gained in your current/last position?

In the last few years, a key project I've been working on is this book with Dean, and I've also recently started a blog. Both of these projects have impressed upon me how much I enjoy writing. And having put in the effort, I now believe I'm pretty good at it.

How did you find out about the field you're in and decide to follow this route?
I've wanted to be a writer for most of my life, going back at least as far as my late teens. I used to pore over issues of *Writer's Digest* magazine regularly and dream of being a freelance writer.

What kind of supervisor do you work best for? Worst for?
I much prefer to be my own boss! But looking back at a few key permanent jobs I've held, I can see that having bosses who recognized my strengths and let me run with them were the best. One supervisor encouraged me to become the lead editor in the technical writing group I was working in. A library director chose me to chair a committee that made major changes to the library's instructional program.

Tell me about a work experience that has been memorable for you. Why was it memorable?
The project I mentioned directly above was memorable, because it involved using many of my best skills. We were charged with taking an underperforming (and overmarketed) library instruction program and making it more effective. It involved lots of writing and editing, and also persuading people that the program needed an underlying philosophy in order to work.

Is your work meaningful to you? How important is work in your life?
My work has always been an important part of my self-concept and idea of success. I do not have children, so that's part of it. I can't, and don't want to, live vicariously through someone else.

What job responsibilities or duties were/are most interesting to you? Least favorite?
Anything that involves working with ideas, and writing and editing, is interesting. Detail work that's not about language, such as checking numbers or graphics or other production details in a document, is less interesting.

If you could have any job you wanted, what would it be?
What I'm doing right now, but with a bit more business savvy to go along with it! Writing a book, starting a blog, working to reestablish the editing side of my business—all are things I enjoy immensely and find stimulating. Making it all succeed is another thing altogether, but I'm working on it!

What are your sources of job satisfaction?
I enjoy thinking and writing and helping people communicate more clearly. I especially enjoy helping people see connections and make the most of their ideas. Even when I'm just proofreading, I always include notes on any unclear or awkward text I see, and suggest ways to fix it.

Describe someone you have admired, appreciated, or respected in your life.
Marcia Yudkin is a marketing expert who was previously a freelance writer and before that a university professor. She is brilliant and a wonderful strategist and wordsmith. Over the years I have purchased several of her books and taken some of her courses.

Personal Questions

What are your thoughts about transition/change/loss?
I'm currently thinking a lot about the idea of reinvention, only in my case it's not so much reinvention but just getting better and more serious about what I've always wanted to do, which is write. Maybe "renewal" is the better word.

When you think about your background and history, who have been the people or what have been the events that have most shaped your life and allowed you to grow?
By far the most important event was attending university for the first time at the age of twenty-eight, which my soon-to-be husband encouraged me to do. Earning a bachelor of arts degree with a major in English opened up a world of ideas I hadn't been exposed to before. My husband supported me through both that degree and a master's degree in library science.

What are your hobbies/interests/leisure activities?
When I'm not writing, my favorite activities are reading, walking, watching TV, and dinners out (pre-COVID-19, that is!) with my husband and close friends.

What are some things that make you happy about life? Upset?
I love the freedom we have to be whoever we want to be and do whatever we're capable of. I do get annoyed when domestic activities, like housekeeping or home maintenance, get in the way of achieving things. (This question is still difficult, by the way!)

Tell me about three accomplishments and/or experiences from your earliest history—those that you were particularly proud of (childhood to age twenty-two).

In elementary school, I twice had the highest standing in the class (grades four and six). I was also into drawing back then. I seem to remember having some of my drawings displayed at a local museum, although much of the rest of the class may have as well! I also vaguely remember enjoying having deep conversations about ideas with people close to me. This makes sense now that I know I'm an INTJ. My memories of those years are pretty dim.

Give me an example of how you go about making decisions for yourself.

This is something I tend to do intuitively rather than systematically. If it feels right, I usually go for it. I also prefer early closure on something rather than agonizing about it.

What value do you bring to the world? Want to bring?

I bring ideas to the world, and help others communicate ideas, through my writing and editing. I especially want to help others like myself who have struggled with establishing themselves career-wise, particularly those who want to work as independent writers and editors. I'm addressing some of those issues in my blog.

What messages did you receive about work while you were growing up?

I grew up in a working-class family that didn't have much money. And at least early on, work was just something that I would need to do until I met the right man.

What are three words that would best describe you as a person?

Cerebral, determined, funny (in a dry humor sort of way).

What was the best piece of feedback you have ever received?

When I was a senior technical writer/editor, my supervisor advised me to simplify my communications to the team, to only give them the information they needed. She helped me understand the importance of focusing one's thoughts and writing to an audience.

What has been a great movie or book that has impacted you? Why?
M. Scott Peck's *The Road Less Traveled*. In it he says something like, "Life is difficult. Get used to it." That was something I was never really taught growing up, even though I did encounter some significant hardships, like the death of my mother when I was ten. Anyway, the book helped me understand better that I was responsible for my own experience of life.

"DEFINING AN IDENTITY" EXERCISE

Dean keeps lots of exercises in his files, and this is one of my favorites. You'll find other exercises in Section 2 of "The Quick-Reference Toolkit."

How do you define yourself?
I am increasingly defining myself as a writer, something I was hesitant to do in the past. What I do for work or as a profession has always been an important part of my identity.

Who are/were your heroes?
Anyone who has been able to make a life as a thinker and writer. Marcia Yudkin, the marketing expert I mentioned earlier, is a current example. Of thinkers and writers of the past, Samuel Johnson is notable, as is Virginia Woolf. My husband, who has put up with me all these years, is a hero and a saint!

Whom do you want as part of your journey?
My husband, who has given his love and support for so many years, and has yet to see a proper return on his investment! He is a big part of what keeps me motivated. My siblings (brother and sister) have also been very supportive of my efforts over the years, even though they have very different interests.

What do you want to achieve in life?
I want to find a way to use my abilities, enjoy my work, and make some money. The biggest failure would be to not use my gifts in a positive way.

If you could do anything in life without barriers, it would be:
Buying any book or taking any course I fancied, or seeking expert advice on my

writing whenever I needed it, without worrying about the costs. Being able to afford the very best in help. Being able to draw expertly without all the practice! (In recent years, I've been trying to take time for sketching again, including a cute bunny character I'm working on that may have commercial potential.)

What is "success" for you?
Knowing who I am and what I have to offer, and doing something about it that has a concrete result.

What is missing from your life?
Right now, it's not making enough money to contribute the way I'd like to our household income. But this is something I'm working on!

People wear various hats in life. Which three hats are most important for you to wear?
Thinker, writer, soulmate.

What is holding you back?
Only myself if I don't make the effort needed.

What's your vision of retirement?
Finally achieving what I haven't up until now, and enjoying life with my husband.

RESULTS FROM FORMAL ASSESSMENTS

In 2000 and 2001, working with Dean, I took several assessments. Then in 2019, I asked him to test me in the California Psychological Inventory (CPI) assessment so I could learn about it for the book. For three of the assessments in the table below—the CPI 434, 16PF Questionnaire, and Values Scale—it was my first time taking them. I had experienced the MBTI assessment in a different format earlier on. When I was a librarian back in 1990, a consultant was brought in who administered an abbreviated version of it to our team. Before that, sometime in the mid-1980s, I took the Strong-Campbell Interest Inventory assessment (an earlier version of the Strong) through a career counselor at the University of Alberta in Edmonton.

Assessment Instrument	Highlights
California Psychological Inventory (CPI 434) assessment	I scored high on what the CPI calls "Achievement via Independence," described this way in the profile: "has a wide range of interests, independent ways of thinking, and a strong desire to do well in settings where ingenuity is favored"; "will show excellent achievement"; and "is intelligent, clear-thinking, and imaginative."
Myers-Briggs Type Indicator (MBTI) assessment	I'm clearly an INTJ (Introverted, Intuitive, Thinking, Judging). My results showed very clear preferences, with only one preference somewhat "mixed." I also tested as an INTJ when I took a version of the MBTI assessment back in 1990, which I mentioned above. What really resonates for me are the component parts of "intuitive" as explained in my Step II report: *abstract, imaginative, inferential* (now *conceptual*), *theoretical*, and *original*. The language of "intuition," as defined by the MBTI assessment, reminds me of how I like to brainstorm and think up ways of packaging and presenting ideas. It helps me make sense of who I am, what I enjoy doing, and why.
16PF Questionnaire	My career development report stated that I'm "comfortable with abstract reasoning and conceptual thinking" and that I'm "probing intellectually." My two top Career Activity Interests were "creating" and "analyzing." The report said I should avoid taking on assignments that don't require creative thought or that don't draw on my intelligence or curiosity.
Strong Interest Inventory assessment	My Holland theme code was AC (Artistic and Conventional). I showed very strong similarity to technical writers and librarians (I've worked as both). I showed "high interest" in reading and writing. The Personal Style Scales showed that I preferred working alone and leading by example, not leading others.

(table continued on next page)

Assessment Instrument	Highlights
Values Scale	My two highest scores on values came under the "Inner-Oriented" category—ability utilization and creativity. Achievement and personal development were not far behind. All of these remain important values for me as I continue my quest to be a writer.

CAREER INGREDIENTS SUMMARY SHEET

Strengths	Weaknesses	Insights
Writing Editing Problem-solving	Detail work Networking Self-absorbed	*What have I learned about myself?* Well-suited for writing. Keep at it!
Environment/Culture	**Personality Traits**	**People**
Work from home Autonomy	Strong INTJ Introverted Independent thinker	*Whom do I like hanging out with, especially at work?* Intelligent people Friendly
Possible Industries	**Possible Occupations**	**Areas of Meaning**
Freelancer Small business Home-based Web content	Writer/editor Blogger Consultant	*What's my purpose?* *What's worthwhile for me?* Make use of my gifts
Career Goals	**Personal Goals**	**Outcomes**
Find success as a writer Blog and write books	Bring in more income to the household	*What results do I want right now?* Blog results in more income, opportunities

CAREER AND JOB COMPATIBILITY MATRIX

Preferred Industries	Preferred Role	Would Rather Avoid
Financial services Health care Life sciences Communications ✓ Media: **Web content** Retail Government Automotive Manufacturing Military Technical/IT ✓ Other: **Publishing/Creative**	✓ Individual contributor Manager Negotiator ✓ Collaborator Decision maker Assistant Partner ✓ Strategist Sponsor Planner Implementer ✓ Other: **Consultant**	✓ Politics Conflict Decision-making Standing out Risk taking ✓ Other: **Routine detail work**
Preferred Sector	**Preferred Company Size/Group**	
Corporate / ✓ Entrepreneur- ial: **Freelance** Nonprofit Government	✓ Small Medium Large	
Preferred Environment	**Preferred People Attributes/ Relationships**	**Other Considerations**

Artistic/aesthetically
  appealing
Modern
Rustic/older
Competitive
Cooperative
Nurturing/warm
✓ Learning/growth
✓ Challenge/results
Team-oriented
✓ Encourages autonomy/
  independence
Quality conscious
Clearly defined/structured
Respectful
Mission-driven
Strong brand identity
Other:
	✓ Professional
	Highly educated
	Customers
	Mechanical/hands-on
	✓ Artistic/creative
	Social
	Quiet/reserved
	Productive
	Male
	Female
	Helpful/caring
	International
	Local
	Humorous
	Inclusive
	✓ Independent
	Appreciative
	✓ Competent
	Other:	

THREE BOOKS I LIKE ON ASSESSMENT

I appreciate and enjoy assessment in any form, and here I want to share with you three books I have found particularly helpful for different reasons. For more complete bibliographical information on these books, see Appendix E.

The Career Guide for Creative and Unconventional People, fourth edition, by Carol Eikleberry, PhD, and Carrie Pinsky. We creative types often have a tougher time selling our strengths and making our way in the world than others with more practical skills. In the book, Eikleberry and Pinsky explain how those who test as "Artistic" on the Holland Codes dislike being defined by others and often find it difficult fitting into more traditional work environments. (If you're not already familiar with them, the six Holland codes, Realistic, Investigative, Artistic, Social, Enterprising, and Conventional, are used in many career assessments, including the Strong Interest Inventory.) What's important about this book, as reflected in the title, is the intense focus it gives creative and unconventional types. I've never really fit well into the conventional workforce, and this book explains why. I can really see myself in this book.

Your Natural Gifts, by Margaret E. Broadley. This book describes aptitudes as measured by the Johnson O'Connor Research Foundation, which has testing centers in eleven US cities: Atlanta, Boston, Chicago, Dallas, Denver, Houston, Los Angeles, New York, San Francisco, Seattle, and Washington, DC. It would be fun to get tested in person, but this book is the next best thing. I found my own most obvious aptitudes in a chapter called "The Creative Arts," which includes writers. Other chapters with titles like "The Executive," "The Salesman," and "The Teacher" (to name just a few) explain the aptitudes needed in those professions. In a handy chart in the back of the book, "Career Suggestions for Various Combinations of Aptitudes," I found a close match in which "inductive reasoning" was linked to "analytical reasoning," which in turn was linked to "editing" and "essay writing."

StrengthsFinder 2.0, by Tom Rath. I bought this book, and used the code inside to take the StrengthsFinder online assessment, in 2003. My signature strengths at the time were Strategic, Input, Intellection, Ideation, and Learner. (I had also taken the StrengthsFinder assessment a few years earlier, in 2000, through my employer. I got the same five signature strengths, only in slightly different order.) In taking this assessment, I was struck by how closely it matched other assessment results I had received when testing with Dean. (See the formal assessment results on page 174.) My StrengthsFinder results also meshed well with the aptitudes from *Your Natural Gifts*. For example, the signature strength "Ideation" is essentially the same as what the Johnson O'Connor system calls "Ideaphoria," or fluency of ideas.

There are many other great books out there that either back up or expand upon formal assessments, such as *Do What You Are*, a book on focusing your career and finding meaningful work based on your MBTI type. For a full write-up of that book, see Appendix B. And for five books Dean has found inspirational and recommends to his career clients, see chapter 2.

SUMMING UP THE ASSESSMENT EXPERIENCE

I began this chapter by talking about Sheila, the career coach who urged me to get out there and look for opportunities back in 1993. In many ways, Sheila was absolutely right, and her approach made perfect sense. After all, she had listened to me say that I wanted to use my writing and editing skills. And she had looked at my résumé and seen evidence that I was a decent writer and had done a fair amount of writing as a librarian. So what was stopping me?

From what I now understand about the INTJ personality type, what others believe about you matters, but not nearly as much as what you believe about yourself. So while Sheila may have seen my potential, I wanted and needed more evidence. If you look at the evidence I've laid out in this chapter—my answers to the structured interview questions and exercise on identity, the results of formal assessments I took with Dean, my notes on the worksheets, insights from books I've read—you'll see a person who wants to be a writer and who is in fact well suited to be a writer, if she just applies herself. To me that's the great value of assessment: the self-awareness and self-confidence it builds through accumulated evidence.

It's often argued that real writers *write*. That's how they prove themselves, not through endless self-analysis. I agree, but only to a point. Career assessment has helped me tremendously in understanding myself better, and I'm hugely grateful for having experienced it.

REFLECTING ON CHAPTER 13:
ASSESSMENT OF A WRITER

Assessment was an important factor for Liz when it came to working with a career coach. While some clients just want to find work and are looking for the fastest route toward that goal, many clients, like Liz, prefer a deeper exploration of their strengths and weaknesses before proceeding. In your work (or in your studies, if you're a student or recent graduate), have you experienced both types of clients? Which type of client might you prefer working with? (See Part 1 of the book for more on specializing in assessment and assessing yourself as a counselor or coach.)

The Strong Interest Inventory assessment suggested that being a librarian might be a good choice for Liz, and in fact she entered a master's program in library science after taking an earlier version of the Strong, the Strong-Campbell Interest Inventory. However, working in a library was ultimately not a good match for her interests, strengths, or temperament. In your work, or in your studies, have you encountered similar mismatches? What does that tell you about the value of using multiple career assessment sources?

When several data sources are used in career assessment, often there are common themes that emerge. In Liz's case, for example, her strength in ideation and conceptual thinking was a common theme. In your own assessment results, or in assessment results of clients or fellow students, what common themes have you noticed in the data?

Uncertainty can often prevent clients from pursuing goals or roles they otherwise would. Have you ever seen assessment results lead to unfreezing clients and giving them that nudge to "go for it"? Has that ever happened to you in your own career? In Liz's case, she long felt uneasy about pursuing a career as a writer, in part because of the impracticality, and along the way, she tried more practical careers, such as library work. After revisiting assessment, however, she knew she had to continue to pursue writing as a goal.

Liz enjoyed the opportunity to reflect when revisiting assessment. When you allow yourself time for self-reflection, you come closer to the truth about yourself. Do you agree with this statement? If so, what does this mean to you? What steps will you take toward greater self-awareness? If you have previous assessments you've taken in your files, consider getting them out and engaging in some analysis. Try answering some of the structured interview questions and completing the worksheets, and see what new ideas and insights emerge.

Chapter 14

. . . .

A CAREER Q&A WITH DEAN

Early on in my career I conducted an informational interview with Lila, a consultant who ran assessment centers for a financial services firm—events designed to help the company select and promote its employees. These centers involved an array of activities: administration of assessment instruments such as the California Psychological Inventory (CPI) assessments and the Watson Glaser (a critical thinking assessment); "inbox exercises" that required clients to solve problems using a specific set of resources; and other techniques designed to assess clients' problem-solving abilities, emotional intelligence, and leadership style. Not only was Lila kind enough to walk me through what she did in her assessment centers, but she also tested me in a couple of the assessments and even had me go through an in-box exercise.

During the interview I learned that Lila and I had something interesting in common: We were both ISTJs (Introverted, Sensing, Thinking, Judging). When I expressed my concern that as an ISTJ, I often felt out of place, and even lacking, around intuitives, she made the point that the kind of detailed assessment work she did in the centers was an excellent fit for an ISTJ. This gave me a boost of self-confidence, and I would later do selection assessment work myself as part of my organizational consulting services.

I tell you this story because reaching out to others through networking and informational interviews—something we encourage our clients to do all the time—is something we need to do more of ourselves. Think of this chapter as an informational interview with me. And if you have further questions, don't hesitate to contact me at dean@innerviewconsulting.com.

Q: How did you get started in career counseling and coaching?
A: In late 1989, I was laid off from a full-time position as a psychologist with a county agency. Not long after being laid off, I learned about a contract

opportunity in outplacement. In early 1990, I landed my first outplacement gig, and I was hooked! I loved helping people in transition, and I knew that this was something I wanted to do from then on.

Working in outplacement was also my first real exposure to doing formal assessment instruments, including the Strong Interest Inventory assessment, Myers-Briggs Type Inventory (MBTI) assessment, and others. What I love about assessment is the intersection between helping people and data analysis—using data to help direct people forward in a positive direction.

Q: Tell me more about that first outplacement position. How did you find it?
A: After getting laid off from my psychologist job, I went into a rather intense period of soul searching, trying to get my bearings and figure out what was next. I returned to school (the University of Minnesota) on a part-time basis, taking courses through the master of arts in industrial relations program (MAIR). I did some job searching and part-time clinical work. I networked with a variety of people, including some fellow psychologists, as well as folks with connections to HR and consulting. At the time I felt that some kind of position in HR or consulting was probably the next best step for me—something that involved helping people, working with other business and professional people, and doing some kind of work requiring data analysis. But things were still pretty vague in my mind.

Then a relative with connections at the outplacement firm mentioned me to one of their senior directors. That got me noticed and started the conversation that ultimately led to my first outplacement gig. Even though I'd had very little exposure to formal assessments up to that point, my background as a psychologist, interest in HR, and enthusiasm for the opportunity encouraged them to take a chance on me. Once there, I had an opportunity to assess clients both on my own and in consultation with more senior consultants.

Working in outplacement definitely led me to starting my own career consulting business. I don't think I would have done that without that experience. It opened my eyes to what was possible. It also served as my training camp and was a great way to ease into the field. If you're looking to break into the career development arena yourself, be open to taking on new projects, even if you think you aren't quite ready. And make time for networking. I believe that's still the best way to break into our field.

Q: What made you decide to specialize in career assessment?

A: That first outplacement project gave me my first real exposure to career assessment instruments, and I really enjoyed it. I gradually built up my knowledge of assessment from there, getting tested myself in different instruments, and adding those instruments to my offerings for clients. As I did that, others began to notice my work and invite me onto their projects as an assessment consultant and specialist. When I served as president of the Minnesota Career Development Association (MCDA) in 2000–2001, I got more exposure for my work in assessment, and things grew from there. So that's a big part of it. You start putting time and effort into something, people take notice, and it begins to pay off. And that becomes an incentive to specialize further. (In chapter 1, I talk about how investing in formal assessments can help you become a go-to person in the field.)

Also, we all need to distinguish ourselves in some way to advance in our careers and realize our potential. As career development professionals, we work with our clients to help them identify their strengths, decide what they most value and are most interested in, and focus on a career direction that makes sense for them. We need to do the same for ourselves! As I grew in my career, I began to realize that helping people in transition was of great interest to me and that assessment was a perfect tool for facilitating that process. Also, having gone through my own transition, I had more insights into what was involved and empathy for others in that position. Gradually career transition and assessment became a kind of dual specialty for me. When clients are going through a crisis of some sort—trying to recover after being fired, changing careers, thinking about reinventing themselves in retirement—the increased self-awareness they gain through assessment can be critical to moving on successfully.

Q: How would you describe your overall approach to working with clients? Is there some kind of underlying philosophy or theory you follow?

A: First, I'm a strong believer in breaking down a daunting task—and helping clients through transition can be daunting—into manageable parts. Assessment isn't a one-time event (like the taking of a test) but a process. To understand my process and its component parts, be sure to read Part 2 of the book. But here's a quick overview: I want clients to have a game plan, which in my program is a set of criteria they need to thrive in their work. To get there we go through a process that includes a structured interview, formal assessments, and further processing of assessment data by the client through worksheets I've developed. So that's a big part of my approach—having a clear process to follow.

Second, for me, career development theory is only of use if you can apply it in some practical way—to turn it into action. If I think back to what I've read and studied over the years, there are a handful of theories that really resonated with me:

- David Cooperrider's Appreciative Inquiry
- Mark Savickas's Career Construction Theory
- John Krumboltz's Planned Happenstance
- Martin Seligman's Positive Psychology/Resilience
- Frederick Herzberg's Two-Factor Theory (Motivation)

Here's an example of how one theory, planned happenstance, plays out in my practice. The idea behind planned happenstance is that when navigating their careers, people should do two things: take advantage of chance events that occur, which are inevitable in any career, and take actions that are likely to lead to other chance events occurring, which they'll then be in a position to take advantage of.

The game plan (discussed in chapter 8) is a good example of how to use planned happenstance. By having clients think about and write down what they most need in their work—a kind of visualization process—the game plan positions them to recognize when chance events are something they should pursue further. Maybe by chance they meet a person of influence in their field while traveling, and then follow up on that by doing an informational interview. Maybe in their game plan action steps they include "enroll in a course." By taking a course, they set themselves up for the possibility of other chance events. Maybe a new interest they develop in that course ends up changing the trajectory of their career.

Q: Who are your clients? Why do you work with the clients you do?
A: My clients come from a range of industries and include both individuals and organizations. I love variety! That said, I do tend to have a preference for folks working in hands-on industries like manufacturing, technology, and health care. That all started with my first outplacement gig. On that project, which was for a large manufacturer doing a major downsizing, I had the pleasure of working with engineers, programmers, and other technical people who

had great skills but who tended to be quite modest—even more so because they had just been let go from what were once stable jobs. They were really hurting. Many were older workers who had been working with systems and software that were no longer current or widely used.

What also struck me about this project was the fact that the outplacement budget was heavily weighted toward executives. Executives were the ones who generally got tested in the MBTI, Strong, and other assessments, while mid- to lower-level managers, technical folks like engineers and programmers, and administrative assistants usually got a lesser package consisting of help with résumés and interviewing. A few got formal assessments, but this was relatively rare. So as I learned to do assessments on this project—I had the opportunity to test some executives and then give feedback to the lead consultants—I began to see the value of assessment for opening up opportunities and increasing self-awareness. After that, I was determined that all my clients would have the opportunity for a full assessment, including formal testing.

While I have worked with executives in the past, I don't target them as clients, unlike many of my colleagues. At one time I thought working in a business environment with high-powered execs would be the ideal path to follow, but my experience on that first outplacement project, combined with other experiences, like growing up on a farm, strengthened my desire to work with regular folks—lower-level managers, individual contributors, and other hands-on people who are willing to work hard to realize their potential. As often happens, folks like that tend to gravitate toward my services, and colleagues tend to refer them to me. (For more on how I work with colleagues with complementary interests and skills, see chapter 1.)

Another key factor in targeting clientele is age. I generally prefer working with folks between thirty and fifty. They're more mature, know themselves better, and tend to be more responsible in taking steps. While I don't mind working with people in their late teens and twenties, I do find that some of them are a bit too self-absorbed, lack motivation, and aren't that responsible. At one point, in fact, I purposely targeted mid-career clients for that reason. These days I'm more open to a range of ages and see myself as a mentor, including to other career counselors and coaches just starting out. As a group, career development professionals tend to be lifelong learners who grow through connections and interactions with others. We're introspective as well as collaborative. All are excellent attributes when it comes to our own career development and helping our clients with their challenges.

Q: How do you ensure that clients are happy with their results after working with you?

A: One of the biggest challenges we have in our work is that clients have unrealistic expectations or have expectations we can't meet. So one of the key things I do is have clients sign my Client-Coach Expectations Agreement (see chapter 4 or Section 1 of "The Quick-Reference Toolkit"). When they work with me, clients know they need to do their part. They're not expecting to get anything handed to them on a platter. So signing an agreement, in and of itself, can go a long way toward ensuring that clients are happy with their results, or at least accept ownership for them. And of course my process as a whole, which ensures that what's most important to clients is gathered and written down, further processed through worksheets, and then worked into a formal game plan, helps to achieve success in a way a looser, less structured process wouldn't, at least for me.

Nevertheless, even when we clearly communicate our process, and even when clients say they understand what that involves and are willing to take part, they may turn on us when their expectations aren't met. I vividly remember one woman who complained at the end of the engagement that the process was too simplistic and that she was expecting something more sophisticated and enlightening. This woman was someone I would characterize as "high-powered." She had worked for a big-city mayor and was used to dealing with movers and shakers. She had taken a few years off to raise her kids and was eager to get back on the fast track. She was a very bright, high-energy person who could multitask and seemed to appreciate complexity.

In retrospect, I believe this was probably just a mismatch. Although I have occasionally worked with executives (and she fit this general type), I prefer working with individual contributors and hands-on managers who are serious about their careers but don't have big egos. A good solution to this type of problem is to have a network of colleagues to whom you can make referrals. It was earlier in my career when I worked with this woman, so I didn't think to refer her elsewhere at the time—and I assumed she was happy with the process we were using. Today I believe I would pick up on the mismatch much earlier and would happily refer her to colleagues who network with leaders and focus on leadership coaching and development. One of my colleagues works with both women returning to the workplace and leaders and high-level managers, and she might have been a much better match. I discuss referrals in more detail in chapter 1.

Despite a few unhappy clients along the way, most of my clients have been pleased with our work together and grateful for what they got out of the process. At least part of that I attribute to my own commitment to helping them. Once I sign on to work with a client, I'm determined to see it through, despite any difficulties we may encounter. Some of this is personality: ISTJs (Introverted, Sensing, Thinking, Judging) are known for their sense of responsibility and doing whatever's needed to get the job done. And while I've had clients who were the same type as me—Sue and Jim in the case studies are both ISTJs, for example—it's not necessary to be the same type to have a good rapport with clients or achieve good results.

Sometimes being a different type can be a distinct advantage. With my client Ed, for example, being opposites—Ed is an ENFP (Extraverted, Intuitive, Feeling, Perceiving)—resulted in an effective partnership. With Ed, I brought my ISTJ sensibilities to the table, helping him take concrete steps he might not have taken otherwise. Ed became a repeat client, checking in with me over the years to share his next challenge or adventure. For more on Ed, see his case study in chapter 12.

Q: How do you handle diversity in your practice? Any suggestions or advice?
A: For years now, I've been working with people with cognitive disabilities and mental health issues as part of my portfolio of services. These are people with real disadvantages in life. Because of their cognitive challenges and lack of social skills, there's usually some level of rejection or at least distancing from others. Often my cognitively disabled clients simply want friends or people in their lives so they're not alone. Some of these clients lack necessary skills for moving forward, while others may be sheltered from taking on opportunities others may view as too challenging. For those with anxiety or depression, fears and negative thoughts can get in their way in moving forward. So my goal for them is to understand their strengths, build a larger social network, and develop better coping skills.

When it comes to other aspects of diversity, I always try to treat clients equally and consistently regardless of their gender, race, ethnicity, economic background, age, sexual orientation, or other social status. I much prefer to think about my clients' potential as individuals than focus on any particular identity group. It's my preferred style as a career counselor and coach, and it also happens to mesh well with my assessment approach, including the use of formal assessments that are regularly vetted by publishers for gender, racial, and other kinds of biases. Still, there are many possibilities for blind spots, both with formal assessments themselves and our personal approaches as career counselors and coaches.

Not too long ago, for example, a colleague shared with me that she had used the Strong Interest Inventory assessment with her transgender client. Her client was disappointed because the Strong does not yet use transgender people as one of its norm groups. For her part, my colleague was embarrassed to admit that our profession hadn't yet caught up with this reality. She was even more disappointed in herself for offering her client an assessment without thinking it through adequately ahead of time. Had she thought about it further, she may have realized that the Strong might have limited usefulness for her client.

In my own practice, although I've worked successfully with LGBTQ clients over the years, one case left me wondering if I could have handled it differently. My client, a young man working for a local media company, felt that his boss (a man twenty years his senior and married) was being especially hard on him, scrutinizing his work more than that of his coworkers and generally giving him a difficult time. But exactly why this was happening was at first a mystery to me. Was it my client's job performance? Was the job a bad fit? Or was something else going on?

At one of our last sessions together, my client told me he was gay; it was clearly difficult for him to come out to me. Although I had a gut feeling all along that he was gay, I didn't ask. He believed his boss was scapegoating him for being gay, and once I got the full picture, I had to admit he was probably right. In any case, it was sad to think that my client may have believed I'd think less of him or not have been supportive had I known he was gay.

What could I have done differently? At the time, I wasn't yet using my Client-Coach Expectations Agreement, which might have encouraged him to disclose more of his situation earlier in the engagement. In addition, I might have asked him a question I sometimes ask clients who appear to be struggling with getting where they want to go: *What seems to be getting in your way?* Ultimately, clients must tell us what they need so we can help them move forward.

Fortunately, we as career development professionals are becoming better attuned to the need for cultural competency in our work, and there's now a wealth of available literature on diversity and related subjects. Included in that category is a new edition (2021) of an important book published by the National Career Development Association called *Gaining Cultural Competence in Career Counseling* (see Appendix E for details on that and other books). Also, if you haven't already read it, see Part 3 of this book, "Assessing the Work Environment," which covers work values and job satisfaction, workplace bullying, and finding a fit at work. As part of our work with clients, we can help them find a work environment that's a good fit for them and that's also welcoming and respectful to all employees, regardless of their background or demographic.

Q: How do you cope with the stress of working with clients who themselves are going through difficult situations?
A: When it comes to combating stress, what's most important for me is owning my own schedule and having balance in my life. Earlier in my career I was something of a workaholic—I assumed that's how the game was played—but that just wasn't sustainable over time. Physical exertion can also ease stress, and that's what does it for me—biking, workouts at the gym or the park, walking. One of my favorite trips is visiting the Boundary Waters Canoe Area in Northern Minnesota with friends. While there we canoe and hike around with heavy backpacks, and it's all very invigorating and stress-reducing. I come back refreshed and ready to face whatever's on my plate.

Another factor for me is knowing myself well and what I need when working with clients. I talk a lot about my assessment process in the book. Having the kind of structure my process provides leads to more predictability, which I find comforting. I enjoy working with a wide variety of clients, and of course each client engagement is different in its own way, but having a process keeps me grounded and ensures that whatever my clients are facing, I have tools in place to meet their needs.

A final thing I would say about coping with stress is to nurture your friendships and your network, including professional associations. In chapter 3, I talk about how professional associations can help you with learning assessment and building a network of colleagues with assessment expertise, but of course there are many more benefits. Support, camaraderie, tips and insights gained—all are benefits of belonging to professional associations and other groups that form from them, like my mastermind group (see chapter 3). When you're frustrated with some aspect of your work or need advice on difficult client situations, these associations can be a great outlet. Knowing that you're not alone out there is one of the best stress reducers I know!

REFLECTING ON CHAPTER 14:
A CAREER Q&A WITH DEAN

There are many paths into career counseling and coaching. For example, my colleague George started in sales and marketing, later specialized in employee assistance programs, moved from there into outplacement, and then started his own company. Pete was in HR for fourteen years before starting his leadership coaching business. Stan, a high school teacher for twenty-five years, switched to career coaching years ago and loves his work. Kate worked with employees and students at a university and later moved into private career coaching work. She's now a recognized expert on clients age fifty and older. Amy, a career expert and newspaper columnist offering career advice, got her start as a freelance writer writing résumés for clients. There's a path for you, too.

Incidentally, I learned most of what I know about my colleagues through networking, which I recommend you do too. To help you with that, read *The 20-Minute Networking Meeting*, by Marcia Ballinger and Nathan A. Perez—one of the best, and most practical, books out there on initiating, conducting, and ending an informational interview.

We all have different approaches to working with clients, and that's what makes it interesting. If you haven't yet worked out your own assessment philosophy or methodology, don't worry, it will come together for you. In the meantime, consider doing some reading and research to get ideas. You'll find plenty to dig into in the book. (See Appendix B for some possibilities.)

Deciding which clients we want to work with is one of the biggest decisions we make. And just as developing an assessment philosophy and approach takes time, so does making decisions about clientele. It can really only come from experience. To help you plan your own path, see Part 1, "Assessing Yourself and your Career."

In the Q&A, we talked about ways to ensure that clients are happy with their results. An important part of that is having a process to communicate to clients so they know what to expect. It's also important to be true to yourself. Clients can sense when we're not being authentic. So think about who you are at your core and how you can relate that to serving your clients.

Part 5

THE QUICK-REFERENCE TOOLKIT

INTRODUCTION TO PART 5

In Parts 1 to 4 of the book, we looked at four different aspects of career assessment in some detail: assessing yourself and your career as a counselor or coach, assessing clients, assessing the work environment, and exploring outcomes of assessment through career stories. In the Toolkit we switch gears and take more of a ready-reference, problem-solution approach. What can you do when clients don't pull their weight? What if your client is feeling down? Where can you find reliable assessment instruments? As career development professionals we're busy and don't always have the luxury of reading an entire book or taking a course in order to solve a problem. Sometimes a simple tool or tip is all we need to get started.

With than in mind, I've organized the Toolkit into three basic sections:

Section 1: Assessment Forms and Strategies. From your first meeting with clients to the end of the engagement, you'll be gathering and managing information. Here are five tools to help you with that process. Section 1 starts on page 195.

Section 2: Exercises to Use with Clients. When clients are feeling down, defeated, fearful, or overwhelmed, simple exercises can do wonders to get them feeling better and moving forward. Here are six you can use as they are or adapt to your needs. Section 2 starts on page 203.

Section 3: Administering Formal Assessments. This section offers tips and checklists on purchasing and administering formal assessments, meeting educational eligibility requirements, and more. Section 3 starts on page 214.

Note that each of the tools in Section 1 is covered in detail in Part 2 of the book, "Assessing Your Clients." So if you'd like more information on how these tools evolved and how they fit into my overall process, you'll want to read Part 2. I've included them in the Toolkit because they're indispensable in my work with clients. Each is designed to meet a different assessment challenge, from ensuring clients take responsibility for their own outcomes to providing them with a plan at the end of the engagement.

Please make the Toolkit your own—use the resources in whatever way makes sense to you, and feel free to copy them as they are or rework them to suit your purposes. And you don't have to use the tool in its entirety to benefit. For example, if you're looking to improve your intake interviews with clients, adding just a few questions from my structured interview list might make all the difference.

I'd love to hear what you think and what you found useful. Let me know at dean@innerviewconsulting.com.

Section 1

· · · · · · · · · · ·

ASSESSMENT FORMS AND STRATEGIES

In the table, if an assessment challenge described in the first column is something you're experiencing in your work with clients, consider using the associated tool. Again, feel free to adapt any of the forms or resources to suit your specific needs or process.

Assessment Challenge	Tool	Page
Are your clients often too passive, expecting you to do all the heavy lifting? Do they lack an understanding of what's expected of them in the process? Are they sometimes late in arriving to appointments or paying their bills?	*Client-Coach Expectations Agreement*	197
Is your current interview process ineffective in building a foundation for working with clients and suggesting next steps? Do your sessions with clients get bogged down in endless discussions of the problem, with no solutions in sight? Do you want your clients to feel more hopeful about their future?	*Structured Interview Questions*	198
After you've worked with clients for a while, do they sometimes ask, "Now what?" Do you wonder what they've learned? Might they benefit from a convenient place to record their insights and process information gathered during assessment?	*Career Ingredients Summary Sheet*	199

(table continued on next page)

Assessment Challenge	Tool	Page
Are your clients unclear or uncertain about what industries, roles, or company environments might suit them or be available to them? Could they use a handy checklist to help them narrow their options? Are they clear on what they *don't* want?	*Career and Job Compatibility Matrix*	200
At the end of the engagement, do your clients have an effective means for planning and making good decisions going forward? Something tangible they can refer to? Something that consolidates everything they've learned during assessment? Can they visualize the kind of career and life they want?	*Game Plan Introduction and Worksheet*	201

CLIENT-COACH EXPECTATIONS AGREEMENT

I greatly appreciate the opportunity to work with you and hope to address as many of your career needs as possible. To help us get started on the right foot, please read this document, answer any questions, and acknowledge by signing and dating below.

A few things I need to know about you:

Are you seeing other counseling/coaching professionals? If so, I need to know so that the help I provide you complements, and doesn't undermine or duplicate, these other services. Please answer briefly here. Example: "I'm seeing another coach for job interview coaching" or "I'm seeing a therapist to deal with anxiety issues."

_____

_____

Will you be responsible for owning your own career progress? That is, are you able and willing to try new things, complete any homework I assign, and take any necessary steps toward meeting your goals? I can assist and encourage you but I can't make you take action; only you can do that. *Please say a few words here about how you plan to assume ownership for your career progress.*

_____

_____

A few things you need to know about me:

I will be open and honest in working with you. I am a strong believer of sharing feedback, some of which will be positive and some of which may be negative, difficult to hear, or perhaps unflattering. Important: I will not reveal confidential information to others in the course of our work together, unless you provide written consent.

I will provide as much support as possible, but you need to communicate your needs and take ownership of the process. We will work together as a team.

I expect courtesy and respect from the people I work with. For example, I expect timely payment when service is delivered and advanced notification of cancellations or the need to reschedule (24 hours is preferred).

By signing this document, I acknowledge that I have read it carefully, answered any questions honestly, and understand our mutual obligations.

_____   _____   _____   _____
Client/Candidate Signature   Date   Coach/Counselor Signature   Date

STRUCTURED INTERVIEW QUESTIONS

Questions are arranged in two categories: Job-Related and Personal. I usually start with job-related questions and move on to personal questions later in the interview.

Job-Related Questions

What were your most recent positions? What positions or roles were you most effective at?

What is it you have gained in your current/last position?

How did you find out about the field you're in and decide to follow this route?

What kind of supervisor do you work best for? Worst for?

Tell me about a work experience that has been memorable for you. Why was it memorable?

Is your work meaningful to you? How important is work in your life?

What job responsibilities or duties were/are most interesting to you? Least favorite?

If you could have any job you wanted, what would it be?

What are your sources of job satisfaction?

Describe someone you have admired, appreciated, or respected in your life.

Personal Questions

What are your thoughts about transition/change/loss?

When you think about your background and history, who have been the people or what have been the events that have most shaped your life and allowed you to grow?

What are your hobbies/interests/leisure activities?

What are some things that make you happy about life? Upset?

Tell me about three accomplishments/experiences from your earliest history—those that you were particularly proud of (childhood to age twenty-two).

Give me an example of how you go about making decisions for yourself.

What value do you bring to the world? Want to bring?

What messages did you receive about work while you were growing up?

What are three words that would best describe you as a person?

What was the best piece of feedback you have ever received?

What has been a great movie or book that has impacted you? Why?

CAREER INGREDIENTS SUMMARY SHEET

Use this sheet to record anything that stood out for you during our initial interview and when reviewing your test results. Feel free to add any additional thoughts that come to mind.

Strengths	Weaknesses	Insights
		What have I learned about myself?
Environment/Culture	**Personality Traits**	**People**
		Whom do I like hanging out with, especially at work?
Possible Industries	**Possible Occupations**	**Areas of Meaning**
		What's my purpose? What's worthwhile for me?
Career Goals	**Personal Goals**	**Outcomes**
		What results do I want right now?

CAREER AND JOB COMPATIBILITY MATRIX

Complete this form by checking or circling items in each category that are most appealing. If you don't see an item listed that comes to mind, add it to the list.

Preferred Industries	Preferred Role	Would Rather Avoid
Financial services Health care Life sciences Communications Media Retail Government Automotive Manufacturing Military Technical/IT Other:	Individual contributor Manager Negotiator Collaborator Decision maker Assistant Partner Strategist Sponsor Planner Implementer Other:	Politics Conflict Decision-making Standing out Risk taking Other:
Preferred Sector	**Preferred Company Size/Group**	
Corporate/Entrepreneurial Nonprofit Government	Small Medium Large	
Preferred Environment	**Preferred People Attributes/ Relationships**	**Other Considerations**

Artistic/aesthetically
  appealing
Modern
Rustic/older
Competitive
Cooperative
Nurturing/warm
Learning/growth
Challenge/results
Team-oriented
Encourages autonomy/
  independence
Quality conscious
Clearly defined/structured
Respectful
Mission-driven
Strong brand identity
Other:
	Professional
	Highly educated
	Customers
	Mechanical/hands-on
	Artistic/creative
	Social
	Quiet/reserved
	Productive
	Male
	Female
	Helpful/caring
	International
	Local
	Humorous
	Inclusive
	Independent
	Appreciative
	Competent
	Other:	

GAME PLAN COVER SHEET

To create a game plan, you'll write down criteria for three aspects of your career and work: *what* you want to do; *where* you want to work; and *whom* you want to work with. (See next page for the game plan worksheet.) When you think about it, having this information to refer to is incredibly valuable. You can use your game plan to:

- evaluate future career and business opportunities
- assess a possible position or project
- clarify a niche or brand for marketing purposes
- develop marketing materials for job-search or business opportunities
- communicate value and fit in a job interview or project presentation
- share goals and ideas with colleagues and networking contacts

As you complete the game plan worksheet, here are some additional questions to think about.

Game Plan Factor	Related Questions
What	What do I want to do with my life? What are my strengths and how can I use them to best advantage? What's available to me? How do my values and lifestyle relate?
Where	Where do I do my best work? Do I want to belong to a large organization, or do I like doing my own thing? What level of control do I need? Does the place have a look and feel that I'm comfortable with?
Who	What kind of people do I want to work with or serve? How important are others to what I want to do? What level of influence should they have? Am I comfortable and safe around these folks? To what extent do they aid my growth? Stifle my growth?

GAME PLAN WORKSHEET

Record your criteria and action steps below. For tips on determining criteria, see the introduction on the reverse side.* If you need extra space, make another copy or add pages as needed.

Game Plan Factor	Criteria
WHAT: What should I be when I grow up (occupation, role, etc.)?	• • • • •
WHERE: The environment, culture, size, pace, of the place I work at.	• • • • •
WHO: The people I want to work with—ideal co-workers, clients, colleagues, etc.	• • • • •

Action Steps

Write down things you can do now to move your job search or business forward.

1.
2.
3.
4.
5.

If desired, include the introduction under "Game Plan Cover Sheet" with the game plan template.

Section 2

......••••••

EXERCISES TO USE WITH CLIENTS

Are your clients struggling with issues that are distracting them and preventing them from benefiting fully from assessment? If so, consider trying one of the suggested exercises in the table below. All of these exercises have facts or variables that can easily be changed, so feel free to adapt as needed.

Client Challenge	Exercise	Page
Many clients in transition get defeated by negative feelings, which can affect their ability to focus and benefit from the assessment work you're doing together. To get them to think more positively, try exercises with that in mind.	*Thinking More Positively: Three Options*	204
When something upsetting happens at work or at home, clients can obsess about what happened and why, replaying it in their heads over and over and often blaming themselves. Thinking things through more objectively can help.	*Restructuring Your Thoughts, Feelings, and Behavior*	205
How clients spend their time has a lot to do with how well they cope with life and navigate career transitions. This is a major challenge for many clients, and reassessing how they use their time can be helpful and, in many cases, transformative.	*The Circle of Connection*	207

(table continued on next page)

Client Challenge	Exercise	Page
Clients who struggle often have a negative story about themselves or their work experience running through their heads. Reaching out for different perspectives can help them see things differently and craft a story based on strengths—strengths they may be underestimating or even oblivious to.	*Multistoried Life*	208
In focusing on the "what" of a job (qualifications, role, tasks, etc.), clients often overlook environmental considerations, that is, how a particular business or organizational culture suits them personally, meets their needs, and fits with their values. This exercise can be done to assess both potential and existing jobs.	*Do You Fit?*	209
Getting clients to move ahead on much-needed changes and goals can be difficult, especially if they lack confidence in themselves and their capabilities, or have forgotten what they're already capable of.	*Getting More Comfortable with Change*	211

For five excellent self-help books to read yourself or recommend to clients, see "Five Key Books on Self-Development" in chapter 2.

EXERCISE 1:
THINKING MORE POSITIVELY

Often clients are in need of more energy and positivity, especially when they're making a shift in their career or feeling frustrated by a protracted job search. If they're feeling down or don't have a clear picture of their strengths and talents, they'll face serious challenges when job searching.

Instructions

Here are three quick suggestions for helping clients think more positively when their self-confidence needs a boost. Try one or two, or all three.

Option 1: Write down at least ten positives about yourself, and as many more as you can think of. (Listing negatives is often much easier for people, so this can be a useful exercise to counteract that tendency.)

Option 2: Ask three to five people who know you well to name one or two strengths or positives about you. If you have tried Option 1, compare what they say to your own list of positives.

Option 3: Find or create some positive affirmations that appeal to you, and read or recite them daily. (A Google search on "positive affirmations" yields a host of good ideas.)

Clients who were raised in a family system in which people focused more on the negative than the positive tend to carry those habits with them until challenged. Trying one or more of the options above can help them feel better about themselves and keep their mind focused on the positive. This helps them face the obstacles and challenges of their journey.

My client Sue is a great example of someone who overcame negative thinking. With Sue, I used a variation on Option 1 by having her list her top "marketing points"—attributes she could highlight in seeking her next position. A perfectionist, Sue always felt she came up short, but she was also highly conscientious in doing her homework. Her list of marketing points was so comprehensive and so impressive that she ended up impressing herself! It was just the spark she needed. For more on Sue's story, see her case study in chapter 12.

EXERCISE 2:
RESTRUCTURING YOUR THOUGHTS, FEELINGS, AND BEHAVIOR

How clients perceive and react to adverse events or incidents in their lives can have a big impact on their self-confidence. This refocusing exercise can help them be more constructive and effective in working out negative situations. For example, if your client is struggling with a boss or another key player at work (see scenario below), this exercise can provide some healthier ways of engaging that person and avoiding the negative consequences of remaining passive or responding inappropriately.

Instructions

For any adverse event your client wants to explore, create a simple table like the one below.

Above the table, indicate the event that occurred.

In the second column, "Initial Response," record the client's initial (automatic) response in terms of (1) what they thought (believed about the event), (2) how they felt, and (3) their behavior (actions they took or didn't take).

In the third column, "Desired Response," restate what happened in terms of the desired (healthier and more assertive) response.

Here's an example:

What Happened: My boss yelled at me in front of my coworkers.

Response	Initial Response	Desired Response
Thought	I thought it was my fault.	I thought my boss was at fault for yelling at me.
Feeling	I felt humiliated.	I felt upset but not humiliated.
Behavior	I never said anything.	I let my boss know that it wasn't acceptable.

Again, repeat this process for any adverse or problematic event you want to discuss with your client.

This exercise roughly reflects an ABC model used in cognitive therapy by Martin Seligman and others to record thought patterns. The *A* stands for "adversity," which is the situation or event that is bothering us: "My boss yelled at me in front of my coworkers." The *B* stands for "beliefs" that form from our initial thinking about the event: "I thought it was my fault." The *C* stands for Consequences. As a result of what we believe, we behave in a particular way: "I never said anything." Rethinking can result in a change of behavior or feeling: "I let my boss know that it wasn't acceptable."

For more on Seligman's approach, see his book *Learned Optimism*. Similarly, David Burns's *Feeling Good: The New Mood Therapy* offers readers ways to counter faulty thinking with more rational thoughts. For details on Seligman's book, see "Five Key Books on Self-Development" in chapter 2.

EXERCISE 3:
THE CIRCLE OF CONNECTION

Work-life imbalance can be a huge issue for many clients. This simple exercise can help them become more aware and intentional about how they're using their time and start to make adjustments. I use this exercise a lot with workaholics or people who have little going on outside of their work life. It's a way of not only becoming more balanced but also gaining energy and expanding networks. People who have difficulty setting boundaries may also benefit.

Instructions

Have clients draw a circle and divide it into slices. Assign work-life categories such as the following (or similar categories of your choice) to each:

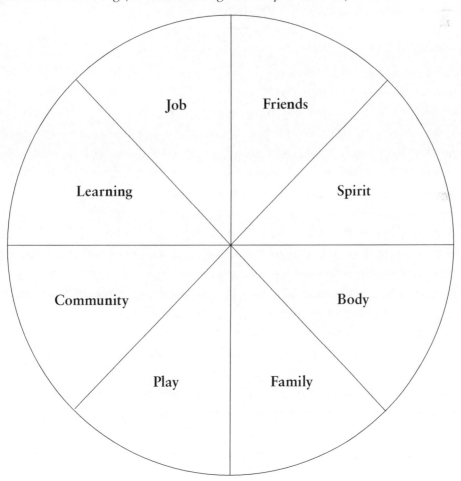

Size each slice—or assign a rough percentage to it—according to how much time you *currently* spend in that category.

Draw a second circle, this time sizing the slices (or assign percentages) according to how much time you'd *prefer* to spend in those categories.

Choose the top three categories in which you would most like to initiate change, and for each category, set at least one goal toward making that change.

The key is to decide on what's most important in your life—and take action that allows you to focus on those priorities. Two books that can help with this, both by Richard Leider, are *Repacking Your Bags* and *The Power of Purpose*. For details on *Repacking Your Bags*, see "Five Key Books on Self-Development" in chapter 2.

EXERCISE 4: MULTISTORIED LIFE

We all have a story—how we explain and summarize our work and our lives—that can influence both our self-confidence and our future direction. Often rewriting that story is the way to greater understanding and self-confidence. And we can rewrite our stories more effectively when we get input from others. How would your significant other tell your story? How would your mentor tell your story? What do assessment results say about you? These are all different versions of your story that can help you see things differently.

This exercise is particularly useful for clients who are feeling negative or depressed about their careers and need a boost of self-confidence. It helps them see the bigger picture. It can also be useful prior to an interview situation. Early on in many interviews, candidates are asked the dreaded "Tell me about yourself" question, which many feel ill equipped to answer. This exercise can aid them in responding more effectively. Thinking about your story can also help shape a personal or professional brand.

Instructions

On a sheet of paper, write down the following items, leaving lots of space under each. Use different or additional items if desired:

Your Story: (*See example below*)

Significant Other's Version:

Mentor's Version: (*See example below*)

Testing/Assessment Version:

Other's (friend's, coworker's, etc.) Version:

For your story, write down some thoughts about how your work, life, and career are going. Then, after seeking feedback from one or more of the other sources listed, affirm or begin to rewrite your story.

My client Karen was a nursing professional who had worked her way up from an entry-level position to an administrator role, earning an RN degree and other credentials along the way. Still, she was unhappy with her career. In Karen's story about herself, the jobs she had held seemed boring, disconnected, and uninspiring. She could point to other RNs and health care professionals whose careers seemed much more exciting, impressive, and more strategically planned than hers.

I'll serve as her mentor for this example. Looking at her work history, I saw a different story. As I looked back at her various positions, I could see some common threads: each job involved providing care and improving people's lives in some way. In a health care setting in particular, both of these aspects are important and valuable contributions. After thinking it through, Karen agreed, and with a new sense of the value she was able to create in her work, she felt invigorated and ready to move forward. She was now able to make more sense of her career and tie it to a purpose.

EXERCISE 5:
DO YOU FIT?

When clients are considering career opportunities such as a new position or thinking about their current position, it helps to consider the various factors that can make for a good match—or, conversely, a poor fit—at work. This exercise is useful for clients who may not be fully aware of the factors that can impact their job satisfaction and effectiveness. It's a way of better understanding if a job role or organizational aspect (values, diversity, corporate culture) is a match or not. I want people to be thorough and thoughtful when making important decisions.

Instructions

Make a four-column table like the one below. In the Factor column, list the factors shown, or substitute factors of your choice.

Factor	Fit	Not a Fit	Notes
Corporate Style			
Values			
Philosophy			
Size/Status			
Communication (e.g., to job applicants)			
Dress Code			
Energy/Pace			
Work Ethic			
Average Employee Age			
Diversity			
Politics			

Have clients check the appropriate column according to whether the factor is a match (Fit) or a mismatch (Not a Fit). If they're unsure about a particular factor, have them mark an X between the columns or leave the factor unchecked. Then, have them make notes for anything that stands out, or for areas where they may be willing to be flexible. For example, if the dress code is more formal than they'd like but most other factors are a good match, they may be willing to compromise.

If you are interested in exploring the idea of fit with clients, try the Career and Job Compatibility Matrix in Section 1 of this Toolkit. I go into fit in more depth in chapter 9, "Work Values Assessment and Job Satisfaction," and chapter 11, "Assessment and Job Fit."

EXERCISE 6:
GETTING MORE COMFORTABLE WITH CHANGE

A common barrier when changing careers (or dealing with other kinds of change) is facing the unfamiliar and getting outside our comfort zones. Here are three steps that can help.

Step 1: Recall Past Successes
Recall changes you made or goals you met in the past in which you were apprehensive at first, but now you are much more comfortable. What steps did you take? At what point did you start feeling more comfortable? Did anyone help you along the way?

Step 2: Identify Changes You Want to Make
List changes you would like to make in your life and career. Rate each change on a scale of 1 to 10, with 1 being least comfortable and 10 being most comfortable. This table has room for eight changes or goals; add more if needed.

Change You Want to Make	Comfort Rating (1–10)

Step 3: Start with a Doable Goal and Take Action

Starting with those areas in which you anticipate the most comfort (ratings of 6 to 10), ask yourself the following questions:

1. What will you do to gain more comfort/familiarity?
2. When do you want this change to happen?
3. Who can help you in this journey?

Now look at areas in which you anticipate the least comfort (ratings of 1 to 5), and ask the same questions again. Just one success in the "more comfortable" category can give you momentum for tackling tougher challenges.

Example

Here's a quick example that Liz, my collaborator on the book, offered relating to relaunching and growing her editing business.

Step 1: Recall past successes

First, Liz recalled how she had learned HTML and later how to use Word-Press to build her first two websites. While she was initially apprehensive about learning these technologies, she found she did very well and enjoyed the process. Part of what helped was taking online classes, which suited her learning style. She has since taken many classes online.

Step 2: Identify changes you want to make

In thinking about relaunching her editing business, Liz recorded the following goals, assigning comfort ratings from 3 to 9.

Change You Want to Make	Comfort Rating (1-10)
Find new editing clients	3
Learn more about the market for editing books	9
Make improvements to my blog/editing website	8
Earn more income by increasing my prices	3
Grow my network	5

Step 3: Start with a doable goal and take action

As you can see from Liz's ratings above, she is very comfortable (comfort rating of 9) with learning more about the book editing market, and it's something she wants to do sooner rather than later. With that in mind, and thinking about her past successes with online learning, Liz enrolled in an online course that's specifically about the book editing market and the opportunities within that market. Through that course, she is making contacts that should help her with less-comfortable goals: finding new clients and growing her network (comfort ratings of 3 and 5, respectively).

Again, starting with a "high-comfort" goal can give you momentum. And recalling your past successes can keep you motivated and working toward your goals.

For more on Liz, see chapter 13, "Assessment of a Writer."

Section 3

ADMINISTERING FORMAL ASSESSMENTS

As I stressed in chapter 1, "Specializing in Career Assessment," having the capability to offer formal assessments to your clients is a major advantage, because many clients have the expectation that you'll be able to offer this service. In addition, having assessments capability can open up many opportunities in selection assessment, outplacement, and other areas.

In this section of the Toolkit, we'll look at some of the questions you may have about administering formal assessments, from where to purchase them to taking advantage of the many resources that test publishers offer. As you'll see, working with the right publishers extends your own capabilities by providing an array of systems and tools, including educational materials for you and your clients.

Question	Topic	Page
What are the best sources of career assessment instruments?	*Test Publishers I Count On*	215
What are the educational requirements for purchasing and administering assessments?	*Qualifying to Administer Assessments*	217
What happens when you administer career assessments online through a test supplier? How complicated is it?	*Administering Assessments: Basic Procedures*	218

Question	Topic	Page
How can I save money on assessments and recover some of my costs?	*Administering Assessments: Costs and Cost Recovery*	219
What are some advantages of working with reputable test publishers? What do they offer their end users?	*Exploring Test Publisher Resources*	221

Note that the emphasis here is on working with test publishers and what that entails. For more general questions on using career assessment instruments, especially when you're just starting out, see the Q&A in chapter 6.

TEST PUBLISHERS I COUNT ON

Whether you're thinking about purchasing assessments for use with your clients or for your own professional development, it's important to know the right (that is, official) publishers. Below are publishing firms I buy from and the assessments I order from each. These firms are long-standing and reputable, and they provide extensive information about their products and services on their websites.

Publisher	Assessment Instruments I Purchase
The Myers-Briggs Company (formerly CPP) themyersbriggs.com	California Psychological Inventory (CPI) assessments* Fundamental Interpersonal Relations Orientation-Behavior (FIRO-B) assessment* Myers-Briggs Type Indicator (MBTI) assessment Strong Interest Inventory assessment Thomas-Kilmann Conflict Mode Instrument (TKI assessment)* Watson-Glaser Critical Thinking Appraisal*

(table continued on next page)

Publisher	Assessment Instruments I Purchase
PSI 16pf.com	16PF Questionnaire (Career Development Report)
PAR (Professional Assessment Products) parinc.com	CASI (Career Attitude and Strategies Inventory) SDS (Self-Directed Search)
PSI Services psionline.com	Employee Aptitude Survey (EAS)*
Pearson Clinical Assessments pearsonassessments.com	MMPI-2 (Minnesota Multiphasic Personality Inventory)** WAIS-III (Wechsler Adult Intelligence Scale)**
Hogan Assessment Systems hoganassessments.com	Hogan Personality Inventory Hogan Development Survey Motives, Values, Preferences Inventory

* Assessments I use in selection assessment when consulting with organizations. (I also use the CPI and FIRO-B with my own career clients.) The Employee Aptitude Survey (EAs) consists of ten different tests covering verbal comprehension, numerical ability, visual speed and accuracy, and other factors.

** Assessments I use in my clinical work. For clinical work I do with people who are cognitively disabled, I use the MMPI-2 and the WAIS-III, along with other tests, including the Symptom Checklist 90-R, Peabody Individual Achievement Test-Revised, and the Peabody Picture Vocabulary Test, 3rd edition. The CPI, 16PF, and Hogan can also detect some possible disturbances or mental health issues.

Note that the table above lists only career assessments and test publishers I work with personally. But of course, there are hundreds of different career assessments available. For an extensive list of career assessment instruments, including information on how to obtain them, see *A Comprehensive Guide to Career Assessment* (seventh edition), published by the National Career Development Association (NCDA). I cover the guide in detail in Appendix B.

QUALIFYING TO ADMINISTER ASSESSMENTS

In order to maintain high standards in the use of their career assessment instruments, the top test publishers have educational eligibility requirements, as well as certification and training services. The Myers-Briggs Company (formally CPP) supplies the majority of formal assessments I discuss in the book, so I will use it as an example.

First, see the educational eligibility page on their site. Eligibility is based on either type of degree (master's level or higher) or licenses or certifications held. Examples of degrees are master's or doctoral degrees in clinical psychology, counselor education, and industrial and organizational psychology. Examples of licenses or certifications are state-licensed clinical social worker (LCSW), state-licensed professional counselor (LPC), and National Certified Counselor (NCC).

Because I earned a master's degree in behavior analysis and therapy in 1983 and became a licensed psychologist (LP) with the state of Minnesota in 1986, I met requirements for administering assessments early on in my work as a career counselor and coach. (Either my degree or my license makes me eligible to purchase and administer assessments.) But I haven't let that limit my learning process (see the next point).

If you do not currently meet the Myers-Briggs Company's educational eligibility requirements, you can still administer assessments if you complete its certification programs. Although I met the basic eligibility requirements, I found that pursuing certification—I completed certification programs for both the Myers-Briggs Type Indicator (MBTI) assessment and Strong Interest Inventory assessment and additional training in other assessments—was both enlightening and helpful to my career.

If you are a counseling student, you are most likely in a master's program and will qualify to purchase and administer assessments once you receive your degree. If you want to study an assessment tool prior to graduation, you would be eligible to enroll in one of the Myers-Briggs Company's certification programs. If you are a working counselor or coach and meet the educational requirements, you can go ahead and use assessments, although I highly recommend you take advantage of training and certification services.

Finally, whether you're a student or a working career counselor or coach, I recommend you take advantage of whatever learning resources are available to accelerate your progress with formal assessments—key texts on the topic, like those in Appendix B, training offered by test publishers, and mentoring and tutoring by experienced colleagues. While the best experience is hands-on work with assessments, you have many learning resources available to you.

Another good example of eligibility requirements is PAR's Qualification Levels page. If you're just starting out with assessments, you can get your feet wet with Level A assessments, which do not require any special credentials to order. A good example of a Level A assessment is the Self-Directed Search (SDS), a classic interest assessment based on the Holland types (Realistic, Investigative, Artistic, Social, Enterprising, and Conventional).

ADMINISTERING ONLINE ASSESSMENTS: BASIC PROCEDURES

If you're just getting started with formal assessments, you may be wondering what's involved in ordering and administering them, so here's a quick overview. Since I purchase the majority of my tests from the Myers-Briggs Company (formerly CPP), I'll use it as an example.

You start by creating an account. Go to themyersbriggs.com, select My Account, then Create Account, and complete the sign-up form. As part of this process, you will enter credentials, which will determine your eligibility to complete an online account and administer tests. (See Qualifying to Administer Assessments for more.)

Once you are an approved test provider with an online account, you can then set up testing for your clients through the company's Elevate test administration system. (Note: I'm assuming you'll want to take advantage of online scoring. For that, you'll need to use Elevate and pay the yearly licensing fee. For more, see Administering Assessments: Costs and Cost Recovery.)

In Elevate, you follow these basic steps to administer formal assessments:

1. Create a project, which consists of the tests you're going to use and the names and contact information for the clients you will send them to. Once you've created a project, you can then send a link for clients to follow to take their assigned assessments.

2. Purchase your inventory. What you're doing here is paying to have the tests you assigned to clients processed so you can download reports.

3. Download reports, and then email results to clients. I generally prefer to hold onto results until I can see clients in person. However, I will email results if we are meeting remotely.

Note that when it comes to purchasing inventory you have two choices. You can purchase as you go or prepurchase assessments and have the inventory available to be used as clients take tests. The first time you use Elevate, however, you won't yet have an existing inventory, so you'll need to purchase the assessments. But once you're established and part of the system, you'll have the option to prepurchase assessments (create an inventory), so you won't need to purchase before each download.

Also, if you didn't keep a copy of an assessment you originally downloaded, you can return to the Elevate website, log in, and download the results again, free of charge. Once you have purchased inventory (and therefore paid for results to be processed), you can download results at any time, usually for up to a year and sometimes longer.

Ordering and administering tests is now very convenient—much more so than in the good old days when tests were still in pencil-and-paper format and delivery was strictly by snail mail and FedEx!

Finally, when making test results available to clients, you generally don't want to provide them with reports too early before meeting with them. If clients read the reports but don't fully understand them, they could become confused or even distressed by the information. If I'm meeting with a client remotely, I will email results ahead of the meeting but ask that they wait to read them until we meet so we can walk through the report or profile together. I want to be their guide throughout this process.

ADMINISTERING ASSESSMENTS: COSTS AND COST RECOVERY

To be a go-to person for doing formal assessments—someone who's set up to deliver them to clients without fuss or delay—you'll need to invest in an assessments infrastructure. An important part of that is purchasing assessments from reputable test publishers and then recovering your costs when billing clients.

Here are some facts and insights on costs and cost recovery based on my experience.

Once again, I will use the Myers-Briggs Company as an example, since I purchase the majority of my assessments from them. As I mentioned in the previous section, I use the Elevate system to manage my assessments. The licensing fee for Elevate is $195.00 per year at this writing. It's well worth it, given the convenience of using a fully automated system that lets you quickly deliver assessments to your clients.

In addition to the licensing fee, I pay for any assessments I purchase, plus taxes. Prices for assessments do change over time, of course. In 2019, I looked back at prices over a five-year period and did a quick analysis of pricing changes. Here's some of what I discovered:

- The MBTI Step II profile went from $24.95 to $34.95.
- The FIRO-B Interpretive Report for Organizations went from $14.95 to $22.95.
- The price of a Strong Interest Inventory profile increased by only 70 cents, from $9.25 to $9.95, over the same period, but it was the exception.

(Prices change, of course, and these are just a snapshot in time. To learn the latest prices for assessment products, check the test publisher website.)

One way to deal with rising prices is to have an inventory of assessments on hand. I try to have approximately three to five of the assessments I use most often in my inventory at any given time (more when I'm working on a large corporate project). Let's say that the price for the MBTI Step II suddenly goes from $34.95 to $39.95. If I have five Step II assessments already in my inventory, I avoid paying that extra $5.00 per assessment, and so I'll be saving myself $25.00. Think of prepurchased assessments like the "Forever" stamps you buy at the post office: when you buy a book of stamps at the going rate, you can still use them even after the cost of a stamp goes up.

The Myers-Briggs Company and other test publishers do offer volume discounts, but because you typically have to purchase a large number of assessments to get a discount (fifty to a hundred or more), they really only make sense for larger organizations. (In recent years, I do recall getting a volume discount for the 16PF Questionnaire through PSI for buying ten at a time, but this kind of discount is relatively rare.)

Finally, let's look at cost recovery. Clients will generally purchase some consulting time as well as pay a material fee for any assessments they take through me. With individual clients, I apply a modest markup, typically 15 to 20 percent, to recover costs. (For corporate clients, the markup would be more.) I find that most clients are more than willing to pay a materials fee given the value they gain.

Note that not all corporate projects require using your own inventory. For example, for a recent outplacement project I did with a business partner (who was managing the project), I was able to use her Elevate account, so no cost recovery was necessary.

EXPLORING TEST PUBLISHER RESOURCES

Through their many resources and services, test publishers can be an excellent source of education and support. Here are some tips on making the most of their offerings.

First, before purchasing from any of these publishers, have a good look at their websites to familiarize yourself with their products, services, certifications, training opportunities, languages used for the assessments, and other resources. Test publisher sites tend to be rich in content, offering case studies, white papers, webinars, educational videos, blogs, guides, and other tools to help you better understand the assessments they offer and their many applications.

One of the most important features test publishers offer is sample reports or profiles. On the Myers-Briggs Company website, go to the Resources menu, and select Sample Reports. From there you can open, save, and print out PDF samples of the many assessment reports the company offers. On the website for the 16PF Questionnaire (16pf.com), you'll find sample reports under the 16pf Overview menu. The ability to review sample reports is a crucial feature, because you will eventually need to decide the best report for your needs among the many available.

Another critical product test publishers offer is user manuals, which were key tools for me when I was first learning to administer assessments. Early copies of my test manuals are dog-eared and full of Post-its, handwritten notes, and highlighted text. They really got a workout! User manuals are generally a separate purchase, but they're well worth it, given their utility and educational value.

In addition to sample reports and user manuals, test publishers offer a variety of supplemental materials you can use to educate yourself and your clients. For example, for the California Psychological Inventory (CPI) assessments, which are key leadership assessments, you can download profiles (norms) for managers, executives, salespeople, law enforcement personnel, and other occupations. If you're planning to do a presentation on a particular assessment, test companies typically have slides or graphs available for downloading. Other support materials, such as booklets and one-sheet handouts, can help you educate your clients on various assessment features, making the task of explaining them easier and more convenient. Once you are registered as a user in the publisher's system, you can download many of these materials free of charge.

Finally, the top test publishers have excellent customer service and regularly reach out to their customers with news and updates. A few years back, the Myers-Briggs Company sponsored a free luncheon for Twin Cities end users to present some of their latest research and product updates, and reps have also presented at our local career development association meetings. In terms of technical support, I have found virtually all of the test publishers I've worked with to be helpful when I've contacted them. A simple phone call is usually all that's needed to clear up a technical issue or question. Larger publishers like the Myers-Briggs Company also have dedicated regional representatives you can contact for help or to give feedback. So find out who the rep is for your area, and add them to your contact list.

Again, make sure to visit the test publisher websites to get a sense of the many services and resources they offer. Exploring these websites, and taking advantage of the free content they offer, can be an education in itself.

AFTERWORD AND ACKNOWLEDGMENTS

As this book gets ready to go to press, we're a year and a half into the COVID-19 pandemic in the US. From the standpoint of writing the book, the pandemic has given Liz and me the gift of time. Before it hit, the book got delayed for any number of reasons—other, more pressing work projects, vacations, family health crises, and other events. Then, in 2020 and 2021, the book finally got the attention it needed.

As you are well aware, COVID-19 has also had a major impact on businesses and professions of all kinds. Many of us in career counseling and coaching, particularly those of us in private practice, have seen our client work slow dramatically as people have taken advantage of the lockdowns to simplify their lives and reduce their expenses. People are also operating more in survival mode these days, with perhaps less thought to personal and career development than in normal times—think Maslow's hierarchy of needs in action.

On the other hand, never has there been a better time to retool and work on personal and professional development. We all need guidance, role models, and specific steps to take in order to move forward, and that's what *Game Plan* is all about. Also, the ideas and tools presented in the book, particularly the use of formal assessments, lend themselves well to the remote work we're all doing more of now. Today more career assessment instruments are available online than ever, and test feedback can be given in a safe and socially distanced manner.

In October 2020, while seeing my dental hygienist, I learned that she planned on quitting a few weeks later. The stress of possible exposure to COVID-19 had finally gotten to her, and she'd had enough. But she wasn't ready to give up working altogether and would need to find a new path. I've worked with many people in health care over the years, and I know the important contributions they make. I've also seen many of them reinvent or reinvigorate their lives and careers through assessment. It's my hope that *Game Plan* has opened your eyes to the value and benefits of assessment, both for you and your clients.

I'd love to hear what you think of the book and answer any questions you might have. You can reach me at dean@innerviewconsulting.com.

* * *

I would not be where I am today, and I ultimately would not be in the position to offer this book, without the help of many close colleagues and others in my network. I want to start by acknowledging some of the key people who were instrumental in helping me grow and shape my career through their thoughtful guidance and mentoring.

Jacki Keagy provided me with my first opportunity to do career work when I joined a Twin Cities outplacement firm as a consultant. Her trust in me provided an opportunity to quickly learn the many career management services offered in the private sector. She exposed me to a career path I had never previously known, and for this I am grateful.

Trudy Canine, founder of Pathfinder, mentored, encouraged, and challenged me when I had little confidence in myself. Her big heart and positive desire to unlock potential in others were an inspiration. Trudy saw more potential in my abilities than I did, and she was generous in sharing insights on being a consultant, navigating corporate politics, and many other issues. Over the years, I've partnered with Trudy in providing outplacement, assessment, and other career services to clients.

Tamara Nelson, a licensed psychologist and owner of CareerMoves, spelled out the power and utility of assessments and how they could provide insights into client growth. Early on in my use of assessment instruments, Tamara tutored me on both interpreting assessments and delivering results to clients. (For more on her tutoring, see chapter 3 of the book.)

Bruce Roselle, founder and principal of Roselle Leadership Strategies, shared his wisdom on selection assessment and offered valuable feedback to make me a more disciplined evaluator. He also helped me hone my report-writing skills while working on selection assessment projects. Having authored several books himself, Bruce provided me with several useful tips on self-publishing.

Richard (Rich) Bents, partner at Future Systems Consulting, showed me how each of us has the power to make positive changes in our lives and helped me see how I could help clients unleash new potential in their own development. Over the years, Rich has shared his deep knowledge of leadership and test development, and we have engaged in several local and international projects together.

Jean Kummerow, owner of Jean Kummerow & Associates LLC, inspired me to use assessment in career counseling back in the 1990s through a training seminar she presented on using the MBTI and Strong Interest Inventory together, through her many publications on assessment, and through her leadership in and enthusiasm for career development.

My mastermind group—George Dow, Tamara Nelson, Carmen Croonquist, Pete Berridge, Molly Conlin, Ann Orchard, and Barb Miller—have been my bedrock of support and confidence, and close friends and confidants I can count on. All have been generous with ideas, resources, and encouragement. They are like my board of directors and are great, special colleagues. Our monthly gatherings have been invaluable and kept us all moving forward in our respective consulting practices.

Special thanks to colleagues who reviewed an earlier version of this book: Bruce Roselle; Vic Massaglia, director, Career and Professional Development at the School of Public Health, University of Minnesota; Tamara Nelson; Michael Stebbleton, associate professor and coordinator of the Higher Education Program, College of Education and Human Development, University of Minnesota; Peter Berridge, owner, Shorebird Coaching and Consulting; and Carolyn Berger, assistant professor, Department of Educational Psychology, University of Minnesota. Their insights and editing suggestions made a significant contribution in helping reshape the content, improve the organization, and smooth out some of the rough edges in presentation.

Finally, Liz and I would like to thank Beth Wright, of Wright for Writers, for her superb work as our publications consultant, editor, and page designer. *Game Plan* would not have been possible without her guidance and expertise.

APPENDICES

Appendix A

. . . .

GLOSSARY

Note that the terms defined below are based on how I use them in the book and in my work, which may differ somewhat from usage you'll find elsewhere. For a broader appreciation of language used in career assessment, I recommend exploring texts such as those listed in Appendix B.

Assessment: Used as a short form for "career assessment." Refers to all of the tools I use in my assessment process, from my structured interview to formal assessments to the game plan. Note that when I refer to "specializing in assessment" in this book, as I do in chapter 1, I'm specifically referring to the practice of assessment in which formal assessments (defined below) are used extensively as part of the overall assessment process.

Career and Job Compatibility Matrix: A worksheet I use with clients to help them process assessment information. Usually employed after formal assessments. See page 73.

Career assessment: See Assessment.

Career assessment instruments: See Formal assessments.

Career Compatibility Scale (CCS): An assessment product I developed with a colleague that measures work values and job satisfaction, weighing what clients want out of work against what they're experiencing.

Career Ingredients Summary Sheet: A worksheet I use with clients to help them process assessment information. Usually employed after formal assessments. See page 72.

Formal assessments: The term used most frequently in the book to describe career assessment instruments such as the Myers-Briggs Type Indicator (MBTI) assessment and Strong Interest Inventory assessment. Also referred to as simply "assessments" or "tests." (Although most formal assessments are not, strictly speaking, tests, the terms "tests" and "testing" are commonly used as shorthand in our field to represent the use of formal assessments.)

Game plan: A simple template I use with clients to help them set criteria for what they need to thrive in their work. Usually employed near the end of an engagement. See page 80.

Mastermind group: A group formed by colleagues to provide advice and mutual support to members on matters of professional and personal development. My own mastermind group is made up of career counselors, coaches, and consultants in private practice.

Outplacement: A service that companies provide to laid-off employees to help them get reestablished in their careers. Often performed by outside consultants utilizing a range of services, including job search assistance, résumé development, and interviewing training. May include formal assessments.

Selection assessment: The use of assessment in the hiring, promotion, and development of employees. Often performed by outside consultants utilizing formal assessments.

Structured interview: My intake interview, in which I used preplanned questions which I ask all clients. Allows me to identify common patterns in client responses, which I use to shape my process. For example, my Career Compatibility Scale (CCS) was created from responses to the structured interview.

Testing, Tests: See Formal assessments.

Appendix B

· · · · · · · · · · · ·

CAREER ASSESSMENT RESOURCES

In this book I've emphasized my own experience with career assessment instruments—the specific set of formal assessments I use in my practice and how I've applied them to help clients; how I've studied assessments over the years and also sought tutoring in their use; and what's involved in purchasing, administering, and maintaining them in my practice. If you're looking for both a broader and a more detailed look at the universe of career assessments, I recommend the resources that follow.

Note that the first two resources cover career assessments more generally and are directed at practitioners. The third resource, *Do What You Are*, is one of my favorite books for a general audience on one of the most popular and widely used assessments today: the Myers-Briggs Type Indicator (MBTI). That's followed by some additional texts you may find of interest.

A Comprehensive Guide to Career Assessment, seventh edition, edited by Kevin Stoltz and Susan Barclay, published by the National Career Development Association (NCDA), 2019. This resource, in continuous publication since 1982, is by far the most detailed and, as the title indicates, comprehensive resource you will find on formal assessments. Some highlights of what you'll find:

- Foundational chapters on the history and use of assessments, current trends, computer-assisted assessments, multicultural considerations, selection of assessments for use with clients, and administration and interpretation.
- Detailed reviews of specific assessment instruments. These reviews outline basic information (purpose of the instrument, target population, scales and scores provided in the test, cost, time needed to administer,

availability of online scoring) and then describe the instrument in detail (history, technical considerations, recommendations for use, and additional references and resources to look to for more information).

- Exhaustive research and documentation. Each chapter includes a substantial list of references for further study. In addition, the editors cite classic resources they drew on for coverage of tests and testing, including *Tests in Print* and *Mental Measurements Yearbook*. Over 175 professional journals are cited in the reviews provided.

The seventh edition of this guide has an online component that's available separately from the print guide. That has allowed the editors to better distribute the information previously available only in print and to expand the coverage to include more global concerns and audiences. It will also allow them to more easily add new reviews and update existing ones.

When I first encountered *A Counselor's Guide to Career Assessment Instruments*, the previous edition of this guide, I was struck by the sheer number of assessments that were available. I also appreciated that one of the first chapters dealt with career assessment standards and competencies, something every effective practitioner needs to observe.

For more on the NCDA, including publications and standards, visit its website, ncda.org. For a concise overview of competencies involved in using formal assessments, select Standards, then Career Counselor Assessment and Evaluation Competencies.

Psychometrics in Coaching: Using Psychological and Psychometric Tools for Development, second edition, edited by Jonathan Passmore, published by Kogan Page, 2012. This resource is similar to the NCDA's guide in that it starts with a basic foundation (chapter 1, for example, is titled "Using Psychometrics and Psychological Tools in Coaching") and then gets into individual career assessment instruments. But it's quite different in that its coverage is more selective, whereas the NCDA's guide is extensive, and its treatment of the various assessment instruments is unique in that it addresses their use from the perspective of a coach's own self-knowledge and interaction with clients.

It provides an accessible and concise overview of some of the technical points coaches must be familiar with when working with formal assessments, including reliability, construct validity, and other factors. This is covered in a section called "The Psychometric Properties of a Psychological Test" in chapter 1 of the book. Also, in chapter 3, "Administering and Managing the Use of Psychometric Questionnaires," the subject of training to do assessments is addressed in detail. While the training options addressed relate to the UK primarily, US training options, which are generally more flexible, are also considered.

In Part 2 of the book, "Individual Instruments and Their Use," the contributors cover a range of tools. Some of these are used more broadly in both career counseling and business settings, including four I cover in this book: the California Psychological Inventory (CPI) assessments; the Myers-Briggs Type Indicator (MBTI) assessment; the 16PF Questionnaire; and the FIRO-B (Fundamental Interpersonal Relations Orientation-Behavior) assessment. But they also cover tools more often used in a corporate setting, such as those for leadership coaching and training and team development. Examples are the Transformational Leadership Questionnaire, instruments developed by Team Management Systems, and the Hogan Development Survey. This is not surprising, given the strong emphasis on coaching in business settings.

One of the most interesting aspects of this book is that for each of the instruments discussed, there's a section devoted specifically to coaches and how the tool relates to them. For example, in chapter 6 on the Myers-Briggs Type Indicator (MBTI)assessment, the authors cite a survey done in the UK that looked at MBTI type distribution among coaches. My own type, ISTJ (Introverted, Sensing, Thinking, Judging), made up only 0.9 percent of coaches, while ENFPs (Extraverted, Intuitive, Feeling, Perceiving), the largest group, made up 18 percent. This explains why I've met only a handful of ISTJ practitioners over the years! They also look at coaching styles based on MBTI types. According to their analysis, an ISTJ coach sees coaching as "an opportunity to use his/her accumulated experience to be of practical help to others," while ENFPs see it as "an opportunity to create and explore new ideas."

Psychometrics in Coaching is one of a series of books published by the Association for Coaching (*Excellence in Coaching* is another). At the end of the book, the authors outline the benefits of membership in the organization and invite readers to join. To learn more about the organization and its publications, visit associationforcoaching.com.

Do What You Are: Discover the Perfect Career for You Through the Secrets of Personality Type, fifth edition, by Paul D. Tieger, Barbara Barron, and Kelly Tieger, Little, Brown, & Company, 2014. By applying the MBTI assessment to the career world, this guide helps readers make better career choices. While this book is written for a general audience, the authors also clearly had career development professionals in mind as well. (See more below on a special chapter the authors wrote especially for us.)

The book provides an excellent introduction to type as it relates to careers and the work world, one that's substantive enough to satisfy career development professionals yet accessible to a wide audience. I've been using this book since it first came out in 1992, and I regularly recommend it to clients, especially those who may not be able to afford formal testing. The early chapters build the foundation: why type is important to career and job satisfaction, how to determine your type, the four temperaments underlying type, and the importance of understanding the strengths and weaknesses of your particular type as they relate to work in particular. After that, each of the types is treated in detail.

It makes good use of client stories, particularly in the chapters covering each of the sixteen types. For each type, you learn about three people who share that type, including a millennial (a new feature in the fifth edition). In each case, you learn why the career the person has chosen works for them and suits their type. These type-specific chapters are also full of practical facts and checklists you and your clients can put to work: the specific characteristics of work that result in career satisfaction for that type, popular occupations for the type, ways to customize a job search using your strengths, work-related strengths and weaknesses, pitfalls to avoid, and more. The combination of client stories and practical strategies in these chapters is invaluable.

It addresses career development professionals directly. "For Career Professionals Only," the final chapter in the book, concerns, among other things, our ethical use of the MBTI. Here the authors stress a critical point about the instrument and our use of it—that we want to focus primarily on what will help the individual rather than being too black-and-white or judgmental about the results. Also interesting in this chapter: how to work with types who are different from ourselves and specific pointers for working with Introverts and Extraverts, Sensors and Intuitives, Thinkers and Feelers, and Judgers and Perceivers. Here, for example, is a tip for working with Perceivers, who like to keep their options open: "Don't force decisions (unless you have to)." This kind of advice can be useful for those of us who are Judgers and prefer closure!

The book concludes with a substantial listing (six pages) of resources. They include professional organizations and associations, as well as an extensive bibliography arranged by the following broad subject areas: General Introduction to Psychological Type, Careers, Children/Education, Counseling/Management, Religion/Spirituality, and Type and Research.

ADDITIONAL RESOURCES ON CAREER ASSESSMENT

The following texts were key to my own learning process and have also been used extensively in educational programs for career developmental professionals.

New Directions in Career Planning and the Workplace, second edition, Jean M. Kummerow, editor, Davies-Black Publishing, 2000. I discovered the first edition of this book, published in 1991, in the mid to late 1990s. I particularly like it because it weaves the work of several notable experts into one volume, including Sunny Hansen's theory of Integrative Life Planning. That theory is something I've believed in for years and apply in my practice: work and family are intricately tied together as part of life, not separate entities. Also, Jean includes her own chapter on using the Strong Interest Inventory and MBTI assessments together, something I do regularly with my career clients. (Using the two together can give greater confidence in one's findings and richer information overall.) Jean was one of my early instructors. I'm one of her biggest fans and have also been privileged to get to know her personally. Jean's an ESTJ (Extraverted, Sensing, Thinking, Judging), so she understands me (an ISTJ) well and has referred clients to me on occasion. In addition to authoring and co-authoring several books, Jean has written user guides on the MBTI assessment for the Myers-Briggs Company.

If you're interested in organizational consulting, two key books are *The Ethical Practice of Psychology in Organizations*, second edition, by Rodney L. Lowman, American Psychological Association, 2006; and *Psychological Consulting to Management: A Clinician's Perspective*, by Lester L. Tobias, Routledge, 1990 (reprinted in paperback in 2015). Lowman's book covers a range of topics, including personnel selection (something I've done through various selection assessment projects), as well as organizational diagnosis and intervention, managing consulting relationships (including how to avoid stepping on landmines), and understanding the limits of testing, particularly as it relates to selecting personnel. Each chapter contains case studies dealing with various ethical dilemmas, which I found particularly useful. Tobias's book offers a straightforward but insightful look at the work psychologists typically do for business organizations, and discusses challenges and mistakes to avoid, such as having dual relationships within the same organization. It also covers some practical business topics, such as running a consulting practice and writing reports.

Three texts by Vernon G. Zunker are useful to explore: *Career Counseling: Applied Concepts of Life Planning*, fourth edition; *Career Counseling: A Holistic Approach*, ninth edition; and *Using Assessment Results for Career Development*, ninth edition, co-authored with Debra Osborn. The first book, used in a graduate-level course I took in career foundations in the mid-1990s, provides a good overview of assessments, but its real strength is its coverage of interviewing. It outlines content areas to inquire about with clients and also discusses interview methods for gathering additional detail and encouraging further client involvement. The second book covers job transition and career development for working adults, issues that are central to my work with clients. The third book provides a comprehensive overview of various types of tests and inventories, including aptitude and achievement, interest, and personality. It also addresses the interpretation of assessments, including ethical concerns, and the integration of formal testing with career counseling.

Appendix C

. . . .

THE CAREER COMPATIBILITY SCALE (CCS): AN INVITATION TO PARTICIPATE

Are your clients dissatisfied with their current role or employer? Do complaints about their workplace dominate your discussions? Are they looking for help in deciding whether to stay in or leave their current job? Are you interested in adding a work values assessment to your own process as a career counselor or coach?

My colleague Rich Bents and I created the Career Compatibility Scale (CCS), an online assessment, to help clients explore what's important to them at work and whether their needs are being met.

While many work values assessments exist, none to my knowledge do what the CCS does: actually weigh what clients say is important to them at work against what they're experiencing in their jobs. It does this based on nine themes: Boss, Environment, Influence, Organization, People, Purpose, Recognition, Task/Challenge, and Team. (See chapter 9 for details.)

As a reader of this book, you have complimentary access to the CCS (it's normally $45.00 to take).

To request to take the CCS, just contact me via email at dean@innerviewconsulting.com. To help me quickly recognize your request, please type "Try the CCS" in the subject line of your email. Once I receive your request, I will assign the CCS to you, and you will receive an email invitation with a link for taking it.

Look for the following message in your email: "You have been invited by Dean R. DeGroot to join ShareOn Corporate Leader Resources and take the CCS." ShareOn, a website on which the CCS and other assessments and leadership resources are housed, is managed by Rich. I've been a ShareOn partner myself since 2000. ShareOn is a collaborative of independent consultants and academics primarily from the United States and Europe who wish to continue to grow, learn, and share their expertise in the development of others.

In return for complimentary access to the CCS, we will ask that you complete a brief, three-question questionnaire, which we will make available to you when or soon after you request to take the assessment.

We think you will find the CCS a useful tool for empowering career change, narrowing the gap between what's important and what's happening at work, and generally fostering growth, self-development, and job satisfaction. At the same time, your participation will help us improve the CCS by gathering more data on what factors seem to be most salient to users.

Thank you in advance for trying the CCS. We value your input. If you have any questions at all about the assessment, please contact me at dean@innerviewconsulting.com.

Appendix D

• • • • • • • • • • • •

WORKPLACE BULLYING: KEY RESOURCES

If you've ever been bullied or suffered through other abuse at work, or if you have helped someone who has, you know that books and other resources can have a healing effect. Reading about others' experiences validates that you're not alone; these things happen to other adults too.

Knowledge of workplace bullying can also be key to doing assessment well. Too often in assessment the focus is simply on *what* clients want to do—*where* they work and *whom* they work with are not examined as thoroughly or as seriously. As a result, clients can find themselves in toxic work environments where bullying and other disrespectful behavior are allowed to thrive unchecked.

I address the what/where/who context of work in chapter 8 on the game plan. And in chapter 10, I cover workplace bullying in detail. In chapter 12, "Client Case Studies," I include a case study on a client who was bullied by her immediate boss.

BOOKS ON WORKPLACE BULLYING AND RELATED TOPICS

Here are twelve books on workplace bullying and related topics, a key website I highly recommend, and information on how to obtain a special presentation I created on bully-proofing the workplace. See Appendix E for full bibliographical details.

The Brain-Friendly Workplace: 5 Big Ideas from Neuroscience to Address Organizational Challenges, by Erika Garms
The Bully at Work: What You Can Do to Stop the Hurt and Reclaim Your Dignity on the Job, second edition, and *The Bully-Free Workplace: Stop*

Jerks, Weasels, and Snakes from Killing Your Organization, by Gary Namie and Ruth Namie

The Complete Idiot's Guide to Office Politics, by Laurie Rozakis and Bob Rozakis

Driving Fear Out of the Workplace: Creating the High-Trust, High-Performance Organization, second edition, by Kathleen D. Ryan and Daniel K. Oestreich

The First 90 Days: Proven Strategies for Getting Up to Speed Faster and Smarter, updated and expanded edition, by Michael Watkins

Learned Optimism: How to Change Your Mind and Your Life, by Martin Seligman

Mobbing: Emotional Abuse in the American Workplace, by Noa Davenport, Ruth D. Schwartz, and Gail Pursell Elliott

The No Asshole Rule: Building a Civilized Workplace and Surviving One That Isn't, by Robert Sutton

Odd Girl Out: The Hidden Culture of Aggression in Girls, revised edition, by Rachel Simmons

Toxic Workplace! Managing Toxic Personalities and Their Systems of Power, by Mitchell Kusy and Elizabeth Holloway

When You Work for a Bully: Assessing Your Options and Taking Action, by Susan Futterman

Any one of the books above is worth exploring, but if you're looking for comprehensive coverage of workplace bullying—research data, guidance on best practices, in-depth discussion of both individual and environmental impact of bullying, and more—consider Gary and Ruth Namie's *The Bully at Work* and *The Bully-Free Workplace.* The Namies, both of whom hold PhDs in psychology, are the founders of the Workplace Bullying Institute (WBI). See below for more on the WBI.

Two other books from the list above I particularly recommend are Robert Sutton's *The No Asshole Rule* and Susan Futterman's *When You Work For a Bully.* Sutton, a Stanford University professor of management science, brings humor to a serious subject (example: "Self-Test: Are You a Certified Asshole?") while painting a clear picture of how people create toxic environments at work. He recommends establishing firm rules for acceptable behavior, rules that everyone involved is expected to enforce. The book includes profiles of prominent workplace bullies, including the late Steve Jobs.

Futterman, a target of bullying herself, provides an excellent, detailed guide for what to do when you've been bullied, such as assessing whether to stay or go, getting legal advice, contacting government agencies for assistance, working with human resources and other corporate departments, managing your finances if you're considering leaving the job, and more. As a former target, Futterman clearly understands the emotional and practical aspects of bullying and brings this experience to the book. In addition to describing her own experience, she includes stories of other targets and how they coped.

THE WORKPLACE BULLYING INSTITUTE (WBI)

If you plan to conduct research into bullying, or if you're simply interested in learning more about the subject, the Workplace Bullying Institute (workplace bullying.org) is a great resource and the definitive destination for information on bullying. The site offers research on a variety of topics, including gender and bullying, race and bullying, target responses, target health, employer policies, barriers to leaving jobs, and more. You can also access WBI scientific surveys through the site.

A SPECIAL PRESENTATION ON WORKPLACE BULLYING

In 2010 I developed a presentation titled "Navigating the Minefield: Bully-Proofing the Workplace," which I delivered to the Minnesota Career Development Association that year. I later revised the presentation and in 2016 presented it to the National Career Development Association. In 2017 I created a webinar based on "Navigating" that's available through the Career Planning Academy (formerly CEUoneStop.com).

If you'd like a summary of the "Navigating the Minefield" presentation (PowerPoint format), just let me know at dean@innerviewconsulting.com, and I'll send you a copy. The webinar itself is available at the Career Planning Academy and costs $35.00; by taking it through the Academy, you can accumulate CEUs.

Appendix E

· · · · · · · · · · · · ·

RECOMMENDED READING

The listing of more than fifty books below includes career development classics from my bookshelves, resources covered in more detail in various parts of this book, and titles that come highly recommended by several of my colleagues. As you would expect from a subject as wide-ranging as career assessment, there's a lot to think about and explore here—from more in-depth, academic texts on career development and career assessment to popular self-help books on career and life transition, networking, interviewing, and job search. If you are interested in learning about diversity, multiculturalism, and cultural competency in assessment, you'll find some key texts in those areas as well.

Bridges, William. *Transitions: Making Sense of Life's Changes*. 40th Anniversary ed. New York: Lifelong, 2019.

Broadley, Margaret E. *Your Natural Gifts: How to Recognize and Develop Them for Success and Self-Fulfillment*. Updated ed. McLean, VA: EPM Publications, 2002.

Buckingham, Marcus, and Curt Coffman. *First, Break All the Rules: What the World's Greatest Managers Do Differently*. Re-release. New York: Gallup, 2016.

Burnett, Bill, and Dave Evans. *Designing Your Life: How to Build a Well-Lived, Joyful Life*. New York: Knopf, 2016.

Burns, David D. *Feeling Good: The New Mood Therapy*. New York: William Morrow, 1999.

Capelli, Peter, and Bill Novelli. *Managing the Older Worker: How to Prepare for the New Organizational Order*. Boston: Harvard Business Review Press, 2010.

Cooperrider, David L., and Diana Whitney. *Appreciative Inquiry: A Positive Revolution in Change.* San Francisco: Berrett-Koehler, 2005.

Davenport, Noa, Ruth D. Schwartz, and Gail Pursell Elliott. *Mobbing: Emotional Abuse in the American Workplace.* Ames, IA: Civil Society Publishing, 1999.

Eikleberry, Carol, and Carrie Pinsky. *The Career Guide for Creative and Unconventional People.* Fourth ed. Berkeley: Ten Speed, 2015.

Evans, Kathy M., and Aubrey L. Sejuit. *Gaining Cultural Competence in Career Counseling.* Second ed. Broken Arrow, OK: National Career Development Association, 2021.

Figler, Howard, and Richard Nelson Bolles. *The Career Counselor's Handbook.* Second ed. Berkeley: Ten Speed, 2007.

Flores, Lisa Y., and Denise H. Bike. "Multicultural Career Counseling." In *APA Handbook of Multicultural Psychology: Vol. 2, Applications and Training,* edited by Frederick T. L. Leong, Lillian Comas-Díaz, Gordon C. Nagayama Hall, Vonnie C. McLoyd, and Joseph E. Trimble, 403–17. Washington, DC: American Psychological Association, 2014.

Futterman, Susan. *When You Work for a Bully: Assessing Your Options and Taking Action.* Leonia, NJ: Croce Publishing, 2004.

Garms, Erika. *The Brain-Friendly Workplace: 5 Big Ideas from Neuroscience to Address Organizational Challenges.* Alexandria, VA: Association for Talent Development, 2014.

Gladwell, Malcolm. *Outliers: The Story of Success.* Reprint ed. New York: Back Bay, 2011.

Grant, Adam. *Give and Take: Why Helping Others Drives Our Success.* Reprint ed. New York: Penguin, 2014.

Hays, Danica G. *Assessment in Counseling.* Sixth ed. Alexandria, VA: American Counseling Association, 2017.

Herzberg, Frederick, Bernard Mausner, and Barbara Bloch Snyderman. *The Motivation to Work.* Abingdon-on-Thames, England: Routledge, 2017.

Hirsh, Sandra Krebs, and Jean M. Kummerow. *LIFETypes.* New York: Grand Central, 1989.

Ibarra, Herminia. *Working Identity: Unconventional Strategies for Reinventing Your Career.* Boston: Harvard Business School Press, 2004.

Jeffers, Susan. *Feel the Fear . . . and Do It Anyway.* 20th anniversary edition. New York: Ballantine, 2006.

Kamphoff, Cindra. *Beyond Grit: 10 Powerful Practices to Gain the High-Performance Edge.* Minneapolis: Wise Ink Creative, 2017.

Krumboltz, John, and Al Levin. *Luck Is No Accident: Making the Most of Happenstance in Your Life and Career.* Second ed. Oakland, CA: Impact, 2010.

Kummerow, Jean M., ed. *New Directions in Career Planning and the Workplace.* Second ed. Mountain View, CA: Davies-Black, 2000.

Kummerow, Jean M., Nancy J. Barger, and Linda K. Kirby. *WORKTypes.* New York: Warner, 1997.

Kusy, Mitchell, and Elizabeth Holloway. *Toxic Workplace! Managing Toxic Personalities and Their Systems of Power.* San Francisco: Jossey-Bass, 2009.

Leider, Richard J. *The Power of Purpose: Find Meaning, Live Longer, Better.* Third ed. San Francisco: Berrett-Koehler, 2015.

Leider, Richard J., and David A. Shapiro. *Repacking Your Bags: Lighten Your Load for the Good Life.* Third ed. San Francisco: Berrett-Koehler, 2012.

Leider, Richard J., and Alan M. Webber. *Life Reimagined: Discovering Your New Life Possibilities.* San Francisco: Berrett-Koehler, 2013.

Leong, Frederick T. L., and Lisa Y. Flores. "Career Interventions with Racial and Ethnic Minority Clients." In *APA Handbook of Career Intervention: Volume 1, Foundations,* edited by Paul J. Hartung, Mark L. Savickas, and W. Bruce Walsh, 225–42. Washington, DC: American Psychological Association, 2014.

Levoy, Gregg. *Callings: Finding and Following an Authentic Life.* New York: Harmony, 1998.

Lowman, Rodney L. *The Ethical Practice of Psychology in Organizations.* Second revised ed. Washington, DC: American Psychological Association, 2006.

MacDougall, Debra Angel, and Elisabeth Harney Sanders-Park. *The 6 Reasons You'll Get the Job: What Employers Look for—Whether They Know It or Not.* Upper Saddle River, NJ: Prentice Hall, 2010.

McClelland, David C. *The Achievement Motive.* Eastford, CT: Martino Fine Books, 2015.

Moses, Barbara. *What Next?: The Complete Guide to Taking Control of Your Working Life.* Third ed. Toronto: DK Canada, 2017.

Namie, Gary, and Ruth Namie. *The Bully at Work: What You Can Do to Stop the Hurt and Reclaim Your Dignity on the Job.* Second ed. Naperville, IL: Sourcebooks, 2020.

Namie, Gary, and Ruth Namie. *The Bully-Free Workplace: Stop Jerks, Weasels, and Snakes from Killing Your Organization.* Hoboken, NJ: Wiley, 2011.

Neukrug, Edward S., and R. Charles Fawcett. *Essentials of Testing and Assessment: A Practical Guide for Counselors, Social Workers, and Psychologists.* Third ed. Boston: Cengage Learning, 2015.

Niles, Spencer G., and JoAnn Harris-Bowlsbey. *Career Development Interventions.* Fifth ed. London: Pearson, 2016.

Osborn, Deborah S., and Vernon G. Zunker. *Using Assessment Results for Career Development.* Ninth ed. Boston: Cengage Learning, 2015.

Passmore, Jonathan, ed. *Psychometrics in Coaching: Using Psychological and Psychometric Tools for Development.* Second ed. London: Kogan Page, 2012.

Perez, Nathan, and Marcia Ballinger. *The 20-Minute Networking Meeting: Learn to Network. Get a Job.* Middletown, DE: Career Innovations, 2016.

Pink, Daniel H. *Free Agent Nation: The Future of Working for Yourself.* New York: Warner, 2001.

Pink, Daniel H. *A Whole New Mind: Why Right-Brainers Will Rule the Future.* Reprint, updated edition. New York: Riverhead, 2006.

Pope, Mark, Lisa Y. Flores, and Patrick J. Rottinghaus, eds. *The Role of Values in Careers.* Charlotte, NC: Information Age, 2014.

Quenk, Naomi L. *Was That Really Me?: How Everyday Stress Brings Out Our Hidden Personality.* New York: Hachette, 2002.

Rath, Tom. *StrengthsFinder 2.0.* Washington, D.C.: Gallup, 2013.

Rozakis, Laurie, and Bob Rozakis. *The Complete Idiot's Guide to Office Politics.* Indianapolis: Alpha, 1998.

Ryan, Kathleen D., and Daniel K. Oestreich. *Driving Fear Out of the Workplace: Creating the High-Trust, High-Performance Organization.* Second ed. San Francisco: Jossey-Bass, 1998.

Seligman, Martin. *Learned Optimism: How to Change Your Mind and Your Life.* New York: Vintage, 2006.

Silsbee, Doug. *The Mindful Coach: Seven Roles for Facilitating Leader Development.* Second ed. San Francisco: Jossey-Bass, 2010.

Simmons, Rachel. *Odd Girl Out: The Hidden Culture of Aggression in Girls.* Revised ed. New York: Mariner, 2011.

Stoltz, Kevin B., and Susan R. Barclay, eds. *A Comprehensive Guide to Career Assessment.* Seventh ed. (includes online component). Broken Arrow, OK: National Career Development Association, 2019.

Sutton, Robert. *The No Asshole Rule: Building a Civilized Workplace and Surviving One That Isn't*. Reprint ed. New York: Business Plus, 2010.

Tieger, Paul D., Barbara Barron, and Kelly Tieger. *Do What You Are: Discover the Perfect Career for You Through the Secret of Personality Type*. Fifth ed. New York: Little, Brown Spark, 2014.

Tobias, L. L. *Psychological Consulting to Management: A Clinician's Perspective*. Abingdon-on-Thames, England: Routledge, 2015.

Watkins, Michael. *The First 90 Days: Proven Strategies for Getting Up to Speed Faster and Smarter*. Updated and expanded ed. Boston: Harvard Business Review Press, 2013.

Wood, Chris, and Danica G. Hays, eds. *A Counselor's Guide to Career Assessment Instruments*. Sixth ed. Broken Arrow, OK: National Career Development Association, 2013.

Zunker, Vernon G. *Career Counseling: A Holistic Approach*. Ninth ed. Independence, KY: Cengage Learning, 2019.

INDEX

ABC model in cognitive therapy, 206

abuse. *See* bullying

academic professional case study, 146–52

achievement motivation, 104

The Achievement Motive (McClelland), 104

active listening, 50

ADHD (attention-deficit/hyperactivity disorder), 141–42

administration of formal assessments, 8, 67–68, 214–22

affirmations, positive, 205

American Society for Training and Development (ASTD), 19, 21

anxiety
  of clients, 110–11, 187. *See also* bullying
  of counselors. *See* fear and anxiety of career counselors

artist case study, 152–56

Artistic type (Holland Codes), 135, 175, 178

arts organization fundraiser case study, 74, 156–63

assessment. *See* career assessment

assignments for clients. *See* homework in career assessment process

Association for Coaching, 233

Association for Talent Development, 19, 26

attention-deficit/hyperactivity disorder (ADHD), 141–42

attitude issues of clients, 62–63, 66, 114–16

Ballinger, Marcia, 190

banking industry professional case study, 138–42

Barclay, Susan, 231

Barron, Barbara, 102, 233

behavioral issues of clients, 62–63, 66, 114–16

Bents, Richard, 19, 95, 96, 237

biases in formal assessments, 187–88

bias for action, 12, 38

Big Five personality traits, 58

blind spots, 188

body language, 51, 108, 111

Made in the USA
Coppell, TX
24 January 2022

72153382R00155